MADE UNDER PRESSURE

A VOLUME IN THE SERIES
Studies in Print Culture and the History of the Book

EDITED BY

Greg Barnhisel
Robert A. Gross
Joan Shelley Rubin
Michael Winship

MADE UNDER PRESSURE

Literary Translation
in the
Soviet Union,
1960–1991

NATALIA KAMOVNIKOVA

UNIVERSITY OF MASSACHUSETTS PRESS
Amherst and Boston

Printed in the United States of America

ISBN 978-1-62534-341-3 (paper); 340-6 (hardcover)

Designed by Sally Nichols
Set in Minion Pro
Printed and bound by Maple Press Inc.

Cover design by Thomas Eykemans
Cover art by Vilen Karakashev and Lila Levshunova, detail from Soviet poster
"Knowledge for All" c. 1972.

Library of Congress Cataloging-in-Publication Data

Names: Kamovnikova, Natalia, author.
Title: Made under pressure : literary translation in the Soviet Union,
1960–1991 / Natalia Kamovnikova.
Description: Amherst : University of Massachusetts Press, 2019. | Series:
Studies in Print Culture and the History of the Book | Includes
bibliographical references and index. | Description based on print version
record and CIP data provided by publisher; resource not viewed.
Identifiers: LCCN 2018019162 (print) | LCCN 2018044430 (ebook) | ISBN
9781613765807 (e-book) | ISBN 9781613765814 (e-book) | ISBN 9781625343413
(pbk.) | ISBN 9781625343406 (hardcover)
Subjects: LCSH: Literature—Translations into Russian—History and criticism.
| Translating and interpreting—Soviet Union. | Soviet
literature—Translations—History and criticism.
Classification: LCC PG2984 (ebook) | LCC PG2984 .K35 2019 (print) | DDC
491.78/04—dc23
LC record available at https://lccn.loc.gov/2018019162

British Library Cataloguing-in-Publication Data
A catalog record for this book is available from the British Library.

Anna Akhmatova's Russian text © by Margarita Novgorodova. Publishing rights
acquired via FTM Agency, Ltd., Russia.

Do you know the Russian metaphoric expression *Sauerkraut is made under pressure?* Well, this is what being a translator meant in those days. The original poets and writers were pressured—think of Akhmatova, Pasternak, Tsvetaeva. And because the original creative activity was impeded, people would go into literary translation.

—Viktor Andreev, translator

CONTENTS

A NOTE ON NAMES, TRANSLITERATION, AND TRANSLATION

Most personal names are given here in the Library of Congress system of Cyrillic transliteration without diacritics. In cases where a particular Russian name has become widely recognized, I preserve its traditional English spelling. For example, I chose to spell the name of the poet Osip Mandelstam in the traditional way; however, I spell it as Mandel'shtam when speaking about the translator Isai Mandel'shtam, although the poet and the translator share the same last name in the Russian language. I also spell Lev Tolstoy and not Lev Tolstoi, Joseph Brodsky and not Iosif Brodskii.

The exceptions also pertain to the names of Russian families of German descent; thus, I use Alexander von Benckendorff and not Aleksandr fon Benkendorf, Arkadii Steinberg and not Arkadii Shteinberg. The names of the Romanov dynasty are presented in their historical spelling, hence Paul I, Alexander I, Nicholas I, and so on. Names of modern Russian writers, poets, and critics, the spelling of whose names has been secured by their foreign publications, are presented here in the way they appear in Western print, for example, Oleg Juriev and not Oleg Iur'ev.

The names of the translators who gave interviews for the book are presented here according to their personal preference, therefore see Witkowsky and not Vitkovskii, Yasnov and not Iasnov.

For the sake of convenience, Russian names are generally presented in the form of the given name plus last name. In the biographies, however, I use the complete forms of Russian names, which traditionally consist of three parts: the given name, the patronymic, and the last name. I also preserve the polite form of the given name plus the patronymic in the quoted interviews and several other instances, where the use of the patronymic is socially and stylistically mandatory. Thus, the students of El'ga Linetskaia refer to her as "El'ga L'vovna," and the students of Efim Etkind call him "Efim Grigor'evich."

All translations of quoted text are my own, unless otherwise indicated.

PREFACE

This book was planned as a study of literary translation under pressure, and state control. It turned out to be a story of passion. Literary translation is known to require concentration, composure, and reserve from those engaged in it. I realized it was the passion of translators for literature, their respect for the written and spoken word, and their desire to share and spread knowledge that gave numerous literary works a second life in a new culture. This commitment to literature and languages made translators choose modern unconventional works of literature and find ways to publish their translations of these works despite all obstacles.

The process of writing this book is also a unique story, which is best described as a story of friendship. I started the project keen on acquiring knowledge. But now I realize that together with knowledge I received another gift: the friendship of many extraordinary and talented people. I thank them for opening up to me—a complete stranger at that time—and for sharing their life histories with me. I thank Irina Komarova, Maiia Kviatkovskaia, Larisa Bespalova, Viktor Golyshev, Viktor Andreev, Inna Streblova, Sergei Stepanov, Mikhail Yasnov, and Evgenii Witkowsky for the memories they shared with me, as well as their kindness, understanding, and encouragement. It is their generosity and encyclopedic knowledge that made this book possible. I grieve the death of Ignatii Ivanovskii, to whom I am grateful for his contribution to this book, for his example of optimism and courage in the face of illness, and for his wonderful poems that he continued to read to me over the phone until three weeks before his death.

I am most indebted to Maria Tymoczko, who told me a book based on interviews could be an interesting project. Her invaluable advice and personal example have been a source of inspiration to me throughout the time I was working on the book.

I owe a debt of gratitude to my dear teacher Irina Arnold, who is very much missed. She would often repeat that the main qualities of a researcher are an interest in other people and the talent of maintaining friendships. This lesson was extremely valuable for this book—as well as all her lessons, which I treasure in my memory.

The extensive library support that I received from my friends and colleagues is inestimable and deserves my special acknowledgment. I thank the extraordinary librarian Tat'iana Borisova for her energy and her almost telepathic ability to find exactly the books I needed even before I asked for them. I thank Outi Paloposki and Daniele Monti-celli for granting me access to their university libraries when I needed it most.

I am deeply grateful to my parents, Galina and Evgenii Kamovnikov, for my wonderful childhood in a house full of books. Two passionate readers, they taught me both the willing suspension of disbelief and the critical ability to read between the lines.

This book would not have been possible without the unfailing support of my two best friends—my husband Denis and daughter Irina, whose love and faith made me a braver and a better person.

MADE UNDER PRESSURE

INTRODUCTION

A Round Unvarnished Tale of the
Whole Course of Love

This book was written in St. Petersburg, Russia—the city of my birth, which has invariably been the main source of inspiration for all my projects. Known all over the world for its architecture, arts, and literature, St. Petersburg is much less known for its translators of literary works, who together with Moscow translators in many respects determined the course of Russian literature, translation, and publishing in the twentieth century. These literary translators of the last century are still living in St. Petersburg, modestly staying in the background, as they have learned to do in their profession. When I realized there were numerous stories waiting to be told about the ways literary translation and publishing worked to make foreign literary works available to Russian readers, I decided to write a book based on the testimonies of the leading Soviet literary translators and editors.

I realized I made the right decision when news of my project started to travel. St. Petersburg translators started introducing me to each other, suggesting their lists of people to whom I should talk. In the course of our interviews, each translator would think of someone who would "remember things better." The field of my research eventually, and quite naturally, extended to Moscow, and three brilliant Muscovites generously shared their memories and ideas with me, making an invaluable contribution to this book. The memories of the interviewed translators were sometimes contradictory, and their views of Soviet politics differed, but what united all these people was their passion for literature, their faith in the powers of literary translation, and their indomitable will, which guided them as they were trying to open the world of foreign literature up to Soviet readers.

Literary translations gained significance for the Soviet readership throughout the entire Soviet period from 1917 to 1991. The chosen political course of the country and later the Iron Curtain to a great degree precluded Soviet citizens from traveling abroad or establishing links with the Western world. In light of this, literary translations in the USSR were sometimes the only way to obtain knowledge about countries other than the Soviet Union. Western literatures were universally read and discussed; people would queue for hours outside bookstores in order to get a rare book; they borrowed them from friends to read overnight and then pass on to others waiting their turn. With freedom of movement and traveling limited, literary translations in many respects played the role of trips overseas, guidebooks, and maps, helping readers to visualize in detail what they could not get in reality. Foreign literature in translation, as Samantha Sherry observes, "not only represented an 'escape' from ideologically correct socialist realism, but was also a desirable object of cultural consumption. . . . Among the educated youth especially, foreign literature represented the idealised world culture of which they wished to be a part, and was treated as high culture rather than entertainment."[1] An annual subscription to literary periodicals like *Novyi mir*, which regularly published translations of modern Western writers and poets, was one of the first things arranged at the arrival of each year. As a child, I always knew that on the day the thick pale blue journal arrived, my parents would probably put me to bed much earlier, and from my bed I would secretly watch them sitting side by side, leaning over the open journal, pointing to this or that line now and then.

Literary translators in those days were perceived of as people of a completely different breed. First, they knew foreign languages—and knew them well. In the Soviet situation, where foreign languages were an obligatory component of a secondary school program, but the approach to language teaching was such that hardly anyone ever learned to speak them, translators produced an unusual effect simply by their extraordinary command of foreign languages. Second, due to their linguistic abilities and occupation, translators had better access to foreign literary sources. Sometimes it was translators who discovered foreign authors and eventually promoted their works for publication. Knowledge of languages and foreign literature contributed to the image of a translator as a person enjoying closer ties with the world beyond the Soviet border. This is why translators regularly attracted the close attention of controlling governmental institutions, which were aware of the latent threat that translators presented to the closed Soviet society.

Leningrad and Moscow were the main centers of literary translation in the Russian Soviet Federative Socialist Republic of the USSR. Moscow as the Soviet capital and Leningrad/St. Petersburg as the old tsarist capital both developed their translation and publishing traditions. Both cities had a great number of academic institutions and therefore were able to educate and train several generations of intellectuals, who later joined the community of literary translators. Some of these translators are still active in the field of translation; they continue to translate prose and poetry, and some of them teach translation at universities, thus passing their knowledge on to the next generations of translators.

When I was planning my first interviews, I thought it would be difficult to persuade the translators to meet me. I knew that most of them were extremely busy translating and teaching, and, to a certain degree, I was prepared for refusals. Yet the eagerness with which the translators responded to my request and the openness with which they spoke for hours, answering all my questions, opening up books for reference, quoting necessary passages, was a life-changing experience for me. Most of the translators invited me to their homes, setting their work and family matters aside for my sake. We would talk about translation, as the manuscripts they were translating at that time were lying open by our sides. Several months later, I would see these manuscripts in bookstores in the shape of translated books, and I would experience an acute sense of déjà vu while taking them into my hands. Distracting themselves from work, the translators gave me the most hearty welcome, treating me to cold drinks on hot summer days in St.

Petersburg or to dinners and tea during my research trip to Moscow in the time of the hardest January frosts, and we would talk until night fell over the city. Sometimes the translators would call or email me the next day, saying that they had realized there was another important thing I should know—and our conversations would continue. It was their time, the outstanding information they generously bequeathed to me, their patience with my at times artless questions, and their warm hospitality that breathed life into this book. The translators shared with me much more than information: they imparted to me the sense of the time, of the space, and of the rules that literary translation had to play by.

This book focuses on the literary translation activity in Moscow and Leningrad in the 1960s through the 1980s. Personal interviews made me aware of the degree of controversy in the literary translators' milieu of the 1960s to 1980s and the complexity of tasks and choices the translators faced in their work. Interviewing as a research method, however, also created a number of difficulties in the analysis and classification of the collected data. These difficulties primarily consisted in the human factor, the natural differences in attitude, life philosophy, educational background, and even the residence of the respondents, as Muscovites and Petersburg-ers/Leningraders demonstrated different views on the literary situation and translation industry of the Soviet period. Naturally, the data provided by translators of prose and poetry also varied, for the approaches, requirements, and translation tools in rendering prosaic and poetic texts differed.

When preparing for each interview, I always compiled two lists of questions: general and personal. The questions from the general list were designed to collect the data that would allow an unbiased description of the translation industry and its requirements in the 1960s through the 1980s. The usual questions that I addressed to all the interviewed translators in some form were the following:

1. How and why did you start to translate foreign literature?
2. When and how did you join the Union of Writers? At whose recommendation?
3. How aware of literary censorship were you? Have your translations ever been censored?
4. Did you always get to choose translation strategies in rendering liter-

ary texts? Have you ever been advised by editors, publishing houses, or controlling organs upon the way your translation should eventually look?

5. Did you know what Glavlit was? Were you aware of its reforms and the restrictions it imposed on publishing houses? Did it in any way affect your translation activity?

6. Did you mainly choose texts for translation yourself, or did you usually get yourself commissioned to do translations?

7. By what criteria were you guided when choosing texts for translation? Did you have a clear understanding of what type of literature would be approved for publication and what texts had no chance of seeing print?

8. Was there a difference between Moscow and Leningrad translators? Can we here talk about two different schools of translation?

Despite the fact that the translators worked under similar conditions and faced similar requirements, the answers to these questions sometimes contradicted each other. Thus, the answers to the questions related to censorship ranged from detailed descriptions of cases of relentless censoring of texts—which sometimes resulted in mitigations, rewording, and omissions—to the attempts of the interviewees to brush off the issue. There was a case when a translator refused me an interview upon hearing that it would include questions on censorship. This refusal I accepted with understanding, for I know that the fear this person experienced was not the fear of punishment or disapproval, but the fear of getting one's whole life ruined by flippant remarks, devalued by political prejudice, besmirched by neglect. By opening themselves up to my interest, the leading Russian translators of the twentieth and twenty-first centuries entrusted me with the history of their lives, which they were living under difficult circumstances—but they were living them in their love for literature and languages and their passion for translation. I take their readiness to share their life experience with me as a great honor, and I shall not here comment upon the translators' views on the political situation and literary activity in the Soviet Union, nor will I dispute their points. Instead of rendering the interviews in my words against the background of facts and numbers, I have decided to let the translators speak for themselves by quoting excerpts of their interviews where possible. The voices will vary in tone, but I hope this polyphony will be able to create if not a complete at least a realistic picture of what literary translation actually was in the last three decades of the Soviet epoch.

Indeed, literary translation under political constraints, as André Lefevere noted, is not done by translators "in a mechanistic universe in which they have no choice. Rather, they have the freedom to stay within the perimeters marked by the constraints, or to challenge those constraints by trying to move beyond them."[2] The Soviet translators, as we shall see, demonstrated great resourcefulness in their attempts to avoid the imposed restrictions. Cases of disobedience also took place in the Soviet translation practice; they ranged from the mere choice of politically inconvenient literature for translation to open protests against censorship.

The list of personal questions that I asked each translator varied depending on the translations that had been made by each particular interviewee. Classical poetry, contemporary prose, political essays, magical realism, fairy tales—the genres of translated texts and individual approaches to translation prompted my questions for each translator. My research curiosity was not the only reason for asking individual questions. At a very early stage of my research, I realized that this book would become a story of love: of the passion of the translators and editors for their work and their desire to share their knowledge of literature with readers. This wish of translators and editors resulted in publications of the most controversial and politically inconvenient literary works. The ways of rendering translated texts were determined by the political and social situation in the Soviet Union at that time, for, as Edwin Gentzler and Maria Tymoczko observe, "Translation . . . is not simply an act of faithful reproduction, but, rather, a deliberate and conscious act of selection, assemblage, structuration, and fabrication—and even, in some cases, of falsification, refusal of information, counterfeiting, and the creation of secret codes. In these ways translators, as much as creative writers and politicians, participate in the powerful acts that create knowledge and shape culture."[3] The cited quotation holds true for the Soviet translators: the very selection of a literary work for translation was not only a literary but also a strategic and a political decision. Such decisions could have adverse effects on the translator's or editor's image and his/her career prospects. Cases of retention of information, including rephrasing, omitting elements of translated texts, or publication of abridged versions, were also not infrequent in the Soviet translation practice, which was subject to the well-developed system of literary control.

Before taking a closer look at literary translation and publishing in the Soviet Union in the second half of the twentieth century, I devote CHAPTER 1 to the description of the general problematic of a closed society, its features, and the ways in which the living principles of a closed society affect translation practices, including selection of literary texts, translation choices, editing, censoring, and publishing. Setting the stage for the detailed study of translation practices in the Soviet Union, chapter 1 dwells on examples of literary translation projects in closed societies of various types of totalitarianism and monarchy. Special attention is given to the terminology employed in the book: loose definitions of the term *ideology* and the psychological inconvenience it regularly creates are able, in my view, to lower the productivity of the multicultural research dialog. This is why I feel the need to complement the term *ideology* with the term *closed society* as understood and described by Karl Popper. This term might prove useful in describing political contexts, as the parameters of the closed society clearly defined by Popper will facilitate the assessment of the degree of control of the state over the activities of its citizens.

CHAPTER 2 gives a survey of the forms censorship and political control took in Russian publishing throughout the centuries. This chapter is important to demonstrate the historical continuity in the use of the main methods of control and intimidation of writers, translators, and publishers in Russia. The system of supervision of literature and surveillance of writers and translators was the legacy of the Russian Empire, the censoring scheme and methods later borrowed and incorporated by the Soviet system. The chapter describes state approaches to the control of literature from the mid-sixteenth century through the beginning of the twentieth century. The examples used in the chapter include cases of censorship and political pressure on such world-renowned Russian writers as Pushkin, Gogol, Dostoyevsky, Tolstoy, and Chekhov.

CHAPTER 3 describes the means of control and subordination that prevailed in the Soviet Union and that affected the course of the evolution of Soviet publishing, literature, and literary translation. Special attention is devoted to the rapid development of controlling organs, which in a very short time united into a complex system of control of all publications. Apart from numerous prescriptions circulated by censoring bodies, publications were also supposed to conform to the main principles of socialist realism, which limited the choice of subjects, attitudes, and approaches to literature.

CHAPTER 4 focuses on the role of literature and translation in the Soviet Union. The active investment of the Soviet Union in literature was motivated both socially and politically. The readers' needs for emotional and aesthetic comfort were increasing, as the state was depriving the citizens of the religion and lifestyle they were accustomed to; at the same time the state saw literature as a mark of national pride and a means of achieving superiority over other states. Literature as a part of the state political program thus became the object of particularly close control. The conflicting tendencies of internationalism and nationalism in literature resulted in multiple literary disputes, which sometimes affected the reputation of translators of foreign literature. Nonetheless, the profession of the literary translator remained attractive to many young people, who made active attempts to enter the field of Soviet literary translation. The state-initiated rise of literary associations in the 1950s contributed to the education of several new generations of literary translators, many of whom attended literary translation seminars chaired by reputed translators. The chapter gives special attention to translation seminars as a special phenomenon of the Soviet culture. Organized officially by local sections of the Union of Writers, translation seminars soon acquired a semiofficial nature, turning into close circles of friends and fellow thinkers.

CHAPTER 5 dwells on the Soviet publishing system and the conditions it offered to literary translators. The scheme of commissioning language specialists to translate texts was combined with the system of individual applications to publishing houses in order to get a translation project approved. The success of individual applications depended to a great degree on the applicant's reputation and publishing history, as well as on his/her membership in the Union of Writers. The chapter studies the requirements of the Union of Writers, the terms and conditions of contracts translators signed with publishing houses, and the difference in literary opportunities in Moscow and Leningrad.

CHAPTER 6 is completely devoted to poetry and poetic translation in the Soviet Union. Poetry traditionally played an important role in Russian culture, and this is why poetry translation attracted the attention of many talented professionals of the twentieth century. Poetry was actively translated not only from major European languages but also from languages of limited circulation, spoken both in the Soviet Union and beyond its borders. Translations from languages of limited circulation encouraged the use of interlinear trots, the active use of which contributed to the popular philosophy of the translator's creative freedom. At the same time, the use of interlinear trots increased the volumes of translated poetry, strengthened the friendly ties between the living poets and their Russian translators, and became an important part of the literary experience of young translators.

The role of censorship and the ways censorship affected literary translation are carefully studied in CHAPTER 7. The absence of clear requirements and the lack of understanding of the system of subordination increased the sense of insecurity and encouraged self-censorship. Despite the lack of clear guidelines, translators and their editors were aware of the reasons for potential rejections. The chapter divides the reasons for publication delay or rejection into three groups: the personal background of authors, contents of literary works, and literary styles. The contents of literary works are studied by subject, namely, political, sexual, religious, national, and anti-Soviet.

CHAPTER 8 is dedicated to the issue of translation activism in the Soviet Union, which took place under the described circumstances. Translation activism manifested itself in different ways, sometimes taking the form of open resistance. However, the mere engagement with literary translation and the decision to mediate Western thought and foreign philosophies should be looked upon here as activism and an act of courage. Translators, editors, and commentators worked together to ensure the publication of new books and promotion of new writers and poets and to create a special space of resistance inhabited by fellow thinkers.

Six of the eight chapters include quotes from interviews with ten Moscow and Leningrad/St. Petersburg literary translators; five chapters are specially structured around these interviews. Short biographies of translators, editors, writers, and critics are listed in appendix B. However, I would like to start my book with the biographies of the ten literary professionals who shared their memories and experiences with me. The stories of these people made the spirit of this book, and it is only fair that their names open the narrative.

ANDREEV, VIKTOR NIKOLAEVICH (b. July 24, 1948). Viktor Andreev is a poet, writer, translator from Spanish, and member of the Union of Writers. He is famous for his translations of prose and poetry of Julio Cortázar; stories of Jorge Luis Borges and Gabriel García Márquez; and poetry of César Vallejo, Miguel Ángel Asturias, Antonio Machado, Miguel Hernández, Rafael Alberti, Juan Ramón Jiménez, and Ramón María del Valle-Inclán. Viktor Andreev lives in St. Petersburg.

BESPALOVA, LARISA GEORGIEVNA (b. January 1, 1933). Larisa Bespalova is a translator, editor, and member of the Union of Writers. She translated *Animal Farm* by George Orwell; *A Handful of Dust* by Evelyn Waugh; *A Gathering of Old Men* by E. G. Gaines (in tandem with Ekaterina Korotkova); *The Leaning Tower* by K. A. Porter; *The Three Dumas* (original title *Les trois Dumas*) by André Maurois; essays by Truman Capote; and stories by Virginia Woolf, Saul Bellow, O. Henry, Agatha Christie, Flannery O'Connor, William Faulkner, and F. Scott Fitzgerald. For fifteen years, Larisa Bespalova worked as an editor for the leading publishing house Molodaia Gvardiia; later she was employed as an editor by *Novyi mir* journal, where she worked for another sixteen years. As an editor of the publishing house and the journal, she edited publications of the works of Kurt Vonnegut, William Faulkner, and Robert Penn Warren. Larisa Bespalova is the widow of the poet, translator, and literary critic Vladimir Kornilov (1928–2002), a famous dissident, with whom she shared the hard years of persecution. She lives in Moscow.

GOLYSHEV, VIKTOR PETROVICH (b. April 26, 1937). Viktor Golyshev is a translator, specialist in American and British literature, and member of the Union of Writers. He is known for his brilliant translations of the cutting-edge novels *Light in August* by William Faulkner, *One Flew over the Cuckoo's Nest* by Ken Kesey, *1984* by George Orwell, *All the King's Men* by Robert Penn Warren, *Breakfast at Tiffany's* by Truman Capote, *The Day of the Locust* by Nathanael West, *Set This House on Fire* by William Styron, *Pulp* by Charles Bukowski, and *Amsterdam* and *On Chesil Beach* by Ian McEwan. The younger generation of the Russian readers is indebted to Viktor Golyshev for *Harry Potter and the Order of Phoenix,* which he translated in tandem with Vladimir Bobkov and Leonid Motylev. Viktor Golyshev is the son of the famous Russian translator Elena Golysheva, who introduced Russian readers to several novels by Graham Greene, *The Roots of Heaven* by Romain Gary, *The Ides of March* by Thornton Wilder, *The Human Comedy* by William Saroyan, and *The Old Man and the Sea* by Ernest Hemingway, and who, as well as her son, was a living lesson in courage for her selection of literature for translation.

Viktor Golyshev remains an active translator of modern prose. He lives and works in Moscow.

IVANOVSKII, IGNATII MIKHAILOVICH (April 1, 1932–August 16, 2016). Ignatii Ivanovskii was a writer, poet, playwright, translator from English and Swedish, and member of the Union of Writers. He was a student of the famous Russian translator of Dante and Shakespeare Mikhail Lozinskii and a friend of poet Anna Akhmatova. Ignatii Ivanovskii is a laureate of the prize of the Swedish Academy for his translations of Carl Bellman; he was also an honorary member of the Swedish Bellman Society. His other translations from Swedish include poems by Gustav Fröding and Nils Ferlin. He also translated English and Scottish ballads; his translations of Robin Hood ballads as well as his translations of Robert Louis Stevenson's poems became the favorite readings learned by heart by several generations of Russian-speaking youth. His other translations from the English language include the poetry of Robert Burns, George Gordon Byron, Percy Bysshe Shelley, and John Keats; he also translated the complete cycle of Shakespeare's sonnets. Ivanovskii is the author of the unique versification of the complete text of the Bible (8,300 poetic lines) and versifications of the sacral texts of other religions. Until his last day, he worked on the translations of these versifications into English. He is the author of the book of memoirs *The Stage Horse*, which got its title from the famous quote of Aleksandr Pushkin that called the translator "the stage horse of enlightenment." In his memoirs, Ivanovskii spoke about the famous translators of the twentieth century and described his personal experience as a literary translator.

KOMAROVA, IRINA BENEDIKTOVNA (b. January 2, 1933). Irina Komarova is a member of the Union of Writers; she is known as the translator of *The French Lieutenant's Woman* by John Fowles (in tandem with Meri Bekker) and *Ann Vickers* by Sinclair Lewis (in tandem with Meri Bekker and Natalia Rakhmanova), as well as stories by Alice Munro, Nathaniel Hawthorne, Rudyard Kipling, Henry James, Edith Wharton, and Daphne du Maurier. She also translated poetry, including poems by Walter Scott and Langston Hughes. Irina Komarova is famous for her unparalleled Russian translations of the poetry of Ogden Nash, with whom she corresponded until his death. She maintained a long friendship with John Fowles, with whom she started to correspond when working on her translation of *The French Lieutenant's Woman*. Irina Komarova has worked all her life as an editor in Leningrad publishing houses and now lives and works in St. Petersburg.

KVIATKOVSKAIA, MAIIA ZALMANOVNA (b. May 9, 1931). Maiia Kviatkovskaia is a poet-translator from French, Spanish, Portuguese, and English and a member of the Union of Writers. She translated the complete works of the great French libertine poet Théophile de Viau. Maiia Kviatkovskaia is widely known for her translations of the poetry of Luis de Góngora, Luís Vaz de Camões, François de Malherbe, José Asunción Silva, and Juan Clemente Zenea. She also translated the poetry of Edgar Allan Poe, Félix Lope de Vega, Jean-Baptiste Racine, Jean de La Fontaine, Paul Verlaine, Jules Laforgue, Rubén Darío, and Germain Nouveau. She lives and works in St. Petersburg.

STEPANOV, SERGEI ANATOL'EVICH (b. December 21, 1952). Sergei Stepanov is actively engaged in poetic translation from the English language. He is a member of the Union of Writers and translator of the poetry of John Donne, W. B. Yeats, T. S. Eliot, Rudyard Kipling, Wilfred

Owen, Robert Frost, and Thom Gunn. He made the complete translation of William Blake's *Songs of Innocence and Experience* into Russian and the complete cycle of Shakespeare's sonnets. He is the author of the monograph *Shekspirovy sonety, ili Igra v igre* (Shakespeare's sonnets, or A game in a game). Stepanov lives in St. Petersburg. Apart from his engagement as a translator, he also teaches literary translation to university students.

STREBLOVA, INNA PAVLOVNA (b. January 24, 1939). Inna Streblova is a great-granddaughter of Anna and Petr Gansen, Russian translators of Scandinavian literature who were famous for their translation of the complete collection of Andersen's fairy tales. Streblova has translated from Danish, Swedish, Norwegian, German, and English. Among her most successful translations are works by Ricarda Huch, Adam Oehlenschläger, and Hermann Broch and children's stories by Astrid Lindgren. She chaired the German translation seminar at the Leningrad Union of Writers in the 1980s. Among her twenty-first-century translations is *The Girl Who Played with Fire* by Stieg Larsson. Inna Streblova lives in St. Petersburg.

WITKOWSKY, EVGENII VLADIMIROVICH (b. June 18, 1950). Evgenii Witkowsky is a translator, poet, fiction writer, editor, and literary critic known for his daring dissident activity in the Soviet times. He is editor-in-chief of the publishing house Vodoley Publishers. He is also a member of the Union of Writers. Evgenii Witkowsky is the founder of the unique website *Vek perevoda* (The age of translation).[4] Defining his profession as that of "translation historian," Witkowsky regularly edits and publishes anthologies of poetic translations, including such famous publications as the series of volumes of *Vek perevoda* (The age of translation), *Strofy veka* (Stanzas of the age), *Sem' vekov frantsuzskoi pojezii v russkikh perevodakh* (Seven centuries of French poetry in Russian translation), and *Sem' vekov angliiskoi poezii* (Seven centuries of English poetry). As a translator, Witkowsky is universally known for his versatility. An exceptionally prolific translator with an active knowledge of German, English, French, Italian, Portuguese, Dutch, Danish, Gaelic, and Afrikaans, Witkowsky has translated Christopher Smart, Robert Southey, Rudyard Kipling, Luís Vaz de Camões, Fernando Pessoa, Rainer Maria Rilke, Theodor

Kramer, Arthur Rimbaud, Paul Valéry, Duncan Ban Macintyre, Iain MacGilleEathain, Dirk Opperman, Gerbrand Bredero, and many others. Witkowsky is a founder of his own translation school; a number of Russian-speaking translators from all across the world recognize him as their teacher. Many of Witkowsky's translations are presented in the recent book of his translations *Vechnyi slushatel': Sem' stoletii poezii v perevode Evgeniia Vitkovskogo* (The eternal listener: Seven centuries of European poetry in the translations of Evgeniy Witkowsky). He lives and works in Moscow.

YASNOV, MIKHAIL DAVYDOVICH (b. January 8, 1946). Mikhail Yasnov is a writer, poet, translator, and member of the Union of Writers. Yasnov is actively engaged in translating French poetry: Guillaume Apollinaire, Jacques Prévert, Paul Verlaine, Paul Valéry, Jules Laforgue, Jean Cocteau, Eugène Ionesco, Maurice Carême, and Michel Deguy. He also translates children's literature and has published his translations of Breton fairy tales and ballads, French children's poetry, and fairy tales by Vercors, Claude Roy, Pierre Gripari, and Jean-Luc Moreau. Mikhail Yasnov is a laureate of the Prix Maurice Wachsmacher for his translation of the Apollinaire collection of stories *L'enchanteur pourrissant. Le poète assassiné.* Mikhail Yasnov has also translated from Swedish and Romanian, as well as Estonian, Latvian, Moldavian, Nenets, and other languages of the former Soviet Union. He is the author of seven books of original poetry and over sixty books of poetry and prose for children. As an editor and literary scholar, he has compiled several anthologies, including Belgian, French, and Quebec poetry collections; he has also compiled a book of translations of Cyrano de Bergerac's prose and the 150th jubilee anthology collection of translations of Arthur Rimbaud's poetry. In 2011, Yasnov was awarded a Chekhov literary prize for his contribution to Russian literature. He lives and works in St. Petersburg.

CHAPTER 1

THE CLOSED SOCIETY AND ITS LITERARY TRANSLATION PRACTICES

L iterature has been an integral part of the stereotypical image of Russia for more than a century. The traditional literary associations with Russia, however, are the classical Russian works of the nineteenth and beginning of the twentieth century. With Tolstoy, Dostoyevsky, and Chekhov universally known to the international reader, most Russian literature of the twentieth century often remains obscure. Revolutionary changes in Russian society deeply affected the political situation and social geography of the world, but their domestic effect was equally strong. Changes in the form of state rule and social order had their impact on all spheres of the public life, including literature, creative writing, and translation. The Russian literature of the Soviet period enjoyed less world popularity due to the cultural situation in Soviet Russia, its strained relations with the West, and the political inability of Soviet writers and poets to publish abroad. Of the twentieth-century Soviet writers who are well familiar to the general international reader, one can mention three Nobel Prize winners—Boris Pasternak, Aleksandr Solzhenitsyn, and Joseph Brodsky—all of whom were politically persecuted in their home country. Two of them—Pasternak and Brodsky—actively engaged in the translation of foreign literature, as they were unable to publish their original works in their home country.

The massive influx of talented and well-educated specialists into literary translation was a distinctive feature of the Soviet period in Russia. Literary translation was often looked upon as a last resort and a steady source of income for people of letters. Generations of Soviet schoolchildren, including the author of this book, were repeatedly admonished by their frightened teachers of Russian literature that Pasternak was not a writer or a poet, but "only" a translator. World literature—from ancient literary texts to contemporary works—arrived throughout the century in translations made by the best writers and poets: Valerii Briusov, Konstantin Bal'mont, Kornei Chukovskii, Marina Tsvetaeva, Anna Akhmatova, Boris Pasternak, Georgii Shengeli, and Mikhail Zenkevich. This literary translation heritage set high standards for new generations of Soviet literary translators, who invariably looked up to the achievements of their distinguished older colleagues.

Whereas the nineteenth century is known to the world as the golden age of Russian literature, the twentieth century in Soviet Russia may well be called the golden age of literary translation. The rapid development of translation coincided, strikingly, not with a time of freedom and the creative opportunities that it might offer, but with years of oppression and fear. And the stronger the fear for one's life and future, the more acute was the desire for self-expression and the longing for difference, for an alternative reality that was often depicted in the works of foreign poets and writers. The literature and translation situation in the Soviet Union falls in line with Maria Tymoczko's observation that "translations are subject to somewhat different rules and expectations from indigenous works of the native literature, being potentially exempt from some of the (oppressive) rules and norms that govern most elements of the literary system."[1] Translation as a source of income and a means of artistic survival became one of the main occupations of the people of letters in the Soviet Union. The tremendous demand for translated literature sustained a well-developed literary translation industry, which set extremely high requirements for translations.

Translation practices in the Soviet Union will therefore be studied here in the context of the political and social situation and the beliefs, fears, and prejudices of Soviet society. And despite the temptation to resort to the term *ideology* at this point, I shall abstain from using it in

this context. Quite the contrary, I shall devote some time here to showing that the overuse of this term can divert the attention of researchers
and their readers from their goals. I am convinced that closer boundar-
ies must be set for the term *ideology* in order to limit the contexts of its
employment. In this terminological revision, I am solely guided by the
intention to make the results of my research useful for further application in classification, comparative analysis, and statistics.

The term *ideology* has been given a variety of definitions, which at
times contradict each other. In his comprehensive study on ideology,
Teun A. Van Dijk attributes the definition of ideology as "a system of
wrong, false, distorted or otherwise misguided beliefs" to Marxist legacy. Van Dijk also draws attention to semantic exclusion contained in
the term *ideology:* "Ours is the Truth, Theirs is the Ideology."[2] The opposition of likeness and otherness, local and foreign often links the term
ideology with politics. The political slant of the term is also pointed out
by María Calzada-Pérez, who ascribes it to Marxist tradition and the
connection of ideology with political domination.[3] Yet Calzada-Pérez
also defines ideology as "a vehicle to promote or legitimate interests of a
particular social group (rather than a means to destroy contenders)," as
"a set of ideas which organize our lives and help us understand the relationship to our environment," and, eventually "the set of ideas, values
and beliefs that govern a community by virtue of being regarded as the
norm."[4] It is notable that these three vectors defined by Calzada-Pérez
are socio-oriented, as she describes ideology as a system of ideas, values,
and beliefs shared by a social group. Van Dijk also actively points out
the social aspect of ideologies, considering them the basis of social rep-
resentations shared by members of a group, identifying them as social
belief systems, and applying a multidisciplinary approach to the studies
of ideology in terms of social cognition, society, and discourse.[5]

Such social and sociolinguistic definitions of ideology make it possible to achieve greater objectivity in translation research. The abovementioned occasional political slant of the term *ideology,* however, seems
extremely undesirable for its ability to create unnecessary connotations
that deprive the word of its terminological quality. This is why in this
book, political definitions of ideology, which might involve pejorative
connotations, will give way to social and sociolinguistic approaches.

By *ideology* I mean the tacit assumptions, beliefs, and value systems that are shared collectively by a social group and that are relevant to the maintenance of power structures within a given language community.[6] Within the field of ideology, translation might be not purely the manipulation of the text, but rather the manipulation of the reader and public opinion. The ideology within which translation is performed determines the translator's approach to the text and the decisions he/she makes in rendering the contents and style of the translated work. But whatever nature the governing ideology might have, no translation, like no exchange of culture, can be free: "there are always economic and ideological interests at play in decisions about what cultural elements are worthy of translation."[7]

This determination of "worthiness" does not solely target manipulation of the reader and the public opinion; choosing texts for translation implies deciding upon the structure of the cultural capital and, ultimately, upon the target culture structure.[8] As Gideon Toury noted, translation starts with "the observation that something is 'missing' in the target culture which should have been there and which, luckily, already exists elsewhere."[9] Therefore the decision regarding worthiness of the original depends on the readiness of the receiving language community to embrace the difference the translation might offer. In case the difference offered by the original endangers the accepted ideology, its chances of being determined worthy of translation and thus joining the realm of cultural capital are considerably lower. This confrontation of the receiving culture with another, different way of looking at life and society was described by André Lefevere as "potentially threatening."[10] The way the receiving culture perceives and reacts to the potential threat is determined by the sociopolitical openness of the receiving language community.

Actively used in modern literary and translation studies and well defined by sociologists and political scientists, the term *ideology* evokes yet a different set of associations with the representatives of different cultures. Initially applied to history, the term *ideology* has expanded so much in scale that Daniel Bell was prompted to observe, in his seminal book *The End of Ideology,* that it is so vast one can hardly "make one's way through this bramble bush."[11] In the Russian language, seventy years of communist rule also made their contribution to the change of the semantic structure of the word *ideology*. The difference becomes clear in a comparison of Russian dictionaries and encyclopedias published at different times. The *Slovar' sovremennogo russkogo literaturnogo iazyka* (Dictionary of the modern Russian literary language) published in 1956 (that is, three years after the death of Stalin) defines ideology as "a system of viewpoints, ideas, opinions that characterize a particular society, a particular class, or a political party."[12] The examples given in the entry are taken from the biography of Vladimir Lenin, and they illustrate the usage of such phrases as *socialist ideology* and *bourgeois ideology*. The *Bol'shaia sovetskaia entsiklopediia* (Big Soviet encyclopedia) of 1972 points out the juxtaposition of Marxist-Leninist and bourgeois ideologies and their "deadly feud," which lies in the basis of Marxism-Leninism. The encyclopedia defines ideology as the "theoretical basis of the communist movement,"[13] which directly links the term *ideology* with the semantic fields *communism* and *socialism*. Enhanced throughout the decades by active use of the term *ideology* in the Soviet context, the association became fixed in the minds of Russian language speakers. The *Bol'shoi rossiiskii entsiklopedicheskii slovar'* (Big Russian encyclopedic dictionary) of 2005 indicates, for instance, that "the term *ideology* is often used for defining a false, delusive, detached from reality type of consciousness."[14]

This historical distortion of the semantic structure of an initially neutral term not only makes the usage of the word *ideology* difficult for a set of contexts, it also creates difficulties in the cross-cultural communication of researchers. Whereas Western researchers mainly employ the word *ideology* terminologically, Eastern European researchers may feel unreasonably targeted, reacting to the term *ideology* as to a marker of their historic and cultural past and a negative experience associated with the society they are representing. This antiterminological emotiveness of the word traditionally used as a term was pointed out by Bell as early as the beginning of the 1960s, when he described ideology as "not simply a *weltanschauung*, a cultural worldview, or a mask for interests, but a historically located belief system that fused ideas with passion, sought to convert ideas into social levers, and in transforming ideas transformed people as well. When it becomes a striking force, ideology looks at the world with eyes wide shut, a closed system which prefabri-cates answers to any questions that might be asked."[15] In this regard, the active use of the word *ideology* within a field other than history and pol-itics is able to create uneasiness among the researchers of different cul-tural backgrounds. World science will barely benefit if the researchers whose countries faced totalitarianism and oppression of any sort in the twentieth and twenty-first centuries felt, in Bell's terminology, recently "transformed" from above. The discreetness I am calling for is especially important for all types of linguistic research, where every word is able to function both as an object of research and a powerful tool.

I foresee objections to my call: indeed, research papers usually indicate quite clearly the type and orientation of ideologies described. For exam-ple, some researchers use the term *communist ideology;* others employ such formulas as *translation under the communist/totalitarian/Nazi/etc. regime.*[16] Lawrence Venuti regularly uses the term *ideology* in his semi-nal book *The Translator's Invisibility*—and almost invariably with adjec-tives: *nationalist ideology, bourgeois ideology, racial ideology, patriarchal ideology, feminist, assimilationist ideology.*[17] The use of these formulas is usually well grounded and contextually motivated; nonetheless, the vari-ety of meanings the word *ideology* acquires once used with an adjective threatens to deprive it of its terminological quality. As one can see from the examples, the majority of connotations generated by adjectives are negative, which implies the antithesis of viewpoints and brings us back to Van Dijk's formula, which defines ideology as an alien feature.[18]

Another question that arises in this regard is the degree of general-ization provided by such formulas as *communist ideology, totalitarian ideology, Soviet ideology,* and so on. Indeed, each of the above-listed designations is able to define notions that can at times prove controver-sial or even contradict each other. For example, the word combination *communist ideology* will effectuate different semantic components when applied in relation to Russia and to China; *totalitarian ideology* of the Third Reich and in the Soviet Union under Stalin, although possessing obvious similarities, had distinctive features and at times quite different manifestations. If we consider the history of the Soviet Union, do we apply the term *totalitarian ideology* to all the years of its existence, or do we use the term *totalitarian ideology* only until the death of Stalin, in

1953, and use the term *Soviet ideology* for a wider historic period? Even the term *Soviet ideology* is far from being definite, because within the USSR, Soviet ideology took different shapes in different socialist republics in each given time span; the difference between Soviet ideologies proves even stronger if we take a closer look at their manifestations in the Warsaw Pact countries. Therefore, additional adjectival specification of the term *ideology,* in my view, leads to blurring of the term, rather than the desired clarification. Adjectival specifications are quite appropriate in describing particular contexts and discourses, as in the quoted works, but they may be misleading in attempts to draw general conclusions.

This necessity to generalize the collected data makes us reconsider the ways the same ideology and regime can be described. Even though different branches of research and science can come very close together, the use of traditional historical terms in linguistic research can prove a distraction from the research objectives. The aim of a translation scholar consists in researching translation trends, policies, and strategies, as well as the activity of translators under different social conditions. The definition of the type of regime by far remains a peripheral task; however, the application of such fuzzy terms as *communist, Soviet,* and *totalitarian* forces researchers to engage in drawing political conclusions. And, therefore, since the studies of social conditions that motivated translation strategies and activities are an integral part of research, the preferred terminology should originate from sociology and sociolinguistics, rather than from history and politics, which provide controversial definitions to seemingly clear terms.

This clarity and uniformity of the terminological nomination of social and political situations is extremely important now that a substantial amount of knowledge has been collected on the issue of translation practices under various social conditions. Impressive statistics and case studies performed by translation scholars, apart from their illustrative and educational function, can play yet another role in the development of translation knowledge—that is, in the establishment of regularities between social contexts and translation practices. Classification of collected data again brings us back to the issue of terminology in which the data will be described and classified.

Therefore, in addition to the term *ideology* we need another term that can embrace the frequently used and overlapping adjectives *communist/ totalitarian/Soviet/etc.* Taking sociology as a point of departure, I find the terms *open society* and *closed society* much more useful for sorting and classifying the collected linguistic material. The terms *open society* and *closed society* were initially coined in 1932 by Henri Bergson in his book *Les deux sources de la morale et de la religion* (*The Two Sources of Morality and Religion*).[19] In 1945, the binary opposition of open and closed societies was carefully dwelt upon by Karl Popper in his groundbreaking work *The Open Society and Its Enemies*. The distinction between open and closed societies consists in the freedom of individual activity, which members of the given society are able or unable to practice. Whereas in an open society individuals are confronted with personal decisions, the closed society delegates authority to institutions, which "leave no room for personal responsibility."[20] Popper characterizes closed societies as rigid and reluctant to change, even where changes are performed in order to provide for the vital needs, for closed societies are "not based upon a rational attempt to improve social conditions."[21] Alongside a complex system of taboos regulating all aspects of social life, members of a closed society are provided with a set of scenarios they are supposed to follow; thus, "the right way" is predominantly determined and seldom disputed. The at times seeming individual responsibility is still part of the collective activity, which has little to do with personal freedom. The lack of personal freedom in a closed society is actively compensated by *tribalism*, which, in Popper's view, holds individuals together "by semi-biological ties—kinship, living together, sharing common efforts, common dangers, common joys and common distress" and prevents the attempts of individuals to rise socially, as individuals in open societies do.[22]

In his detailed account of Hegelian philosophy, Popper lists the fundamental ideas employed by authoritarian movements in human history, which will prove very useful in our studies of translation, text manipulation, and manipulation of public opinion.

1. Nationalism as the incarnation of Spirit or Blood, which results in the domination of a state-creating nation or race.
2. The state as the natural enemy of all other states, asserting its existence in war.

3. The exemption of the state from any kind of moral obligation.

4. Collective utility as the sole principle of personal conduct.

5. The "ethical" idea of war and the elevated status of war, fate, and fame.

6. The creative role of the Great Man—an individual who is ascribed deep knowledge and great passion and is seen as an unchallenged authority.

7. The ideal of the heroic life full of dangers and struggle and of the "heroic man" as opposed to the petty bourgeois and his life of shallow mediocrity.[23]

It should be noted that closed societies may take different shapes, and the proportion of the listed features can vary from one closed society to another. The openness or closedness of a society does not directly follow from its self-identification: constitutionally declared democracy does not necessarily imply openness, just as monarchy does not always mean closedness. The extent of openness and closedness of a society can also vary at every stage of societal development, with the change of social and legal practices and the degree of accepted social freedoms. It is also true that adoption and further cultivation of at least one of these fundamental ideas by a society will eventually result in the adoption of the other ideas, for all of them are closely bound and mutually causal. However, it is quite clear that no society can be labeled completely open or completely closed: there will always be manifestations of the alternative form performed by those individuals and social groups that oppose the community's *status* quo. In this regard, Popper's list is extremely convenient for this research devoted to translation and language: free from the necessity to use political terminology and therefore express certain political judgments, I can solely concentrate on translation practices, using the items of Popper's list as reference points. Application of Popper's approach to translation studies can also be useful in establishing correspondences between the degree of closedness or openness of a society and the nature of its translation practices at each stage, the intensiveness of translation activism and resistance, and the types and genres of literary works preferred at different times. The neutrality of the term and the clarity of the description of features of a closed society will contribute

to the systematization of the collected data on translation under different conditions. By suggesting this approach I am far from calling it a
universal systematizing method; nonetheless, I think the development
of such a method is essential now that translation studies avail themselves of substantial material on the subject of translation and ideology.
I shall now go through all seven features of Popper's list and link them
to existing research on translation and ideology to demonstrate that a
projection of Popper's list onto translation would give us understanding
of the direct influence of social conditions over translation practices and
translators and would permit drawing parallels between different cases
that describe the interdependence of translation and ideology.

The idea of nationalism and the domination of a state-creating race,
for example, results in the growth of status of one nation, which in most
cases is but one of the multiple nations compiling an ethnos. Elevation
of a single nation involves elevation of a single national language, other
languages of the ethnos losing their status to the extent the elevated
language achieves dominance according to the asymmetric principle of
multilingualism. This linguistic dominance can result in the dominant
language acquiring the role of a lingua franca or even becoming the
high-status language in a diglossic situation.[24] This linguistic imperialism naturally gives rise to cultural imperialism in linguistic and nonlin-
guistic forms, as well as social imperialism relating to the transmission
of the norms and behavior of a model social structure. Among other
forms of manifestation, cultural imperialism can demonstrate itself in
literary translation.[25] In a situation of growing linguistic asymmetry, the
majority of literary works will in all probability be written in the dominant language, and translations will be primarily made into the dominant language as well. Translations into other languages of the community will be possible, but translations into the dominant language will
arrive earlier, their status will be better recognized, and the number of
translated versions performed by different translators and the number
of editions will be considerably higher.

In this regard, interesting statistics have been collected by Daniele
Monticelli, who observes that the preponderant share of literary translations made in Estonia after World War II was restricted to nineteenth-
century Russian literary classics and Russian-language writers of the

twentieth century. The share of translated Russian literature in Estonia exceeded 60 percent of all literary publications in some years of the 1950s, and with about a 10 percent share of translated Russian language literature of the Soviet period, there remained very little space left for Estonian-language literature and translations into Estonian. Monticelli comments upon the influence the Russian-language dominance exercised over the Estonian literary system: according to Monticelli, translations from Russian provided matrixes for Estonian literary works in order to bring Estonian literature in line with the canons of socialist realism, thus adopting "solid realistic positions," as an Estonian Communist Party official wrote in 1950.[26] The beginning of the fifties was also marked by what Monticelli calls the *erasure*, which involved a ban on a substantial part of original Estonian literature and many translations published in Estonian before the war.[27]

The perilous fate of Ukrainian literary translation in the Russian Empire (see chap. 2) and in the Soviet Union is closely linked with the efforts of the Ukrainian-speaking population to achieve recognition of Ukrainian as the official language. Despite the Ukrainian language gaining an official status in the Ukrainian Soviet Socialist Republic, it continued to be looked down upon by many Russian speakers, who saw it as a rural dialect of the Russian language. An egregious example of this rejection of the Ukrainian language took place in 1927, when the Russian writer Maksim Gor'kii, whose individual writings were genuinely respected by readers and whose endeavors in developing a Russian translation tradition and a corpus of high-quality translations are still highly appreciated in the country, openly demonstrated disbelief in the literary powers of Ukrainian. When a Ukrainian editor requested Gor'kii's permission to translate his novel *Mother* into the Ukrainian language, Gor'kii responded irritably: "It seems to be that the translation of this novel into the Ukrainian dialect . . . is also not necessary. I am very surprised by the fact that people setting the same goals not only affirm the difference of dialects—they try to make a dialect into a language, but also discriminate those Russians who are a minority in the area of this dialect."[28] Maksim Strikha correctly observes that this undisguised irritation of a respected Russian writer is mingled with a clear understanding of the nation-forming role translation historically played in Ukraine.[29]

Another example of the role of language and translation in the promotion of nationalistic ideas comes from the time of the French Revolution, when the National Constituent Assembly issued decrees in support of translation into local languages and salary increases for bilingual teachers. France enjoyed the granted freedom for a year; in 1791, the Jacobins called for a unified and centralized state, which resulted in the rise of monolingualism, which was supposed to ensure the ability of the peoples of France to communicate, and for the idea of universal education to be implemented.[30]

Nationalistic ideas and active promotion of one dominant language can combine with overt imitations of multilingualism and multiculturalism. Such attempts will be described in detail in the second part of this book, where I shall talk about literary translation in the 1960s through the 1980s in the Soviet Union. A historically earlier example is the notorious case of pseudotranslations into Russian of the works of a Kazakh poet, Dzhambul Dzhabaev (or just Dzhambul), in the 1930s in the Soviet Union. The involvement of celebrities from the national republics of the Soviet Union was a popular measure in the maintenance of the Soviet system and its widely propagated concept of multinationalism. The figure of Dzhambul fitted perfectly with the state policy: an aged Kazakh elder glorifying the Soviet state, the party officials, and especially Stalin. Dzhambul enjoyed popularity and was actively published and quoted, despite the fact that, although existing as an individual, Dzhambul was fictitious as a poet, his Russian translations being produced from manipulated or fictitious originals.[31]

Linguistic suspicion can also result from the aggression of the state upon other states and its belligerent policy. This linguistic suspicion consists in an apprehension of the effects foreign ideas and texts might have upon their readers, with this apprehension resulting in the close control of the form and content of these texts and the development of the system that would be able to supervise the process of text selection, translation, editing, and publication. These methods target prevention of ideas alien or hostile to the receiving language and its community. The approval of purism is generally clad in the myth of a special mission of the nation, its unique social, revolutionary, or religious role in the development of mankind. Active purist policy, for example, was a distinct feature of

Nazi Germany, which strongly objected to active penetration of ideas by means of foreign literature. As a booksellers' journal proclaimed in 1939, "In the years since the National Socialist revolution, German literature has been thoroughly cleansed, and all the elements alien to the German character have been eliminated. But today we are faced with a new development that in many cases tries, using the indirect route of foreign translated literature, to familiarize us with exactly the same negative values that we have just spent so much effort in removing from German literature."[32] The war imposed additional limitations on the import of literature; publication permissions were granted in accordance with their usefulness to the war effort.[33] This usefulness, in Ine Van Linthout's observation, was mainly limited to military propaganda and to creating a strategically convenient image of translated nations and literatures.[34]

The exemption of the state from any kind of moral obligation manifests itself in the impunity of the controlling organs in their approval or disapproval of foreign language texts offered for translation, their acceptance of already existing translations, and the dependence of this acceptance on social and political factors. Thus, for instance, the personality of the translator can become an important factor in the publishing process. Translators favored by authorities enjoy higher chances of getting their translations published, whereas other translators are assigned minor roles, and their position and income are unstable.

The exemption from moral obligations of a closed society manifests itself in the case of Johannes Semper, an Estonian translator whose tragic fate was described in detail by Monticelli. Once expelled from the Communist Party on accusations of cosmopolitism, Semper was never able to publish his translations again. His previous works were banned, his name removed from the histories of Estonian literature and inked over on title pages of existing publications.[35]

Released from the responsibility to account for its actions, the state acquires infinite power. Declaring its own inherent value, the closed society asserts its purpose in serving the nation, the collective. Collective utility therefore becomes a reference point for any personal decision or activity. In translation, collective primacy affects the individual methodology employed by translators. Literary and translation methods officially approved of by official institutions dominate other approaches.

Deviation from the prescribed methodology can result in general disapproval and even vilification of translators, which results in the inability of these translators to continue their literary practice. Guidance by collective utility can also result in the careful selection of subjects of original and translated literary works. Some subjects can be declared socially destabilizing, demoralizing, and dangerous. In the course of this book, we shall study multiple examples of this seeming social orientation of literary translation, as the Soviet system actively used literature for social manipulation. Literary translation shared the fate of original literature and was looked upon as a tool of social influence.

The "ethical" idea of war comes alongside the ideal of the heroic life full of dangers and struggle and of the "heroic man." This propaganda of ideas affects the selection of literary texts for translation: military subjects and descriptions of heroic deeds and courageous efforts are given preference. Stories of noble overcoming of hardship, poverty, and treason are also looked upon favorably. The extolled role of heroic actions and exaggeration of their frequency in everyday life contributes to the manipulation of public opinion by controlling institutions. The adopted literary pattern can later be used to argue against texts, methods, subjects, and translators who for some reason are considered threatening to the state. Any literary work, its contents, translation approach, or translator, can be labeled bourgeois, mediocre, underdeveloped, or even hostile to the society on grounds of nonconformity with the adopted ideals. Such labeling can also result into publication bans and individual persecutions.

The ideological demand for literary heroic images raised special interest in Shakespeare's *Coriolanus* in the 1920s in Italy. As Alessandra Calvani observes, the desire to exalt the grandeur and force of Rome and its heroes found its concrete implementation in *Coriolanus*, a "virile" man—the adjective *virile* actively used at the time, defining a feature desirable for a true citizen of the country.[36]

A demonstrative case of a translation ban for reasons of antiwar propaganda is described by Jonathon Green and Nicholas J. Karolides in their account of the perilous fate of Erich Maria Remarque's novel *All Quiet on the Western Front*. The novel faced its first ban in the author's native Germany, the grounds for the ban being those of collective utility:

in the beginning of the 1930s, National Socialists found the novel slanderous of Germany, and therefore demoralizing, depriving the Germans of their national spirit. As a result, all Remarque's works were consigned to bonfires. Whereas in Germany the ban was ascribed a collective purpose, the ban imposed on the Italian translation of the novel was motivated in a different way: in Italy, *All Quiet on the Western Front* was banned because of its antiwar propaganda.[37] Indeed, antiwar moods were extremely inconvenient for the Italian state in the 1930s, which are entered into Italian history as the years of its aggressive foreign policy, marked by the seizure of Ethiopia in 1935, Spanish intervention in 1936–39, and the signing the Pact of Steel in 1939. Therefore, the novel of Remarque clearly did not fall in line with the military activity of Italy and the buildup of the Mussolini dictatorship.

The history of the suppression of Byron's *Manfred* in Socialist Bulgaria described in detail by Vitana Kostadinova presents us with an example of a ban for an insufficiency of heroism in a book. In Kostadinova's view, the distorted image of Manfred owed a lot to the monograph by the Sofia University professor Konstantin Stefanov, who "declared Manfred a *Bolshevik* who undermined social order, religion, and culture, and had no respect for law, freedom of conscience, marital ties, or motherland."[38] Described in antisocial terms, the image of Manfred evoked apprehension in publishers, who preferred to abstain from publishing the work of such controversial content.[39]

The figure of the Great Man with unchallenged authority is seen as the sole possessor of ultimate truth in the closed society. Among other actions, approvals and bans of originals, translations, and translators can be done in the name of the symbolic figure, which might by the time have already lost its historic features. Curiously enough, the Great Man can be ascribed infinite knowledge in different fields, including literature, linguistics, translation, and publishing. The name of the Great Man can also be manipulated as the last resort in confrontations with persistent individuals (writers, translators, editors, publishers) who aspire to challenge the existing institutions and to remonstrate against criticism of their work. Attempts to dispute the power of the Great Man or to evoke doubts of his goodness are naturally suppressed by his adherents. This suppression can affect translation as well. For example, Brian James

Baer talks about the ban on staging the Russian translation of *Hamlet* in 1762, which was the year that Catherine II ascended the Russian throne in a coup. The subsequent murder of Catherine's husband, the crowned tsar Peter III, was treated as a nonevent by silent agreement of the coup participants. The subject of a royal murder in *Hamlet* could trigger associations with Catherine's rise and was therefore considered unwise for stage productions.[40]

Active implantation of images of Great Men by means of translation regularly took place in Soviet Ukraine. Whereas literary and scientific translation into Ukrainian was suffering a tremendous decline, Ukrainian translations of Marx, Engels, and Lenin, as well as proceedings of plenary sessions and congresses of the Communist Party, were duly made and circulated. It was these translations that were later declared the highest achievements of Ukrainian translation, and multiple brilliant literary translations were thus ignored at the official level.[41]

The figure of the Great Man does not necessarily imply a sole ruler; this formula of Popper can be used in defining a group of people or a class clad in great authority. Thus, for instance, an eighteenth-century Russian censor motivated the temporary ban on Swift's *Gulliver's Travels* by Swift's criticism of the whole class of state officials. This criticism, in his view, interfered with the public image of a statesman: "The author of the book tries to ridicule different court institutions, as, for example, he says quite acidly at page 305, that rope-jumping is done only by people of power."[42]

The listed examples demonstrate a direct proportional dependence of the degree of closedness of a society and the influence of the patronizing institutions over the selection of originals, control of translations, and distribution of translation orders among available literary translators. Patronizing institutions can take the shape of publishing houses, universities, and granting agencies, as well as writers' and translators' unions and governmental organizations specially created for control and guidance of literary activity within a community.[43] A closed society with a well-implemented system of the described fundamental ideas would possess a stronger network of patronizing institutions that would dictate its requirements for the form and content of literary translations.

The impact of ideology on translation and literature can take many shapes; active participation of the state in initiating translation and literary projects may target the maintenance of the governing ideology, as the promoted works employ favored subjects, use conventional language, or praise people, actions, or lifestyles officially approved of. However, strategies applied in translation, as with any discourse strategies, are never exclusively ideological and do not have the sole purpose of reproducing an ideology.[44] This is true even if the translator shares the governing ideology and genuinely believes in its worth. The engagement of the translator in the translation process is primarily introverted, text oriented, and language bound. A considerable number of text manipulations are performed unintentionally, the translator him-/herself being part of the receiving culture and the beliefs this culture is manifesting.

The influence of the closed society over its translation activity is never absolute, however strong its pursuit of absolute power might be. As Tymoczko points out, power can seldom be viewed without opposing forces that target its resistance and contestation.[45] In the hands of governing political powers, translation can be a significant tool for achieving social domination; however, at the same time, translation can be used by opposing forces and become a way of contesting and undermining this domination.[46]

Political and social activism of translators does not reduce itself to resisting the socially imposed literary limitations; activism can acquire different shapes depending on the social and cultural situation in the given language community and the personality of the translator. Tymoczko notes that a translator can exercise politicized and ethical agency on any level of translation choices.[47] These choices can vary from unconventional approaches to rendering the form and content of originals to the selection of literary originals, promotion of translations, interacting with editing and censoring institutions, writing prefaces and commentaries to published translations, and presenting translations and their authors at public occasions. The paths and shapes activism can take in the field of translation also fall in line with Popper's classification of fundamental ideas of closed societies. Thus, for example, in opposing nationalism, translators can choose to translate texts into the minority languages of the community. When translating from minority languages into the dominant language, translators intentionally demonstrate the difference of the translated original from the domestic literary and social practices. Such text foreignization can be a means of propagating minority languages, language variations, and cultures.[48]

A striking case of translation activism was described by Dimitris Asimakoulas, who made a detailed analysis of the Greek translations of Bertolt Brecht's works produced by Dionyses Divares in 1971 under the Greek military junta regime. Divares pays special attention to the translation of the Christmas message of Rudolf Hess and the speech by Hermann Göring on the crushing defeat of communism. In the original, these speeches are arranged in two columns—one containing the speech as such, and the other, the reconstructed meaning behind Nazi discourse. In rendering Brecht's design, the translator resorted to the use of sociolect code-switching. Thus, in Divares's translation the speech column is rendered in *katharevousa*, the purist variety of Greek championed by the junta. Conversely, the "reconstructed meaning" column was rendered in *dhimotiki*—the spoken variety of Greek.[49] Associated with religion and "high" culture, *katharevousa* gave way to *dhimotiki* by the 1960s, when a modified type of *dhimotiki* with elements of *katharevousa* was eventually made the language of public schooling. However, the Regime of the Colonels declared *katharevousa* to be the only acceptable and "educated" form of Greek.[50] By opposing the two language forms, the translation of Divares drew a bold parallel between the purist policy of the Greek junta and of the Nazi government.

As a closed society continues propagating its special mission and demonstrates reluctance to accept new ideas and forms of expression, translators can actively search for literary texts of considerable novelty both in form and content. Translators can also experiment with new forms of rendering the selected texts, thus avoiding traditional translation techniques. In this regard, the nineteenth-century Ukrainian translation of *Hamlet* made by Mikhail Staritskii is an interesting case of translation activism. The very selection of the play can be classified as a social action: Staritskii was translating *Hamlet* during the time when Ukraine fell within the scope of the imperial Ems edict, which suppressed publications in the Ukrainian language. Both the language of the translation and the undesirable political associations it was able to evoke made the translation unacceptable for publication, which became possible only after the derogation of the edict in 1881. The publication took place the next year, in 1882, presenting the Ukrainian reader with the translator's unconventional experimentation with the prosody and style of the original play. The bold experiments of Staritskii evoked controversial feelings that critics were never tired of expressing, even eighty years after the publication of the translation.[51]

Shakespeare's *Hamlet* historically is one of the literary works that regularly find themselves as the focus of political attention. As in the case of its ban in the Russian Empire during the rule of Catherine II, it was frequently used as a counterweapon in the political struggle by opposing forces. Thus, the Russian translation of *Hamlet* made by Boris Pasternak in the middle of the twentieth century was banned from the stage for several years in the Soviet Union. After its staging was eventually permitted, the play in Pasternak's translation enjoyed tremendous popularity with the Russian intellectuals: audiences broke into applause at the line "There is something rotten in the state of Denmark," taking it as an allusion to the situation in the USSR.[52]

Pasternak's translation of *Hamlet* implicitly channeled disagreement, thus evoking the stormy reaction of the audience. Interestingly enough, it was not the initial intention of the translator but rather the ultimate reaction of the target audience that contributed to the political image of the translation. This case successfully proves Van Dijk's statement that within an ideological communication, the way the discourse comes across and is interpreted is as important as the initial intention of the sender.[53]

A peculiar form of activism was described by Sibelan Forrester, who pointed out an unexpected rise of interest of Serbian and Croatian translators in twentieth-century Russian poetry, which took place in the 1970s and 1980s, when the image of the Soviet Union had already been tarnished and the popularity of Soviet literature had suffered a tremendous decline. This interest especially concerned the Soviet poet Vladimir Mayakovskii—a poet favored by the communist regime, extolled as the poet of the revolution, and officially chosen for compulsory reading at all levels of education. As a poet, Mayakovskii was literally imposed on readers; he was quoted on official occasions and so actively praised that it killed interest in his works better than censorship could. In 1970s and 1980s, however, as Forrester puts it, "Yugoslav readers . . . were not forced to read his work," which gave them a chance to find pleasure in his innovative style and futurist experimenting.[54] We can call such a phenomenon *rebounding translation activism,* with translators turning to the works of literature that were socially important in the past but have lost their influence and social role.

The exemption of the state from moral obligation can also be challenged by translators. The very decision of a translator to work with literary material unknown to or disapproved of by governing institutions indicates the readiness of this translator to take up responsibility. Throughout history, translators have been resolute in protecting their translations and the originals, as well as their individual literary and translation methods, in the face of danger coming from influential literary and political institutions. Translators are known to have signed political petitions and open letters in defense of fellow thinkers, as well as literary methods and approaches; they have insisted on the artistic merits of foreign works, writers, and poets they translated. Open protests against bans and interference of censors take place more rarely, for any rebellion is a comparatively rare manifestation—but the cases of Irina Komarova and Viktor Golyshev described in this book give us splendid examples of a translator resisting the publishing system and eventually winning the battle.

Selection and promotion of unconventional forms and subjects contest the idea of collective utility as the sole principle of personal conduct. The quest for new forms of self-expression and their representation in translation is an individual activity that targets the reconstruction of an alternative way of thinking. Unconventionality is therefore opposed to collective uniformity, which makes the translator's social position precarious in the face of potential collective disapproval of his/her activity. Selection of alternative subjects for literary translation rather than those automatically approved of by a closed society can also be taken as a form of translation activism. A curious way of fighting conventions and therefore promoting new forms and literary subjects is the intentional disguise of the translated literary texts as patriotic or socially oriented by equipping them with misleading prefaces and reviews, as well as with biographies of their authors. Thus, for instance, the popular four-volume edition of the works of Jack London in the Soviet Union had a lengthy preface, which described in detail the hardships Jack London faced in his life, the miseries of his childhood, his interest in the writings of Karl Marx, and the high opinion Maksim Gor'kii had of Jack London's writings.[55] The mention of Karl Marx, albeit in passing, was a popular means of securing the political reliability of the publication, which allowed publishers to promote works of controversial form and content. Take, for instance, *The Sea-Wolf*, which the same preface describes as the result of London's study of Marx and Nietzsche[56]—Marx mentioned here clearly in order to distract from the name of Nietzsche, as well as to justify the interest of the compilers toward the novel.

The figure of the Great Man can thus be used as a weapon against the adepts of his own teachings. Figures of Great Men are hard to shake even by the collective effort of translation activists; nonetheless, their images can be contested in the course of translation practices both in the choice of texts for translation and in the application of translation techniques. An interesting example in this regard was provided by Susanna Witt, who presented a case study of Boris Pasternak's translation of Goethe's *Faust* into Russian made in the beginning of the 1950s. The application of the "free" translation approach to Goethe's text allowed Pasternak to encode the name of Stalin into the demonic context of *Faust,* thus sending an encrypted message to his fellow thinkers.[57]

Translation activism, overt or covert, is always rooted in a personal dream of a different way of living, working, and creating. The choice of an alternative approach to translation, or a new author, or an unconventional subject indicates a desire for change. As Forrester puts it, "Translation works as a particularly strong way to locate and recreate one's own literary forebears and interlocutors."[58] In other words, we can see engagement in translation activity as a claim for freedom—and, consequently, as a claim for power.[59] At the same time, translation activism is exercised within the confines and priorities set by translators themselves. By making choices about values and institutions to support and to oppose, they also make choices about the translation strategies that will be applied to each text. In the following chapters we shall see this choice-making process as described by the Soviet literary translators who were actively involved in translation at that time and who are still living and working in the two Russian capitals at present. In describing the translators' activity, we shall mainly concentrate on the three parameters defined by Tymoczko as the determinative factors of the political agency exercised by translators: the locus of the action, the nature of the activist community, and the types of textual products involved.[60] I shall first speak about the political and social tendencies that determined the literary situation first in imperial Russia and then in the Soviet Union as the direct heir of the imperial legacy; after that I shall take a closer look at the Soviet literary translation community and the nature of the tasks the translators were allotted to do.

CHAPTER 2

CENSORSHIP AND THE RUSSIAN PUBLISHING SYSTEM THROUGH HISTORY

A well-developed system of censorship and political control existed in Russia long before the socialist revolution of the twentieth century. It was formed long before the turmoil of the October Revolution of 1917 and the selection of the political course by the Soviet government. The sequence of tragic events of the Soviet period gives an impression that the powerful machine of control was created to suit the needs of the initiators of the power shift. This image, though well rooted in the minds of many, is true only to an extent. It did not take the leaders of the October uprising much time and effort to incorporate the tsarist system of censorship and control into the new social conditions. The leaders of the Russian Revolution, who mainly came from a middle-class background and who had received a substantial education, had a good knowledge of tsarist policy and political measures; therefore, censorship and total control in the Soviet Union was not invented or newly introduced but was inherited from the old regime.

Well incorporated into the Soviet system of control, censorship was officially denied in the Soviet Union. Throughout the seventy years of Soviet power, historians and specialists in literature wrote and spoke a lot about censorship in tsarist Russia, as well as bourgeois and capitalist censorship abroad, but barely related the term to the realities of the domestic culture. This refusal to admit the existing cultural reality and dismissal of the tsarist heritage contributed to the popular opinion that it was the Soviet system that bred a monster the likes of which Russia had never seen before.

In fact, the first Russian document that legalized censorship and approved of its use was produced during the rule of Tsar Ivan IV (Ivan the Terrible) in 1551. A council of Russian bishops, summoned by the tsar, made one hundred decisions, which were listed in the volume entitled *Stoglav*.[1] The decisions mainly concerned the issues of religion and monarchy, as well as the role of the tsar and the Russian Orthodox Church in worldly life. *Stoglav* proclaimed the necessity of revising all existing religious books in order to define the degree of their correspondence to the sacred originals. It also entitled the religious authorities to select and confiscate the manuscripts proposed for publication. This means that *Stoglav* introduced both preliminary censorship and postpublishing censorship, which have never lost their importance for Russian publishing, despite the subsequent transformation of Russian censorship from religious into secular.[2]

The legalization of censorship in the middle of the sixteenth century came along with the introduction of the printing press in Russia. The two phenomena, now often looked upon as antipodal, were initially supposed to serve the same purpose. Religious censorship was introduced as a means of improving existing books, which, rewritten by hand, accumulated numerous errors. Once purged of blasphemous literature, the existing libraries needed to be replenished with carefully selected and edited books of sacred content. The provision of such a large corpus of sanctioned literature was only within the power of a machine—a printing press—which produced the first Russian printed book, *Apostol*,[3] in 1564. Ivan Fedorov, the Russian pioneer printer, ended *Apostol* with an afterword, in which he praised Tsar Ivan IV and Metropolitan Makarius for their wisdom. Initially approved of and sponsored by the tsar, Ivan Fedorov soon, however, fell from grace and had to flee to Lithuania, and later to Ukraine, persecuted for his "dangerous thinking" and close associations with reform seekers.[4] Living abroad, Fedorov continued to work as a printer and publisher, producing books of both religious and secular content—one of them being the famous *Azbuka,* or the Slavic alphabet employed in Russia and Ukraine, which was later used as a sample for Russian spelling books for many years. This is how the second half of the sixteenth century in Russia created the outline of the relations between the state and the publishing system. The perilous fate of Ivan Fedorov became prognostic of the destiny of publishers who continued to be persecuted and exiled, and who, if spared, resumed their work abroad, creating an alternative for Russian-printed publications.

Persecutions for storing foreign-published literature in homes continued in the sixteenth and seventeenth centuries, including the period after the enthronement of the Romanov dynasty in 1613. This concerned not only Catholic religious literature, or any religious literature on doctrines other than the Eastern Orthodox, but also foreign-printed literature in Slavic languages and even Greek religious books printed abroad. These church persecutions of heretics faced vehement opposition by both clerics and laypeople, which led to armed revolts, including those in monasteries. It was after Peter I (the Great) ascended to the Russian throne that the religious and the worldly power became split into two separate branches, with religious authorities in charge of censoring religious literature. Secular censorship regulations remained quite loose and unsystematic until the rule of Catherine II (the Great) in 1762–96. The first half of the eighteenth century from the reign of Peter the Great to the reign of his daughter Elizabeth was later described as a lost paradise due to the liberal attitude of the authorities toward printed literature.[5] The relatively loose requirements for publishing were put an end to by Catherine the Great, who was the first of the Romanovs to embark upon a consistent policy of information control. The political measures taken by Catherine in this regard ranged from official regulations of publishing activity to creating the official journal,[6] by means of which Catherine channeled her official position to the general public. The biggest competing publisher and mason Nikolai Novikov was eventually thrown into prison in 1792, with 18,656 volumes of books printed by him burned at the stake.[7] Soon afterward, a couple of months before her own death, Catherine, due to fear of the French Revolution, issued a decree on censorship of all published literature written or translated in the Russian Empire. This document defined censors as state officials, which was the next step toward building up the system of publishing control in Russia.[8]

The successors of Catherine the Great persevered in developing censoring institutions and practices. The first censorship statute was signed by Tsar Alexander I on June 9, 1804. The statute appointed the Central Administration of Schools of the Ministry of National Education as the central censoring organ, which resulted in total censorship of university study materials and mass dismissals of university professors in 1821, with their books simultaneously removed from libraries.[9] Consolidation on statehood and its bureaucratic apparatus reached its peak during the rule of Nicholas I, whose ascent to the Russian throne started with the Decembrist uprising at the end of 1825. After the death of Alexander I in December 1825, the troops refused to swear allegiance to Nicholas I, having already sworn allegiance to his elder brother, Constantine, who had by then already voluntarily removed himself from the line of succession. A group of Russian officers, mostly from noble background, took this moment to interdict the troops from pledging to the tsar, aiming at the establishment of a new constitutional state and the abolition of serfdom. By calling for radical political changes, the Decembrists followed the constitutional projects that had been developed by the Russian secret societies, known as the Northern Society and the Southern Society. The Decembrist revolt was soon put down, and its leaders were either exiled or hanged despite their noble descent. This tragic start of his rule convinced Nicholas I of the necessity of the close political control of the country.

His memory of the constitutional projects of the Northern and Southern Societies clear, Nicholas I actively engaged in lawmaking; as the result of his efforts, the Code of Laws of the Russian Empire amounted to fifteen volumes in the edition of 1833. Regulations on censorship and control of published literature were entrusted to the minister of spiritual affairs and public education Alexander Shishkov, who undertook the state post with an incredible zeal and eventually initiated the new censorship statute of June 10, 1826, which was nicknamed the "cast-iron statute" for its comprehensive nature and such attention to detail that it created confusion in censorship activity. Consisting of nineteen chapters and 230 paragraphs, the statute regulated every activity of censors and gave prescriptions on censoring texts of different content and practical orientation. The statute proclaimed the importance of channeling the published literature in a direction "useful, or, at least, harmless for the good of the motherland" and defined the job of a censor as a demanding and important activity "which cannot be combined with another position," thus defining the censor as a professional in the service of the state.[10] According to the statute, censorship remained within the sphere of the Ministry of National Education. Within the ministry, however, the administrative functions were delegated from the Central Administration of Schools to the Central Administration of Censorship.

The cast-iron statute proved impracticable within a year and was later revised and considerably abridged first in 1827 and then in 1828, when the new statute simplified the structure of the censoring system but increased the number of censors. Consistently created in the statutes of 1826–28, the censoring scheme remained the basis for further modifications of censorship in the Russian Empire.

However self-contained the structure of the Russian censoring system might have looked in the second quarter of the nineteenth century, it was not in itself independent but subject to personal decisions of the autocrat—Tsar Nicholas I, who went down in Russian history as the "censor of censors." His personal control of authors and publications at times took the shape of reprisals, as in the case of poet Aleksandr Polezhaev, who was arrested at night and tried by the tsar himself for his satirical poetry. The trial took place fifteen days after the execution of the leaders of Decembrist uprising and half a year before the coronation of Nicholas I. As the result of the trial, Polezhaev was exiled to the Caucasus, which was the center of military activity at the time. Nicholas I made regular enquiries about Polezhaev's fate until the death of Polezhaev of tuberculosis at the age of thirty-three.

In his attempts to control most spheres of social life in the country, Nicholas I was to a great degree guided by his personal preferences and dislikes. Such was the case of Aleksandr Pushkin (1799–1837), which deserves our close attention. In the twenty-first century, Pushkin remains for many the greatest Russian poet, playwright, and novelist due to his substantial contribution to the Russian language and literature. The large body of his work, his tragic death at the age of thirty-seven, and the response it evoked in the literary circles fostered the image of Pushkin as a tragic hero.

The image of a genius cut off in his prime was artfully manipulated in the twentieth century. At that time the figure of Pushkin assumed many features of the national symbol, which suited Stalin and his national policy.[11] But much less is spoken about the autocratic patronage granted to Pushkin by Nicholas I in September 1826, that is, three months after the cast-iron statute came into effect. The royal patronage gave Pushkin unparalleled privileges in publishing and promoting his works. Pushkin was well aware of these privileges, as is clearly seen from his correspondence.[12] He also enjoyed the right of approval of epigrams and satires that targeted him personally. In his letter to writer and poet Ivan Velikopol'skii, who made critical remarks regarding his *Eugene Onegin*, Pushkin wrote, "Bulgarin showed me your very lovely stances to me, written as a reply to my joke. He told me that censorship would not pass them without my approval. Unfortunately, I could not agree."[13]

Taken as a courtier by Nicholas I himself, Pushkin was given access to archives, where he could engage in the historical research required for his writings. He actively protected his right to be censored by the tsar personally, even in his correspondence with the universally feared head of the Secret Police Alexander von Benckendorff. Pushkin also succeeded in publishing his works, with the Russian crown picking up the costs; in his letter to Pavel Nashchokin of March 1834, Pushkin mentions that the publication costs of *The History of Pugachev* were covered personally by the tsar.[14] In his critical essay "Journey from Moscow to St. Petersburg," Pushkin openly approves of censorship, describing it as a feature of a civil society designed to prevent criminal actions at the point they emerge in the human mind.[15] "The law does not only punish," wrote Pushkin, "but it also precludes. It is even its beneficial side. The action of an individual is instantaneous and isolated [*isolé*]; the effect of a book is multiple and universal. Laws against misuse of publishing do not achieve the aim of the law, they do not prevent the evil, and seldom suppress it. Only censorship is able to do both."[16] Curiously enough, this article was first published only posthumously in 1841, carefully censored and with extensive deletions.[17]

In the 1840s, censorship affected Nikolai Gogol, who in 1841 submitted the manuscript of his *Dead Souls* for consideration to the censorial committee in Moscow. The title of the book, as well as its contents, immediately raised the suspicions of censors. In his letter to Petr Pletnev, Gogol gave a detailed account of the way the Moscow committee reacted to his work.

> When Golokhvastov, who was the president [of the committee] heard the title *Dead Souls,* he cried out in a voice of an ancient Roman: "No, no, I shall never allow that: the soul is immortal, the soul cannot be dead, the author takes up arms against immortality." At long last, the smart president realized that it was about census records. Once he and other censors got on the point that *dead* referred to census records, there was even more commotion . . . I omit here other small remarks, like the mention of a landowner who ruined himself by trying to decorate his house in Moscow in a fashionable manner. "But, indeed, the tsar is now building a palace in Moscow!" said a censor. Here on this subject, the censors started a conversation, which is unique in the whole world.[18]

The described complications made Gogol withdraw the manuscript and submit it to the censorial committee in St. Petersburg in 1842. The attempt made in the capital was more successful and resulted in the publication of the novel. St. Petersburg censors, however, insisted on the change of the title: the novel was first published as *The Adventures of Chichikov, or Dead Souls.* Some parts of the novel were removed by the censors, including one element of considerable length—"Tale of Captain Kopeikin," presented in the novel in the form of an anecdote of an invalid who came to St. Petersburg to get his pension for his faithful military service. Describing the tale of Kopeikin as "one of the best parts" of his novel, Gogol thought it was "better to change than to lose." He rewrote the tale thoroughly, omitting some parts and worsening the character of Kopeikin, making him look more stubborn and unruly in order to justify the officials who eventually removed Kopeikin from the capital.[19]

It has been noted that the degree of involvement of Nicholas I in censorship issues varied depending on his personal judgment of the potential political danger to the monarchy. Censorship in Russia toughened with the revolutionary events in Europe in 1830–31 and in 1848, when censorship in Russia welcomed informants and political denouncers.

The years 1848–55 entered the history of Russian publishing as "the epoch of censorial terror."[20]

The state control over publishing also included careful detection and withdrawal of unofficially circulated forbidden writings. One such forbidden work was the famous letter of critic Vissarion Belinskii to Nikolai Gogol. In criticizing Gogol's new book *Selected Passages from Correspondence with Friends*, Belinskii wrote a letter to Gogol on July 15, 1847. The correspondence was soon made public and came to be perceived as a manifesto of progressive thinking. "What she [Russia] needs," wrote Belinskii,

> is not sermons (she has heard enough of them!) or prayers (she has repeated them too often!), but the awakening in the people of a sense of their human dignity lost for so many centuries amid dirt and refuse; she needs rights and laws conforming not with the preaching of the church but with common sense and justice, and their strictest possible observance. Instead of which she presents the dire spectacle of a country where men traffic in men . . . The most vital national problems in Russia today are the abolition of serfdom and corporal punishment and the strictest possible observance of at least those laws which already exist.[21]

Forbidden in Russia for its dangerous liberal content, the letter was circulated in handwritten copies within the progressive circles in Russia. One such circle was the Petrashevskii circle in St. Petersburg, organized for literary readings and discussions by Mikhail Butashevich-Petrashevskii. Literary Fridays at Petrashevskii's place were attended by the most progressive people of the time, including the twenty-six-year-old Fyodor Dostoyevsky, writer Mikhail Saltykov-Shchedrin, and poets Aleksei Pleshcheyev and Apollon Maikov. Members of the circle shared the ideas of Fourier and Proudhon and discussed prospects for the future development of Russia during the gatherings; and despite being branded as rebels by some contemporaries, very few members of the circle were truly revolutionary minded. Members of the Petrashevskii circle were also engaged in the compilation of the *Pocket Dictionary of Foreign Words*, which gave definitions of the terms employed in the existing theories on socialism, materialism, and democracy. "There was not a single 'monster' or 'scoundrel' among the Petrashevskii circle," wrote Dostoyevsky later. "But there were not many of us who could resist that well-known cycle of ideas and concepts that had then taken such a strong hold on young society. We were infected with the ideas of the then theoretical socialism."[22] The arrests of the members of the Petrashevskii circle took place after their denouncement in April 1849; the charges brought against them were mainly reduced to misprision and circulation of Belinskii's letter. Out of thirty-two arrested circle members, two died in prison and twenty-two were tried by military court, which sentenced twenty-one persons to execution by a firing squad. Due to the fact that most of the circle members repented during the trial, the execution by a firing squad was secretly substituted by a mock execution and exile. The condemned, however, were not informed of the reprieve and went through the whole procedure of the preparation for the execution sure of their imminent death. "We of Petrashevskii Circle stood on the scaffold and listened to our sentences without the least bit of repentance," recalled Dostoyevsky in *Writer's Diary*. "The sentence of death by firing squad that was read to us at first was certainly not pronounced as a joke; almost all the condemned were convinced that the sentence would be carried out and underwent at least ten dreadful, infinitely terrible minutes expecting to die."[23]

The death penalty of Dostoyevsky was commuted to a four-year exile to a hard labor camp in Omsk, Siberia, followed by compulsory military service. Dostoyevsky described his prison experience in his blood-chilling novel *The House of the Dead*, which he published in 1861–62 in the journal *Vremia*[24] that he was running together with his brother Mikhail. The publication was carefully censored; a section of substantial length where Dostoyevsky dwelt on the feeling of the loss of freedom was crossed out by the censors.[25] Dostoyevsky published another novel in *Vremia*, titled *Humiliated and Insulted*. The political engagement of the journal and its focus on social issues led to the censorial ban of the journal and its closure in 1863.

The reforms of Tsar Alexander II (1855–81), who is mostly known for the liberation of the serfs in 1861, also included the censorship reform of 1865. The reform was preceded by the delegation of the responsibility for censorship control to the Ministry of Internal Affairs in January 1863. This transfer of responsibilities and the control of censorial activities by the Ministry of Internal Affairs meant that censorship was seen as a defense measure, maintained to safeguard the interests of the Russian Empire. The danger of revolutionary movements attended by risks of terrorist attacks as well as the active liberation movement in Poland increased the desire of the Russian government to control public activity in the country.[26] The rise of the Ministry of Internal Affairs immediately affected the literary and publishing situation in the country.

Half a year after the assumption of censorial responsibilities by the Ministry of Internal Affairs, Minister of Internal Affairs Petr Valuev issued the notorious decree that became universally known as the Valuev's circular. The circular suspended all publications in the Ukrainian language apart from those falling into the category of belles lettres. The negative effect of the circular on Ukrainian language and literature was enhanced by the Ems edict, signed by Alexander II in May 1876 in Bad Ems. The edict limited the use of the Ukrainian language in everyday life and education by banning translations into Ukrainian, the import of Ukrainian-language books from abroad, theater performances in the Ukrainian language, and even musical scores with Ukrainian text. The only Ukrainian texts that remained appropriate for publication were historical documents and original literary works, the imposed limitations thus impairing the status of the Ukrainian language in the Russian Empire and the status of the Ukrainian speakers accordingly.[27]

The linguistic situation that followed the Ems edict was defined by Jaroslav Rudnyckyj as linguicide.[28] The ban on translations had a tremendous impact not only on the literary but also on the social situation in Ukraine, evoking multiple protests of Ukrainian intellectuals and increasing Ukrainian emigrant activity in Europe.[29] For example, in disregard of the edict, translations of Shakespeare by Mikhail Staritskii and Panteleimon Kulish were published in 1882. Kulish continued translating the Pentateuch, the Psalter, and the Gospel, which he had started in 1860. Jointly with Ivan Puluj and Ivan Nechui-Levitskii, Kulish was able to produce the first complete translation of the Bible into Ukrainian, which was published by the British and Foreign Bible Society in 1904, seven years after Kulish's death.

Ricarda Vulpius suggests that the issue of the Valuev circular itself was triggered by the complete Ukrainian translations of the New Testament by Pilip Morachevs'kii.[30] Morachevs'kii's translation, completed by 1863, followed the publication of the New Testament in a contemporary Russian translation in 1862. And even though the direct connection of Morachevs'kii's translation with the Valuev circular has been disputed, the influence of the Russian Orthodox Church over publishing in the Russian Empire cannot be underestimated.[31]

The translation of the Bible into the contemporary Russian language also faced difficulties throughout the nineteenth century. The Russian Biblical Society first attempted to translate the Holy Scripture into contemporary Russian in the 1820s with the permission of Tsar Alexander I himself. The resistance of the Russian Orthodox hierarchs to the idea of the translation of sacred texts, however, was so strong that several hundred thousand printed copies were burned almost immediately. It was only in 1859 that the Holy Synod granted permission for the complete translation of the Holy Scripture into contemporary Russian as opposed to the already existing Old Slavic texts. The translation of the New Testament was published in 1862, and the complete translation of the Bible— the so-called Russian Synodal Bible—was first published in 1876, which, notably, was a year after the publication of the first translation of Marx's *Capital* into Russian.[32] The Synodal Bible has been used for by Russian Orthodox congregations since 1876; however, the Church Slavonic language remains the language of the liturgy.

Secular and clerical censorship in Russia were officially separated in 1743, as of which time clerical censorship was supposed to engage in controlling books of religious content. The difference between the two censorships, however, became at times insignificant, especially when it concerned the issues of virtue and public morals. A striking example in this regard is the confrontation between Lev Tolstoy and the Russian Orthodox Church, which lasted for many years and eventually resulted in Tolstoy's excommunication by the Holy Synod ruling of February 20–22, 1901, for Tolstoy's radical views on the role of religion in human life, as well as his denial of the Holy Trinity, Immaculate Conception, and the necessity of religious sacraments. But already a decade earlier, Tolstoy had had to go to great lengths to publish his polemical work—*The Kreutzer Sonata*—in which he sought to show the controversy between Christian love and the relationship between the sexes.

The Kreutzer Sonata was banned in 1890 by imperial censorship with the intervention of religious censoring organs, namely, Ober-Procurator of the Most Holy Synod Konstantin Pobedonostsev. Publication finally became possible in 1891, after an audience of Tolstoy's wife, countess Sofia Tolstaia, with Tsar Alexander III.[33] In total, around forty works by Tolstoy were banned at different times throughout the writer's life, with the bans imposed by both secular and religious censors.[34]

Maintenance of morals and virtue by censorship also affected the life of Anton Chekhov in 1896, when he submitted his *Seagull* for censorship revision. Writer Ignatii Potapenko, who took up the task of corresponding with censors, wrote to Chekhov on this account: "A little bit of a problem with your *Seagull*. Contrary to all expectation, it got caught in the nets of the censorship, but not so badly, so it can be rescued. The whole trouble is that your decadent has a lax attitude to his mother's love life, which the censor's rules do not allow. You'll have to insert a scene from Hamlet: 'A bloody deed! almost as bad, good mother / As kill a king and marry with his brother.'"[35] In his letter, censor Litvinov made the reason for the rejection of the play quite clear: "The point is not that the actress and the writer live together, but in the son and brother taking it quietly."[36] Chekhov took up the task of altering his play reluctantly; he eventually made changes to make Treplev look more hurt by the affair of Arkadina and Trigorin and took out the scene where Dr. Dorn confesses to being Masha's father.[37] The censors eventually found the changes sufficient, and *Seagull* was staged and first shown in St. Petersburg on October 17, 1896. However, Chekhov restored the precensored text when publishing his play in the journal *Russkaia Mysl'* two months later in December 1896.[38] The confession of Dr. Dorn remained unrestored; the theme of his fatherhood now lingers in the text of the play in hints and described sensations as, for instance, in Masha's words, "I don't love my father, but my heart turns to you. For some reason, I feel with all my soul that you are near to me," or in Dorn's emotional reply, "What can I do for you, my child? What? What?"[39]

As one can see, censorship in Russian literary and publishing practice under the monarchy was so extremely well developed and rooted in the system that it was naturally taken over by the new government as a ready-made operating system. Soviet literary hierarchy adopted the time-tested scheme of literary control and subordination, which compelled writers, translators, and editors to self-censorship. The officially declared policy of the Soviet Union, however, was built on claims of openness and transparency, which resulted in the denial of censorship as such, despite the fact that the existing prerevolutionary practices of literary control were embraced almost immediately after the October events of 1917. This continuity in the use of controlling techniques contributed to the strengthening of the Soviet system of censorship and control, providing it with proven methods of intimidation and subjection.

CHAPTER 3

THE PYRAMID OF SUBORDINATION

Literary Translation and Means of Social Control in the Soviet Union

For many years, Soviet literary translation has been the focus of atten-tion of research specialists of both Soviet and Western background. Some researchers took up the task of describing the general translation tendencies in the Soviet Union, whereas others concentrated on transla-tion practice in different socialist republics at different periods of Soviet history and addressed such issues as selection of originals, translation strategies, and readership reaction. A panoramic classic study of Rus-sian and Soviet literary translation history was conducted by Maurice Friedberg in his book *Literary Translation in Russia: A Cultural His-tory,* where he gives a detailed description of Russian translation history from the times of Kievan Rus', through the golden age of translation in the nineteenth century, to the Soviet period.[1] Brian James Baer takes a close look at the history of translation in Russia and the Soviet Union in his *Translation and the Making of Modern Russian Literature.*[2] Baer also coedited a comprehensive anthology, *Russian Writers on Transla-tion,* which equips researchers with the texts that reflect the evolution of views on translation from the eighteenth century edict of Peter I—*On the Preparation of Translators of Books for Instruction in the Sciences*—to the articles written in the twentieth century by Soviet translators, writers, and critics.[3] Impressive case studies on Soviet translation were made by Vitaly Chernetsky, Anne Lange and Daniele Monticelli, Natalia Kaloh Vid, and Susanna Witt; detailed research on Ukrainian translation was presented by Maksim Strikha in his monograph *Ukrains'kii khudozhnii pereklad: mizh literaturoiu i natsietvorenniam (Ukrainian literary translation: between literature and nation-building).*[4] The variety of subjects described and approaches applied to the studies of translation in the Soviet Union allow me to omit some issues that have already been presented in complete detail. I shall limit the material of my research both in terms of time and location. I shall here concentrate on the period between 1960 and 1991, that is, from the Khrushchev Thaw to the fall of the Soviet system. I also limit my research to the literary translation situation in the Russian Soviet Federative Socialist Republic—namely, in its two major cities—Moscow and Leningrad (currently St. Petersburg). I limit my research to this time and place for the following reasons.

1. The literary situation was undergoing rapid changes throughout the seventy years of the existence of the Soviet Union. Censorial restrictions on literature and publishing and the demand for literature and translation varied with every decade. For this reason, I found it important to concentrate on the relatively recent events of Soviet translation history, for which I was able to collect firsthand material.

2. The same is true for the literary situation in different Soviet republics. Within the same decade, requirements for literary translation in different republics diverged considerably. Despite obvious similarities, situations in different republics were far from being uniform: bans and permissions for publications in the republics corresponded to the local language policy and educational situation, as well as to the degree the local community was compelled to use the Russian language. To avoid broad conclusions, I find it important to concentrate my research on a smaller regional segment.

3. Moscow and Leningrad, apart from being major publishing, and therefore translation, centers of the Soviet Union, were also known for their literary translation schools, which educated several generations of talented and highly qualified translation specialists.

4. One of the main sources of the material for this research was the firsthand interviews of the translators still living who were actively engaged in literary translation in 1960–91. It is my deepest regret that I was unable to interview the older generation of translators. Recent years have been merciless to the Soviet masters of literary translation of all generations: translator Aleksandra Koss passed away in 2010; Aleksandr Revich, in 2012; Vasilii Betaki and Viktor Toporov, in 2013; Vladimir Vasil'ev, in 2014; and the brilliant literary critic and editor Nina D'iakonova, in 2013. In the context of these tragic losses, I felt it especially important to collect the living memories of people who were eager to share their experience with me.

A contradictory social and political situation in the Soviet Union in the 1960s through the 1980s has made the perception of the period extremely emotional, especially because eyewitnesses of the period are still very active and willing to share their memories. The emotional aspect, invaluable for understanding the social context of the period, needs to be presented alongside a detached analysis of the situation described. In this regard, the evaluation of the degree of openness/closedness of Soviet society at different years will, in my view, contribute to the unbiased assessment of the described approaches and case studies. From 1960 to the mid-1980s, social practices of the Soviet Union remained in tune with the general political course of the state, yet in terms of the scope and strictness of political persecutions, the situation looked much more favorable in comparison to the previous decades. In this chapter, I shall describe the literary situation in the country, paying special attention to the parameters of the closed society described in chapter 1. This description will require additional explanations and digressions into the earlier Soviet history, which will be done for the sake of clarity and completeness of information. The parameters of a closed society will be studied here purely through the prism of literature, publishing, and to an extent education, leaving aside economic and foreign policy parameters that are also very important in the description of the degree of closedness/openness of a society but may be distracting from the general theme of this book.

The development of publishing and literature in the USSR invariably mirrored the political situation in the country, responding to political regulations and decisions taken on the highest levels of the Soviet government. The Soviet history of censorship officially began with the legalization of censorship by the Decree on Press on November 9, 1917. The Decree on Press was signed on the third day after the revolution and became one of the first decrees of the Soviet government alongside the Decree on Peace and the Decree on Land. Issued in a moment of universal hope for freedom and new life, the Decree on Press in itself was oriented toward the construction of a closed society as it legalized the powerful tool of control and restraint. The decree called for closing all publishing organizations that "(1) call for open resistance or insubordination to the government of Workers and Peasants; (2) wreak havoc by apparently slanderous distortion of facts; (3) call for apparently criminal, that is penal, actions."[5] This formula reflects two fundamentals of a closed society, the first of them being exemption from moral obligation, which is shown in the vague and general wording of the decree: the meaning of such words as *resistance, insubordination,* and *distortion of facts* were not specified and therefore were subject to a variety of interpretations. The second fundamental built into the decree is the establishment of "collective utility"—the Decree on Press even announced its temporary nature until "the arrival of normal conditions of social life."[6]

It took over seventy years for these "normal conditions of social life" to arrive, for the Decree on Press never was cancelled under the Soviet regime. In the meantime, in 1918–19, private publishing houses were nationalized. Nationalization arrived as a natural consequence of the Soviet constitution of 1918, which proclaimed the exclusive power of workers and peasants. "In this moment of resolute struggle of the proletariat against its exploiters, the exploiters may not find a place in any governmental body. . . . In accordance with the interests of the working class in general, the Russian Socialist Federative Soviet Republic deprives individuals and separate groups of the rights that are exercised by them to the prejudice of the socialist revolution."[7] It was at this point in 1918 that the principles of collective utility and exemption of the state from moral obligations were joined by the third fundamental—the self-declaration as a warring state. The use of the word *struggle* in the text of the constitution is extremely demonstrative in this regard. In the following years it would be a leitmotif in documents and regulations issued by the state, sometimes substituted by synonyms. Thus, for example, Vladimir Lenin wrote about merciless suppression of the bourgeois press and especially indicated the warring nature of the Soviet press in the struggle with bourgeois ideology.[8]

The year 1922 was marked by the emergence of a new institution under the name Main Administration for Literary and Publishing Affairs (*Glavlit*) at the RSFSP People's Commissariat of Education.[9] Throughout sixty-nine years of its existence the institution regularly changed its name. Thus, in 1953 it turned into the Main Administration for the Protection of Military and State Secrets in the Press under the USSR Council of Ministers. It finally became the Agency for the Protection of State Secrets in the Mass Media under the Ministry of Information and Press of the USSR in July 1991—less than six months before it finally ceased to exist. But at all times, despite the regular name change, it was universally known as the powerful *Glavlit*. Glavlit was meant to become a stable and universal organization to control all information undergoing publication. Already in 1922, a Sovnarkom regulation on Glavlit defined its main responsibilities, which were predominantly reduced to prepublication control of all literature and issuing lists of banned literature.[10] By the end of the same year, a circulated regulation on Glavlit sent a clear message regarding censorship as a state-approved approach to publications. "Censorship of printed works," it stated, "consists in (a) preventing all articles clearly hostile toward the Communist Party and Soviet power from being printed; (b) preventing all works presenting an ideology hostile to us on issues of primary importance (society, religion, economics, arts, etc.) from being printed; (c) removal from articles of particularly critical points (facts, figures, characteristics) that may discredit the Communist Party and Soviet power."[11] This is how within five years from the October Revolution in 1917 censorship became a centralized strategy in publishing and, consequently, in literature and translation.

The further inclusion of the Russian Socialist Federative Soviet Republic with the Ukraine Socialist Soviet Republic, Belarus Socialist Soviet Republic, and Transcaucasian Socialist Federative Soviet Republic (consisting of Georgia, Azerbaijan, and Armenia) into the Union of Soviet Socialist Republics (USSR) on December 30, 1922, strengthened the positions of

Glavlit. Glavlit gradually developed a well-coordinated network of vertical architecture. If described from top down, it consisted of the central office of Glavlit of the USSR at the top, followed by Glavlits of the Soviet Socialist Republics of the Soviet Union at the lower level, and finally followed by Glavlits of the autonomous republics of the Soviet Union and regional Glavlits.[12] The Russian Federative Republic was the only one that did not have a republican Glavlit; therefore its publishing was controlled directly by the central Glavlit of the USSR. However, Glavlit had large representational offices in the biggest cities of the Russian Federation—Mosgorlit in Moscow and Lengorlit in Leningrad—which ensured close control over the literary activity in Russia's largest cultural centers.

Glavlit was primarily engaged in close control of literature and publishing in order to detect all ideologically harmful, politically suspicious, or dangerous texts, subjects, or authors, even though the existence of censorship in the country was denied by the Soviet government. At the same time, the Bolshevist approach denied the political neutrality of the arts. Such terms as "party literature" and "party press" were already operated by Lenin, who called for bringing literary and publishing activities in line with the adopted policy. "Down with nonparty writers!" wrote Lenin. "Literary activity must become part of the all-proletariat activity, a 'wheel and cog' in the single great social-democratic machine."[13] Lenin did not consider party control to be an obstacle to creativity; quite the contrary, he looked upon it as a contribution to the development of the liberal arts. The party, in Lenin's view, would be able to encourage writers and journalists to serve the state by providing them with financial support.[14] The direct dependence of arts on the state and state regulations became a distinctive feature of the Soviet period till the end of the 1980s.

With minor exceptions, all mass information was to be approved by Glavlit. Its influence over publishing and literature could not be underestimated: in fact, any printed material from a book or a journal to a postcard, playbill, or a picture on a box of matches was to be officially approved by Glavlit. For example, in his book *Kak eto delalos' v Leningrade* (The way it was done in Leningrad), Arlen Blium describes an episode where an invitation to an evening event held by the Philharmonic Society and the Union of Composers was criticized by censors because the wine glass painted on it looked "way too large."[15]

As an organization, Glavlit was much more than a purely censoring organ. With its prescriptive, controlling, and preventive functions, it originated as a progressive phenomenon of its time that aimed at a revolutionary change in the thinking of citizens of the new state.[16] Decisions of censoring organs were not merely limited to bans—they bore a prescriptive and "optimistic" character and dictated to the authors on the form and content of their writings, thus interfering in the creative process. Noncompliance with the prescribed poetics, form, and style became a reason for rejection or removal from general access of many literary works on neutral and politically unbiased subjects.[17] Active interference of the Soviet controlling organs with writing activities targeted exclusion of any unnecessary "otherness" in accordance with the newest Communist Party regulations. Mikhail Zelenov observes that initially in the 1920s the exclusion of otherness was a means to highlight the distinct differentiating features of the USSR. "Otherness" was seen as an "enemy," and the elimination of one type of otherness was always followed by the search for the new other to fight with, which ensured the longevity of Glavlit.[18]

The deputy head of Glavlit in 1985–91, Viktor Pribytkov, states in his memoirs that despite the tremendous impact Glavlit had on literary activity in the USSR, its staff was surprisingly limited, amounting to 430 employees in the central office and around two thousand employees across the country. The central office of Glavlit, unlike ministries and other institutions, did not run smaller departments and limited its activity to control and censorship of printed media and publishing houses. Censors worked directly on site—that is, in publishing houses or radio or TV stations—and read all information to be released.[19]

Designed to control information, Glavlit, in its turn, worked on the principles of underinforming and holding writers and publishers in suspense. The absence of clearly formulated norms and requirements for literary works made writers and publishers feel insecure, with censors feeling their own impunity at the same time. Any work of art could be declared ideologically harmful on the grounds of personal taste, dislike, or nepotism.[20] Marianna Tax Choldin describes this situation as *omnicensorship*, introducing the new term to define the system that permeated the society thoroughly and affected everyone.[21]

Evgenii Witkowsky, who was active as a translator and a participant in the dissident movement since the 1970s, says that even in cases where Glavlit was directly contacted by publishers for information and guidelines, it provided extremely evasive, misleading, and intimidating answers.

> EVGENII WITKOWSKY: If Glavlit was asked for particular instructions, it would just ignore the request. If there was a direct question asked, Glavlit officials would often answer: "What do you think?" It was the favorite reply of Boris Stukalin, who headed Glavlit for a long time. Another possible reply was that the strategy, approach, or book "could not be recommended." Or Glavlit would just reject the publication altogether, if one asked too many questions.

The information regarding the internal structure and activity of Glavlit remained classified long after the fall of the Soviet Union. As late as 2005, Blium stated that the process of declassification was going very slowly and had almost been frozen in the 1990s. Blium also pointed out that the archive of Mosgorlit had been almost completely destroyed, as well as other regional archives that were severely damaged when the Soviet system collapsed.[22] Descriptions of Glavlit's activities vary in different sources; memories of its activity also vary, which is why the description presented here is not intended to be exhaustive and is subject to further additions and revisions.

Going through a series of approvals, any book or other publication could be rejected at any stage. Efim Etkind described the scheme of the publication approval in the following way:

> (1) Editor → (2) managing editor → (3) editor-in-chief → (4) first reviewer → (5) second reviewer → (6) director → (7) censor (Glavlit employee) → (8) regional committee of the Communist Party of the Soviet Union → (9) Committee for Print of the Russian Soviet Federative Socialist Republic (Glavlit regional department) → (10) Committee for Print of the USSR (Glavlit) → (11) Department for Propaganda or Department of Culture of the Central Committee of the Communist Party of the Soviet Union → (12) KGB.[23]

As one can see from the list, the first three stages of manuscript approval took place within the publishing house. In most cases, editors of publishing houses were extremely well educated and had a high expertise in literature, arts, and foreign languages. Editors did the difficult job of proofreading and text editing. Editors-in-chief, in their turn, were often selected from active Communist Party members—this fact often being explanatory of their rigor in ideological editing.

Publication of a book also required two positive reviews by the reviewers suggested by the publishing house. The process of reviewing created favorable conditions for rejecting the manuscript at any stage without making the reasons for rejection clear to the applicant. The method frequently employed in such cases was nicknamed "passing it on." It consisted in passing it from one reviewer to another, collecting negative reviews sometimes, instead of rejecting the manuscript officially. This approach was resorted to in cases where publishers were reluctant to publish the manuscript or did not want to deal with an author of questionable reputation. Since the reviews were anonymous, the author was at the mercy of the publishing house, unable to find out the reasons for negative reviews. Sometimes the number of negative reviews reached ten, and the author would finally give up on the publication or publish the book illegally in the underground press.[24]

Commenting upon Etkind's scheme, Evgenii Witkowsky noted that not all the stages listed by Etkind had equal importance in the process of publication. Some of the stages listed by Etkind, in Witkowsky's view, were rather more typical for the Leningrad publishing system, which was more complex than the publishing system in the Soviet capital.[25]

EVGENII WITKOWSKY: Long before the editor saw the text, it had been self-censored. There were two types of self-censorship. First, the very choice of the text for translation was self-censored. This was hard to accept yet unavoidable. Translators had to find texts for translation themselves, because orders from publishing houses came quite rarely, and this is why translators had to choose texts that would not annoy editors. The second type of self-censorship took place within the translation process; sometimes translators were directly requested to mitigate some elements of the original. As for Etkind's description, it is quite obvious that he was describing the scheme from his memory, which is why it is not quite the way it was in reality. And it is a Leningrad scheme, too. In Moscow, the number of stages was smaller, and the publishing process was much more straightforward.

1. *Editor.* The editor dealt only with the text. If the editor was a graphomaniac, he/she would start to interfere with the text just for the sake of interfering. I had cases when my translations of the same literary work would get published in different versions by different publishing houses at approximately the same time.
2. *Managing editor.* Managing editors compiled publishing plans. They interfered with translators' work extremely seldom. They had power to cancel or deny the publication, but their attitude was mostly very mild.
3. *Editor-in-chief.* The editor-in-chief confirmed the publishing plan. If the editor and the managing editor liked the translator, the editor-in-chief did not interfere with the translation process at all. But it was mainly the editor-in-chief (or, in some cases, the director), who instructed the editor that this or that translator should be hired. They could demand that particular translator be given a job.
4. *First reviewer.* The reviewers were mainly used for prose, rather than poetry. And one could fight the will of the reviewer. One could demand a second opinion, and the publishing house would find two other reviewers. Therefore, reviewers could only advise but were not a decisive factor.
5. *Second reviewer.* See above.
6. *Director.* The director signed contracts. If the text for translation was not very long, the contract was not necessary, and then the director worked with payment documents.
7. *Censor (Glavlit employee).* The censor had the power to ban or grant the approval of the text. The managing editor knew who the censor was, but he/she would never disclose this information to translators. However, the managing editor could tell the translator the opinion of the censor. At times, there was no censor to check the translation.
8. *Regional Committee of the Communist Party of the Soviet Union.* There had to be a unique case for this institution to interfere. I would say, Etkind is rather assuming this. This could be a very Leningrad thing, too.
9. *Committee for Print of the Russian Soviet Federative Socialist Republic (Glavlit regional department).* This could also be an exclusively Leningrad phenomenon. In Moscow, this stage did not exist.
10. *Committee for Print of the USSR (Glavlit).* This was an absolute must, of course.
11. *Department for Propaganda or Department of Culture of the Central Committee of the Communist Party of the Soviet Union.* This existed, too; they issued instructions.
12. *KGB.* As far as I was concerned, this institution never interfered with my publications.

13. What Etkind does not know is that there also was the Committee for Control that was above the Committee for Print[26]. It was even entitled to check the actions of KGB. But this mainly concerned books by foreign authors.

What Witkowsky calls the Committee for Control is seldom described or referred to in books on Soviet publishing due to the extreme closedness of the institution and the lack of information on its activities. The institution as such, indeed, existed: Inga Shomrakova and Iosif Barenbaum speak of "ideological departments of the party" that had different names at different times in Soviet history: Agitprop, Cultprop, Ideological Department, and so on. These organizations instructed the censoring bodies and signaled the beginnings of different political or ideological campaigns, to which censoring institutions duly responded.[27]

Publishing houses were required to compile annual or five-year publishing plans (also called *templans,* that is, thematic plans). These plans were revised and approved by different party organizations, including regional committees of the Communist Party. In the course of these revisions "unimportant" authors could get crossed out along with authors of "doubtful reputation"—that is, those who participated in protests, signed open letters, or maintained contacts with dissidents. The party organizations paid close attention to every detail and advised on the number of copies, making sure that politically dangerous authors like Anna Akhmatova or Osip Mandelstam would get published to appease the intellectuals but would at the same time get a very limited circulation.[28] The inclusion of the literary work into the publishing plan was an important step; to be included, the original author or the translator of the prospective publication needed to write a well-motivated application. Literary translators who had already proven their skills and qualifications actively applied to publishing houses for the literary works they wanted to translate.

It is important to point out that copyright of foreign authors was completely ignored by the Soviet Union. The first decision regarding copyright was made in November 1918, when the Council of People's Commissars issued the Decree on the Scientific, Literary, Musical, and Artistic Works, which stated that any published or unpublished work could be declared property of the state (at that point—the Russian Soviet

Federative Socialist Republic), disregarding the original ownership. The decree proclaimed that translations of literary works published both in Russia and abroad could be "declared the monopoly of the Russian Soviet Federative Socialist Republic."[29] By the mid-twentieth century the state monopoly for publishing all existing literary works became an unquestionable fact. Authors from outside the USSR were often aware of the fact that their works were being translated and published in thousands of copies in the Soviet Union, but they were barely contacted for permission and hardly got any royalties.

Therefore an application by a translator was often sufficient for the publishing house to initiate the translation process. However, an application by a translator had better chances of getting approved if submitted alongside the recommendation of a well-known critic or literary specialist who, in the case of the application approval, could later be appointed executive editor for the translated volume. Editors and anthologists themselves could create individual applications for anthologies and collections of works; in the case of application approval, these editors had an important say in the choice of translators for the compiled volume.

The translator and the process of translation were located seven stages away from the censor and ten stages away from Glavlit itself. Needless to say, memories of Glavlit have faded by now, especially for literary translators whose translations were not subject to severe censorship or those who did not have to deal with Glavlit as an organization. Evgenii Witkowsky, however, shared his clear memories of Glavlit activities. A translator from many languages, Witkowsky was even contacted by Glavlit directly to be commissioned to do a job.

EVGENII WITKOWSKY: The cases when Glavlit worked directly with translators were extremely rare. However, translator Andrei Sergeev and I happened to receive orders directly from Glavlit. Such things happened when Glavlit was instructed by the Central Committee of the Communist Party that it should publish works of a particular author that the committee considered politically convenient. Usually, the translators did not even get to see the translated book in print. And it is not surprising: in such cases, the book would be published in ten copies only, and nine out of ten would be presented to the author himself. This is how I got to translate the book of poetry of Senator Eugene McCar-thy[30]. Andrei Sergeev, in his turn, was commissioned to translate the works of some Indian female poet, who was, as I remember, the wife of an Indian Communist Party official. We were paid the maximum price but never got to see the translations in the shape of books. And I know our cases were not unique: there were other translators who got such orders from Glavlit.

Having gone through a series of internal reorganizations in the 1950s and 1960s, Glavlit was a solid screen between literature and its readers, as it imposed strict limitations on the activity of publishing houses, which remained nationalized throughout the whole Soviet period. In terms of translations and foreign literature publishing, the most influen-tial publishing house was Khudozhestvennaia Literatura. It was founded in 1930 under the name Goslitizdat, which later merged with Akademiia publishing house in 1937 and was renamed Khudozhestvennaia Liter-atura in 1963. The publishing house had its departments and printing shops both in Moscow and Leningrad and was the biggest publisher of foreign literature, including the famous series Biblioteka vsemirnoi literatury (Library of world literature). Another publishing house, Izda-tel'stvo Inostrannoi Literatury, was founded in 1946, later splitting into the publishing houses Mir and Progress in 1963–64. In 1982, Raduga (or Raduga Publishers) sprang from Progress, being the last to join the list of the main publishing engines in the Soviet Union.

The only alternative to state-owned and Glavlit-controlled publish-ing houses was the underground press called *samizdat* (literally, self-publishing), whose active development took place during the period of the so-called Khrushchev Thaw, the start of which is traditionally dated February 25, 1956, when Nikita Khrushchev openly denounced and con-demned the personality cult of Joseph Stalin in the Twentieth Congress of the Communist Party of the Soviet Union. The subsequent loosening of state control over the press encouraged the increase of underground literary activity, which reached its peak in the 1970s and 1980s. Informal in its nature, samizdat engaged in publishing literary works that could not or for some reasons had not passed the official publishing selection process and were therefore considered ideologically harmful. Samiz-dat was not an organization; it was the name for the illegal publishing activity and its products. For getting access to forbidden or restricted-access literary works, Soviet readers resorted to photocopying, microfilming, and even retyping and making carbon copies. This is how Russian readers would get acquainted with *The Master and Margarita* and other works by Mikhail Bulgakov, the poems of Nikolai Gumilev and Osip Mandelstam, *Requiem* by Anna Akhmatova, the works of Aleksandr Solzhenitsyn, the memorandum of Andrei Sakharov, and numerous poems and songs of Aneksandr Galich, Bulat Okudzhava, and even Vladimir Vysotskii, who was worshipped by millions of Soviet people.

Samizdat was a serious interference with the state publishing monopoly and a means of circulation of unwelcome thoughts and ideas. This is why any samizdat activity and publications attracted the close attention of the KGB. The state policy was also directed against *tamizdat* (literally, there publishing)—that is, works by Soviet writers first published abroad in violation of the state-declared right for the first publication of all literary works written in the Soviet Union before they could be published anywhere else in the world. Published outside the Soviet Union, tamizdat was illegally imported by mail or brought through Soviet customs by risk takers. Publications in tamizdat could have extremely negative consequences for authors; thus, the publication of *Doctor Zhivago* in Italy in 1957 and the subsequent Nobel prize award in 1958 resulted in the bullying campaign against Boris Pasternak.

The creative role of a Great Man as a feature of a closed society also affected literary activity in the USSR. The figure of absolute worship was Lenin: his presence in the life of Soviet citizens was akin to a religious cult, his images and citations employed in almost all spheres of social life. Lenin was traditionally depicted as part of a trine along with Marx and Engels, and it was the three leaders of Marxism-Leninism whose publications were presented in the best way in the Soviet Union—both in Russian and foreign languages. Thus, for instance, the complete works of Marx and Engels were published in fifty volumes in English by Progress publishing house in 1966. At the end of 1960s, the complete works of Lenin were released in Russian in fifty-five volumes in two hundred fifty thousand copies, which were replenished in 1976 by another two hundred thousand copies. The centenary celebration of Lenin's birthday in 1970 required the active involvement of publishing houses; the leading role in this regard was played by the abovementioned Progress publishing house, which duly published a forty-five-volume collection of Lenin's works in English, French, Vietnamese, and Finnish, as well a collection of Lenin's selected works in Spanish, Arabic, Swahili, Urdu, Hausa, Hindi, and Japanese.

In the context of multiple restrictions and bans imposed on literature in the Soviet Union, there existed particular requirements that Soviet writers and literary translators were supposed to conform to at all times. These requirements were set out in the first half of the twentieth century, however, their observance remained mandatory after the end of World War II, throughout the period of the Khrushchev Thaw, and afterward, in the period of the 1960s through the 1980s, which later came to be called the "stagnation." Definitions of these requirements varied throughout Soviet history; here we can conventionally break them into two groups.

1. Clarity requirements. These requirements look very well grounded in the light of the universal education established by the Soviet government. Nonetheless, the call for clarity did not reduce itself to achieving plainness and explicitness, which would ensure understanding of literature by less educated readers. Quite the contrary, the call for clarity in literary translations was first made to ensure the improvement of the quality of translations in terms of their stylistic and grammatical conformity to the rules of the target language. For instance, writer and thinker Maksim Gor'kii wrote of the necessity to avoid the automatic transfer of foreign grammatical structures and foreign words into the Russian translation without substantial grounds.[31] Thus clarity of translation for Gor'kii was its correspondence to Russian speech and language norms.

2. Socialist realism requirements. Recognized as the dominant literary approach in 1932, socialist realism postulated three requirements that were supposed to apply to all works of art and literary works. The first of the three was national spirit (*narodnost'*) which implied both the clarity of art for the average citizen and the adherence of works of art to the Russian tradition with its images, traditional language, and methods. Second, socialist realism called for ideological commitment (*ideinost'*), that is, representation of everyday life and activities of common people, their struggle for a better future and happiness.

Third, works of art were supposed to conform to the requirement of specificity (*konkretnost'*), which meant materialism and direct reference of art to reality.[32]

The increase in the number of requirements affected the literary translation of both prose and poetry. Thus, for instance, the requirement of specificity could either result in overly detailed explanations within the text or an attempt to explain the places that the author left unexplained in the original. The requirement for national spirit led to text distortions, especially in form and style. With the orientation of translations toward target-language cultural values, we can here talk about the gradual establishment and further maintenance of domesticating practices.[33] The concept of "form" was regularly neglected, since national spirit, ideological commitment, and specificity were not directly related to the form of the literary work.

Socialist realism requirements therefore contributed to the construction of the concept of "free" translation, which eventually became very well rooted in the Soviet literary tradition. "Translation is creative obsession with the translated work and its author and not the cold-blooded rendering into another language, even though performed on a high professional level," wrote the Armenian researcher Khachik Dashtents in 1968.[34] The issue of artistic creativity almost came to equal quality in translation of literary works, especially after the influential translator and literary critic Kornei Chukovskii published his bright and tremendously witty book *Vysokoe iskusstvo* (A high art) devoted to literary translation and translation approaches in 1964. Not devoid of controversy and subjectivity, the book created a vivid picture of the translation situation of the 1960s.[35] The book became widely popular among professional and nonprofessional readers interested in literature and translation; it enjoyed multiple re-editions and continues to be read and reprinted in Russia to this day.

Chukovskii sees literary translation as a creative activity. "I understood," wrote Chukovskii, "that a good translator deserves respect in our literary community, because he is not a craftsman, nor a copyist, but an artist. He does not photograph the original . . . but recreates it artistically. The text of the original serves him the material for difficult and often inspirational creativity. The translator is primarily talent. To translate Balzac he has to some extent become Balzac, adopt his temperament, get inspired by his ideas, his poetic feel of life."[36]

Numerous followers of this romantic opinion shared the belief that the translator transformed into the translated author and embraced his/her way of thinking and that the translator recreated the original in the new language the way the author would have done it had he/she known the Russian language. This concept of the creative freedom of translators gradually became the governing principle in the light of which excessive attention of a translator to the formal features of the original could lead to being labeled a formalist. For a Soviet translator, accusations of formalism *(formalizm)* and literalism *(bukvalizm)* were extremely dangerous, however far etymologically these two terms were from being pejorative. The word *formalism* traditionally existed in the Russian language to define "any formal approach or formality."[37] The word acquired an additional meaning in the middle of the 1910s when the Russian formalist movement and the Russian Formal School of Literary Studies came into being, calling for putting the text in the focus of literary research rather than dwelling upon the extralinguistic features of literary works.[38] Adherents of formalism did not call their approach an aesthetic theory as they sought "to create a separate literary discipline on the basis of specific features of the literary material."[39] The formalist approach was severely criticized in the 1920s, but the importance of the formalist movement was nonetheless acknowledged by critics and language specialists. The *Bol'shaia sovetskaia entsiklopediia* (Big Soviet encyclopedia) of 1936 dedicated over ten pages to the description of formalism, including formalism in philosophy, music, arts, and cinematography. The section devoted to literature defined formalism as an idealistic approach placing the highest value on the form. Being generally descriptive and neutral in its tone, the entry of 1936 ended with the following remark: "The general development of the Soviet literature was following the path of Socialist Realism, which has nothing in common with the recipes of Formalism."[40] The remark is demonstrative of the general tendency: the word *formalism* was gradually turning into a swear-word used to define the primacy of form over content. Twenty years later, the postwar edition of the *Bol'shaia sovetskaia entsiklopediia* defined formalism as an "artistic method hostile to realism" and overcoming formalism—as one of the most important tasks of world art.[41] Thus the term *formalism* eventually came to define technical complexity, deviation from the requirement of specificity and other requirements imposed on literature by the socialist realism.[42] Rendered forms and styles of original works could be in conflict with the Soviet vision of the functions of art and literature. Putting a high value on the formal features of the literary work and giving the formal features of the original the highest priority in literary translation placed translators at the risk of being accused of formalism and disregard of the official course of the Soviet literature.[43] The evolution of the term in the course of less than fifty years is striking: what was clearly associated with the word *form* came to mean "formal," "rigid," or "dry." This tragic discrepancy in terminology was later hinted at by Viktor Shklovskii, one of the key figures and theorists of Russian formalism. In 1983, when dwelling on the issues of formalism and structuralism, Shklovskii carefully noted, "All names are always false."[44]

Unlike formalism, the term *literalism (bukvalizm)* in the Russian language always had a negative connotation and was used to describe a formal approach to an activity.[45] In the middle of the twentieth century, literalism in translation was looked upon as a "formalist" feature consisting in the mechanic rewording of the original as opposed to the emotional empathy and creativity employed by those translators who strove to recreate translated originals.

Works of people of letters, literary critics, and practicing translators regularly dwelt on the issues of creativity in literary translation. This general outcry in favor of creativity resulted in the attempt to develop a strict methodology, which was undertaken by the Soviet theorist Ivan Kashkin, the famous translator of Chaucer, founder and chair of one of the translation seminars in the Moscow department of the Union of Writers. Calling for creativity in literary translation, Kashkin at the same time saw the main function of literary translation as educational. Kashkin called for realistic translation, which was in line with the socialist realism guidelines and, in Kashkin's own words, resulted "not from the words and forms that depict the subject or describe the activity, but from the subject and the activity as such, as seen by the author and as it must be seen by the translator."[46] Calling the literary text "a conditional verbal sign," Kashkin expressed his admiration of the translators who were able "to see the original together with the author, through the author's eyes, and represent what they saw by means correctly chosen from their native language."[47] At the same time the translator, in Kashkin's view, was supposed to observe "the right to read the original through the eyes of our contemporaries in the light of their socialistic, revolutionary view of the world."[48] The call for so-called free translation fell in line with the socialist realism philosophy with its tendency toward national spirit and condemnation of the elitism; it perfectly fit in with censorship, which ideologically predisposed modifications of the source text.[49]

Enjoying wide popularity, Kashkin found his opponent in the person of Andrei Fedorov who was the first in the Soviet Union to declare the supremacy of the linguistic approach to translation over the literary approach, inspiration, and other extralinguistic phenomena.[50] His book *Vvedenie v teoriiu perevoda* (Introduction to translation theory) first published in 1953 saw several editions and evolved into an even bigger monograph *Osnovy obshchei teorii perevoda (lingvisticheskie problemy)* (Fundamentals of general translation theory [linguistic problems]).[51] "The linguistic approach to studying translation," wrote Fedorov,

> touches upon its very basis—the language, beyond which no functions of translation are possible—neither social and political, nor cultural and cognitive, nor its artistic meaning, etc. At the same time linguistic studies of translation, that is, its studies in view of the comparison of two languages, allow us to be specific, as we operate objective factors of language. Any research and speculation as to how the content of the original reflected in the translation and what role it played in the receiving literature would be groundless unless based on the analysis of the linguistic means employed in the translation. Translation theory as a special field of philology is primarily a linguistic discipline. In some cases, however, it is closely linked with literature studies—literary history and theory where it borrows some data and ideas, and with the history of the nations whose languages are used in the translation process . . . But the close connection of the translation theory with these disciplines does not change its specifics as a linguistic discipline.[52]

The new approach declared by Fedorov had a revolutionary effect. First published in 1953, the book attracted universal attention not only due to its outstanding novelty, but also because *Vvedenie v teoriiu perevoda* was the first book on the subject of translation published in the Soviet Union after World War II and was therefore separated by twelve years from the prewar books dedicated to translation problems. Several manuals on translation practice were published after the war, but the theory was first addressed by Fedorov, and it was done in such a new and daring way that it created substantial grounds for disputes for the decades to come.

The novelty of Fedorov's approach conflicted with the views of the key linguists of the USSR. Fedorov was aware of this; thus, for instance, in his *Vvedenie v teoriiu perevoda*, Fedorov openly disputed the opinion of the well-known linguist Aleksandr Reformatskii who deemed the mere existence of translation theory practically impossible.[53] The resolution of Fedorov naturally evoked anger and resentment, as well as the wave of criticism from the adherents of the "realistic" approach to translation. Whereas Fedorov believed the linguistic approach to be a substantial basis for translation practice, for "any creative activity requires theoretical generalization,"[54] Fedorov's opponents accused Fedorov of indifference to the aesthetics of the original. Ukrainian scholar Oleksei Kundzich described this situation in his notes, which were partly published in 1968. "Invariably sensitive to literary matters, I. Kashkin exercised great composure in straightening up the line of the theory of our art," wrote Kundzich, "but his remark upon the extremity of Fedorov's linguistic judgment was overly exaggerated in publications and speeches of other writers. It even came to the point that the 'linguistic slant' started to be identified with literalism."[55] To illustrate the perception of Fedorov's linguistic theory, Kundzich quotes the words of the distinguished Soviet writer and translator Nikolai Zabolotskii: "A translator who follows the linguistic approach is like a bug that crawls over the text and examines every word through a huge magnifying glass. In such translation, words are translated correctly but it is difficult to read the book because literary translation is not the same as the translation of words."[56, 57]

Such a perception of Fedorov's research is demonstrative of the general attitude to literature and literary translation in 1960s and 1970s. Nonetheless, the linguistic approach to translation proclaimed by Fedorov eventually outweighed the literary approach advocated by

Kashkin. In response to Kashkin's criticism, Fedorov himself noted that the linguistic theory did not exist for the sake of providing ready-made "recipes" for practicing translators, but "for the sake of studying regularities that exist objectively between languages . . . and stylistic systems of the original and translation."[58]

Among other distinguished researchers of the time was another Leningrad scholar, professor Efim Etkind, who in his seminal monograph *Poeziia i perevod* (Poetry and translation) studied the key issues of translatability, transfer of the implied meaning and formal features of the original, and personality of the literary translator. "There is no universal criterion to measure the faithfulness of the translation to the original," admitted Etkind. "Faithfulness is a changeable notion."[59] At the same time, Etkind severely criticized Kashkin's approach and disputed every argument of Kashkin's theory of realistic translation and his perception of the literary text as a conditional verbal sign.[60] "It is insufficient to understand the reality 'in its directed development, in its revolutionary development,' as Kashkin demands—one must be able to read the original," ruthlessly summarizes Etkind at the end of his ten-page long criticism of Kashkin's approach.[61] Needless to say, such outspoken criticism and sarcastic remarks about the revolutionary approach contributed to Etkind's image of a rebel and in some regard predetermined his future as a political exile. But although translation theory was gradually shaping up as a linguistic discipline in the Soviet Union, debates over literalism and creativity in translation remained stormy throughout the twentieth century.

The growth of Fedorov's influence over linguists and translation specialists, bold statements of Etkind, and ironic comments of Kundzich reflected new moods that were arising in the 1960s. It was the 1960s that created a new social phenomenon—a generation of people called *shestidesiatniks* (people of the sixties). Born between 1925 and 1945, shestidesiatniks inherited respect for communist ideas from their parents, some of whom had been participants in the October Revolution and the civil war. It was mainly the generation of the parents of shestidesiatniks who were victims of Stalin's repression; many shestidesiatniks themselves were veterans of World War II. Memories of war and political repressions turned shestidesiatniks into active thinkers who declared honesty of perception and expression as their main philosophy.

Shestidesiatniks as a social phenomenon came about with the Khrushchev Thaw, which started with the denouncement of the cult of Stalin. This public deposition of the recently deceased tyrant detonated a stormy reaction of the general public: people engaged in active disputes on their recent past, openly expressing their opinions and sharing their painful memories. The awakening of the people of the Soviet Union to new knowledge and their new ability for self-expression became distinctive features of the beginning of the 1960s, which gave the period the metaphoric name of the *Thaw*. Shaped under new, rapidly changing circumstances, shestidesiatniks would later openly join the dissident movement, protest against the Soviet occupation of Czechoslovakia, and organize the Moscow Helsinki Watch Group—the human rights organization founded in 1976 to monitor compliance of the Soviet Union with the Helsinki Accords of 1975. In their majority, shestidesiatniks demonstrated lenience toward dissidence, even though most of them never actively engaged in opposing the state openly. As the Russian economist and a shestidesiatnik Evgenii Iasin noted, shestidesiatniks were all those people who had no power to change the existing circumstances but who were getting together in kitchens, sharing their ideas, and "waiting for their time to come."[62] As people with university education, shestidesiatniks fulfilled themselves in science, engineering, medicine, cinematography, music, and theater, but it was literature that became the central theme of the 1960s and 1970s. The growing awareness of and active interest in the world beyond the borders of the Soviet Union determined the rise of the universal interest toward creative writing, which fell in line with the Russian cultural tradition of self-expression in literature.[63] The literary boom manifested itself both in the original literature of Viktor Nekrasov, Iurii Bondyrev, Vasil' Bykov, Vladimir Voinovich, Fazil' Iskander, and many others and in literary translation, which was also experiencing a tremendous rise. The effect foreign literature had on shestidesiatniks was comparable to a revelation: a portrait of Hemingway or Remarque was a common picture on the wall of the living room in the house of an intellectual in the 1960s.

Nonetheless, manifestations of freedom were closely monitored by the Cultural Department of the Communist Party and creative unions.[64] The seeming awakening of freedom made uncomfortable the conservative representatives of artistic circles, who felt threatened by the new opportunities provided to young progressive artists and writers. Trying to keep a tight rein on literature and arts, the Communist Party circulated letters and regulations reminding the citizens of the actual state of things. Thus, the letter entitled "On increasing party organizations' political work with the population and on suppression of raids of anti-Soviet hostile elements" made it quite clear that the indulgence of the Soviet government with manifestations of freedom was a mere flirtation with democracy. "We cannot be of two minds regarding the hostile Rump and how to fight it," the letter said.[65] "The dictatorship of the proletariat must be merciless toward the anti-Soviet elements."[66] This resolution of the Communist Party to maintain its position and influence came into full force during the campaign against Boris Pasternak, which resulted in the writer's forced denouncement of the Nobel Prize for Literature in 1958.

Therefore, the Thaw barely weakened the influence of the state over the literary activity in the country. Glavlit continued to perform its censoring functions, informing the Central Committee of the Communist Party or KGB of all anti-Soviet activity in arts and literature. The imminent danger of becoming an object of political censorship and repression gradually made self-censorship a natural strategy and a means of self-preservation. In this regard, the restrictedly circulated regulation of the Central Committee of the Communist Party of the Soviet Union "On raising the responsibility of the press, radio, television, cinematography, and culture and arts institutions for the ideological and political level of published materials and repertoire" of January 7, 1969, strengthened the importance of self-censorship by calling it a natural trait of Soviet art and declared authors and editors personally responsible for the contents of their publications.[67] The regulation raised the level of tension in the Soviet publishing houses, which began to pay even closer attention to the choice of texts, authors, and translators.

Political control of published literature and literary activity, requirements of socialist realism, and politically disapproved alternatives to state-owned publishing houses were therefore the important features of Soviet literary life in 1960–85. Literature as a cultural segment could not develop independently from the domestic and foreign policy of the

Soviet state. Changes in the political course led to changes in the attitude of the state toward subjects, characters, and styles of literary texts.
But despite the varying political affiliations and ambitions of the Soviet
Union, the fundamental principles of the closed society remained viable
in the strategic orientation of Soviet literature and literary translation:

1. Nationalism as a guiding principle in selection and publication of literary works remained part of the general state policy, despite the fact
   that nationalism ran counter to the federative principles of the Soviet
   constitution. Russian language and culture continued to dominate
   other languages and cultures of the Soviet Union, enjoying greater
   publishing and literary translation opportunities.

2. The promotion of the image of the Soviet Union as a warring state
   taking part in the battle for the good of humankind was an important
   and highly effective manipulative technique that helped to cultivate a
   sense of national pride in Soviet citizens. The alliance with the Communist bloc of the Warsaw Pact presented a logical collective antithesis to the Western world, and the Communist Party of the Soviet
   Union continued to implant the fear of war into the minds of the
   nation that had already seen the terrors of war and sustained tremendous losses.

3. Despite the general fear of war, war enjoyed elevated status in the Soviet Union. The Soviet Union regularly engaged in military actions,
   including military conflicts in Africa, the War of Attrition, the invasion of Czechoslovakia, Sino-Soviet border conflicts, the Soviet-
   Afghan War, and the Nicaraguan civil war, as well as the Cold War, in
   which the Soviet Union portrayed itself as the nuclear danger defense
   screen. Soviet citizens were presented with the image of their state
   administrating justice and making sacrifices for the good of humankind. For this reason, elevated military subjects and literary images
   of warriors and freedom fighters never lost their importance and enjoyed active promotion in publishing.

4. The fighting policy of the Soviet Union encouraged and even de-
   manded individual and social heroism from its citizens, both in their
   social responsibilities and in their individual endeavors, including
   creative work.

5. The state continued to feel exempt from moral obligation. Development and growth of censoring institutions, show trials of poets and writers, public baiting, compulsory psychiatric care, prison sentences, and exiles of inconvenient social figures continued to take place even in the relatively lenient years of the Thaw.

6. Collective utility continued to be propagated as the main guideline for personal conduct. Principles of collectivism were not always possible to combine with individual creativity and personal aspirations of people engaged in literature and arts, which is why individual creative approaches and methods were regularly suppressed and self-censored by writers and translators, so that they could continue to work within the field of literature.

7. The creative role of the Great Man in 1960–85 remains to be ascribed to Lenin. Stalin's image, which had claimed its share of the universal adoration, was shattered and cast down in 1956, leaving the role of the semideity to his predecessor, who, along with Marx and Engels, formed a trine of unchallenged authority. It is also specific to the pyramid of subordination of the Soviet society that every superior official was potentially ascribed more wisdom and expertise than his/her inferiors.

The described parameters demonstrate a high degree of closedness of Soviet society in the studied period. Closedness manifests itself at all points in the above list, and despite the relative loosening of control and gaining of new freedoms, Soviet society remained separated from the rest of the world. It is against these parameters that I am going to study Soviet translation in the following chapters.

It is notable that the rise of creative writing and literary translation in the Soviet Union was especially dynamic in the 1960s, which, albeit insufficiently, provided both information and leniency toward novelty. The ability to gain new knowledge and make conscious choices found expression in a variety of social manifestations—from literary engagement to dissident protests. Different in their nature, all these manifestations had their purpose in the discovery of new knowledge and further sharing of this knowledge with the rest of the world. Sharing knowledge with others could take the shape of a social action, an open protest, or just a translation of a foreign novel.

The Soviet translators who are going to be the focus of our attention in this book mainly belonged to the generation of shestidesiatniks and were actively influenced by the ideals of freedom and unconventional thinking. Some of the translators whom I interviewed were born after 1945 and therefore technically belong to a younger generation, the *semi-desiatniks* (people of the seventies), whose subculture originated from the ideas of the shestidesiatniks. The shestidesiatniks and semidesiat-niks worked closely together in art and literature; their literary methods, although different in artistic vision, were marked by the acute feeling of longing for freedom of expression. Literary translators were politically engaged merely because they were part of Soviet literary life: literature as an activity required courage, especially after Khrushchev's dismissal and the arrival of the new government, which resumed tightening the control of arts and literature. Some translators were political activists and dissidents, but even those who never openly engaged in politics had to resist censorship, control, and restrictions of the freedom of speech in their literary work. In fact, more than half of the interviewed translators denied their involvement in activism of any kind, but, as we shall see the activism inspired by political and social factors sometimes takes place when the translator remains unaware of his/her social contribution.

CHAPTER 4

THE MAKING OF A TRANSLATOR

Old Controversies and New Friendships

Throughout the centuries, literary translation in Russia remained a carefully supervised activity. The development of the Russian state and the spread of influence of the Russian Orthodox Church required focusing on domestic affairs and local religion. The state and the church made regular attempts to reduce the number of channels of information about other cultures. Interest in foreign literature, both original and translated, sometimes had unpleasant or even tragic outcomes. One of the famous records of such repression dates back to the beginning of the seventeenth century, when Prince Ivan Khvorostinin was accused of heresy for his interest in European art and for his collection of "Catholic" books and paintings. After the official seizure of his library and arts collection, Khvorostinin was tried for his alleged denial of Christianity and exiled to a monastery.[1] In the eighteenth century, imported literature raised concerns for Catherine II, and in the second year of her reign she issued a special decree in which she called on the Academy of Sciences to command closer control of imported literature, especially such books whose contents were "against the law, good manners, ourselves and the Russian nation."[2] Censorship reform of Paul I in 1800 culminated in his decree that stated, "Since different imported foreign books abuse faith, civil law, and good manners, we hereby order until the special decree to forbid the import from abroad into our state of all sorts of books, disregarding their language, without exception, and also music."[3] Strengthening of the censorship apparatus in the nineteenth century also affected translation (see chap. 1). Translation also became a point of dispute in the nineteenth century when the clergy split on the issue of translation of the Holy Bible into the contemporary Russian language, as opposed to Old Slavonic (chap. 2).

In its worldly sense, translation was seen as a source of knowledge and, therefore, of an alternative point of view. With the Russian monarchy and the Russian Orthodox Church highly protective of their power, alternative visions of the world were regularly looked upon as interference with national stability and morals. It is no wonder therefore that throughout Russian history translators were carefully watched for their professional "foreignness." The stereotypical image of a literary translator as a semiforeigner engaged in creative activity remains alive in Russia to this day.

Disapproval of "foreignness" in Russian culture alternated with periods of remission, when interest in foreign works and translations was initiated from above to a certain extent. Such a rise of interest, for instance, took place in the beginning of the eighteenth century, when Peter the Great encouraged his subjects to embrace Western thought and philosophy by getting familiar with the achievements of the West. The practical need for high-quality translations increased the requirements for all publications, bringing Russian literature to a new level.[4]

Literary translation remained one of the major vehicles of literature production in the nineteenth century, presenting a good platform for literary experimenting. The nineteenth century brought original creative writing and literary translation closer together. As Brian Baer observes, "polylingualism, combined with the enormous prestige of Western European culture in Russia, the idea of translation as service to the nation, as well as the unfortunate reality of repressive censorship restrictions on original writing, led the most canonical Russian writers of the nineteenth century—and many of the twentieth century, as well—to engage in translation work in a serious and sustained manner."[5] Distinguished Russian poets, writers, and journalists engaged in literary translation and led heated discussions of translation approaches, techniques, and philosophy.[6] Prominent figures such as Vasilii Zhukovskii, Aleksandr Pushkin, Mikhail Lermontov, Ivan Turgenev, Aleskei Pleshcheev, and Fedor Dostoyevsky translated foreign literature at different stages of their literary career for different reasons ranging from desire for experimentation to financial motives. This active engagement of original writers and poets in translating others gradually created a stereotype of a literary translator as a cocreator of a literary work in a new language. This stereotyping was enhanced by incessant nineteenth-century debates between the adversaries of "free" and "faithful" translation, which was modified over the years and reverberated, as we shall see, in the twentieth century.

The twentieth century in Russia continued the history of literary translation experimenting, which, with the advent of the October Revolution of 1917, had to adapt to the new social order and its practical demands. Literature was allocated a new important role in Soviet Russia: it was supposed to become the basis for the education of new generations of the new monarchy-free state.[7] The orientation of literature toward education increased the demand for literary translation. Foreign literature was actively published in the Soviet Union from the very first years the new state came into being. Already in 1919, writer Maksim Gor'kii initiated the publication of the literature series Vsemirnaia literatura (World literature) that was to consist of two parts—the main one, of 1,500 volumes and twenty printer's sheets each, and the so-called people's library of 2,500 volumes and two to four printer's sheets each.[8] Despite the unfavorable economic situation in the country, the publication of the series lasted only until 1927, eventually amounting to 120 volumes of the works of European, North American, and South American literature. "The Russian nation in all its mass," wrote Gor'kii, "must know the historical, sociological, and psychological characteristics of those nations, with which it is now striving towards the construction of the new forms of social life. Literature, the living and graphic history of deeds and misdeeds, contributions, and errors of our ancestors, wielding a mighty ability to influence the organization of thought, softening the crudeness of instinct, nurturing the will, must, in the end, fulfill its planetary role—a role of power, strongly and profoundly uniting nations from within through a consciousness of a communion with their sufferings and desires, a consciousness of the unity of their strivings towards the improvement of a free and beautiful life."[9]

The series prided itself on the translations done by the best translators of the time who remained in the Soviet Russia after the revolution and who readily became involved in the Vsemirnaia literatura project. These were famous poets Aleksandr Blok, Valerii Briusov, Nikolai Gumilev, translators Anna Gansen and Wilhelm Sorgenfrei, literature specialists and critics Fedor Batiushkov, Aleksandr Smirnov, Viktor Zhirmunskii, and other distinguished scholars who provided the published works with detailed commentaries and extensive forewords. Such engagement of well-known poets, translators, and critics in the Vsemirnaia literatura project was important to manifest the readiness of the literati to get involved in the universal education process and share their knowledge with readers of all social strata. At the same time, this massive participation of original poets and writers in a big literary translation project largely contributed to the stereotype of the translator as an independent creator, engaged in the process of cocreation with the author of the original.[10]

Another achievement of the series was the approach of its editors to the quality of translations, which created substantial grounds for calling this series "the cradle of the Soviet literary translation school."[11] Forty years later, the well-remembered success of the Vsemirnaia literatura series encouraged the publishing house Khudozhestvennaia Literatura to initiate the series Biblioteka vsemirnoi literatury (Library of world literature)—a collection of two hundred volumes of literary works, which was published in 1967–77. Out of the two hundred volumes of the series, 160 were dedicated to foreign literature. The series prided itself on the high quality of print, excellent illustrations, and in-depth commentaries and introductory notes written by distinguished researchers and literature specialists of the time.

The immediate investment of the Soviet state into literature in the second year of the existence of the Soviet power is characteristic of the emerging trend, which would remain viable in the subsequent decades. As Katerina Clark explains in detail in her *Moscow, the Fourth Rome*, claims of superiority over other states required substantial proof, which in the early years the Soviet Union could not be found in its technology or military potential. The Soviet state hence chose culture as the main argument for preeminence. The purposeful activities of the Soviet state in promoting culture eventually resulted in culture becoming an area defining the Soviet identity, with Soviet citizens taking particular pride in the national literature, architecture, and ballet.[12] The empowerment of culture in the Soviet context was facilitated by antireligious persecutions, which resulted in frustrated believers addressing their unused religious zeal to arts and reading. This shift in emphasis could be clearly observed already in the 1930s, when, as Clark puts it "culture began to take off both as a value for its own sake and as emblem of national glory, achieving a cult status in a cultural turn."[13] This particularly concerned literature, which, in its nature relating to intellectual and spiritual rather than material wealth, met the readers' needs for emotional comfort.

In this context, foreign literature played an important role in Soviet culture. Foreign literature was a tangible link to the outside world and a proof of the Soviet involvement in the widely propagated internationalism, which, as Clark correctly observes, was "a euphemism for the cause of Soviet ideological hegemony throughout the world."[14] The notion of "world literature" went far beyond the name of the successful literary project; it eventually came to define an ultimate goal. Embracing world literature meant both eager acceptance and appropriation of the world cultural heritage, which symbolically appointed the Soviet state the custodian of the world classics and the inspirer of modernity. Clark refers to the revival of pre-Soviet Russian culture in the 1930s as a part of the Great Appropriation.[15] This appropriation process continued long after the 1930s into the second half of the twentieth century. Literary translation was one of the spheres actively employed in appropriation. As a result, the Soviet epoch produced a unique collection of literary translations of the works of all centuries, genres, and cultures. This overwhelming translation heritage was both a cause for national pride and a reason for silent bewilderment of the Soviet readers.

> *Mikhail Yasnov:* Efim Etkind would repeatedly say that the Soviet Union felt itself a rightful heir to the world literature. This is why the Soviet Union had an urge to translate everything. Apart from religion and eroticism, of course. The Soviet Union developed a unique culture of translation and translation editing. In 1950–60, there were published brilliant

sets of collected works of different writers that are hard to match even now. The translations themselves, commentaries to them, the printing quality—everything was brilliant. There were also such books as "European seventeenth-century sonnets." I showed it to Etkind when we met in Paris, and he was amazed. "How can one publish such a book?" he exclaimed. "It is absolutely cost-ineffective."

The claim of the Soviet Union to being the world literature successor resulted in several distinctive features of Soviet publishing. Thus, disregard for copyright law, as we have already seen in chapter 3, resulted in numerous translations and publications of foreign authors without obtaining the permissions of these authors or their legal heirs or paying any royalties. The Soviet Union never joined the Berne Convention; the Russian Federation signed it only as a separate state in 1995, thus taking up obligations to observe international copyright legislation.

> *Irina Komarova:* In the Soviet Union, the whole notion of copyright was ignored; authors abroad knew they were being translated in the Soviet Union but could not do anything about it and would not get a penny from the Soviet publishing houses. For instance, John Fowles knew that Meri Bekker and I were translating *The French Lieutenant's Woman.* Fowles and I corresponded, he advised me on how the translation should be done, but he never tried to get any money from the Russian publication of his novel.

Claims for world literature also resulted in another important feature of Soviet publishing. Being a legitimate heir implied not only ownership of all rights, but also a tremendous responsibility for the preservation of world literature. The requirements set for the quality of literary translation were extremely high. Despite the severe control by censors who at times could hardly be called literature specialists, Soviet publishers paid the closest attention to the quality of translations. Literary translation in the Soviet Union could be called an industry, yet an industry with the assembly line producing handmade products.

> *Mikhail Yasnov:* What I found amazing about the Soviet publishing houses like Khudozhestvannaia Literatura is that apart from editors they also used to have *svershchiks,* that is, cross-checkers. A *svershchik* was a

person who knew many languages and who was hired to compare translations against their originals. The cross-checker was interested in how the two texts differed and how much was missing in the translation. This mainly concerned prose rather than poetry.

Such open manifestations of responsibility for world literature taken by the state attest to the degree of importance ascribed to literature and arts. This internationalism, which required openness to new trends, authors, literatures, and points of view, clashed with bellicose nationalism, which was intrinsic to the Soviet policy and was a feature of a closed society. Literary trends and styles that did not fit in with the program of national state building were relentlessly rejected for reasons of insignificance and seeming triviality.[16] This clash of opposing tendencies was reflected in the instance of literary translation. Whereas the state openly initiated literary translation and publication activities, literary opportunities in the Soviet Union were getting increasingly limited due to the centralization of the publishing business in the country, closures of private publishing houses, and growth of state control over translators, their translations, and political engagement. The advent of socialist realism in the 1930s automatically affected the process of selection of originals and approaches to literary translations, for nonconformity with its requirements was seen as lenience toward bourgeois philosophy, defection, and latent hostility toward Soviet ideals. These constraints of a political nature set technical bounds on creative choice. Indeed, translators were supposed to render the poetic features, style, and implications of the original, and at the same time they were required to ensure clarity and specificity and, if possible, create a possible ideological link; thus they faced an incredibly vast number of tasks and had to make choices in favor of the imposed requirements at the expense of form and content.

This compulsive compromise was directly connected to the much-discussed dilemma of "correct" and "faulty" understanding of the original. Texts and authors classified as appropriate or friendly to the Soviet reality were expected to conform to the local values. This resulted in the emergence of several literary personality cults, like the cult of Aleksandr Pushkin, George Byron, or Charles Dickens, each of them ascribed a special role in the education and liberation of humankind.[17] Such a rise of literary personalities took place alongside the promotion of particularly suitable works and ideas of favored authors.

This approach found its advocates, who looked upon the notions of "correct understanding" of the message of the original and the necessity of representation of this message in the translation not as a limitation of the professional freedom but as the ultimate freedom of creative thinkers. For example, Ivan Kashkin, an accomplished translator who educated an impressive number of literary translators of the Moscow school (Evgeniia Kalashnikova, Vera Toper, Olga Kholmskaia, Natalia Volzhina, Nina Daruzes, Mariia Lorie, and Mariia Bogoslovskaia), wrote with enthusiasm in 1954, "Approaching the literary work as an ideological-literary unity and subordinating all its parts to the correctly understood whole, the best Soviet translators achieve faithfulness to the original . . . They achieve historic specificity which guarantees the avoidance of approximation of any kind and which ensures the correct transfer of the features of the time and space. They introduce vividness and relevance into their translations thus ruling out any dryness of idealistic abstractions."[18] This absolute faith in the inviolability of the Soviet requirements made Kashkin rise in arms against anyone whose approach to translation clashed with his own. The influence of Kashkin as an accomplished translator, theorist, and educator over the minds of critics and readers was strong enough to impair the reputation of those whom he selected as a target of his criticism.

One of the targets of Kashkin's anger was Georgii Shengeli (1894–1956), a distinguished Russian poet and translator, who in 1947 produced his translation of Byron's *Don Juan*.[19] The attempt of Shengeli to preserve Byron's style, rhyming scheme, and images was strikingly foreignizing in the context of the translation situation in the Soviet Union, which gave Kashkin substantial grounds to vilify the translation and the translator himself in the article "Traditsiia i epigonstvo" (Tradition and epigony) in 1952.[20] "The text [of the original] is falsely read and mistakenly interpreted," wrote Kashkin. "This translation is principally corrupt in its artistic basis, in its methodology."[21] In his article, Kashkin dissected Shengeli's translation, accusing the translator of using too much detail that could not be clear to the Soviet reader and of distorting the social purpose of the poem. But the main blow to the translator was the accusation of besmearing the name of the great Russian general Suvorov (1730–1800) whose portrait in *Don Juan* was depicted by Byron with much detail. Even until today, the figure of Suvorov continues to be one of the few in Russian history that Russians see as "perfect," and his name has remained unspotted in the course of history. This is why the Byronic description indeed does not seem respectful enough to the Russian hero of the Ottoman campaigns as would any description done by an outside observer. In translating the parts related to Suvorov, Shengeli preserved the tone and wording of the original, which allowed Kashkin to deal the fatal blow to the reputation of the translator. Shengeli was severely criticized for the preservation of the definition of Suvorov as a "Harlequin in uniform" in the last line of the stanza—the strong position where the textual element is most visible to the recipient. As well, Kashkin expressed special indignation at the fact that Shengeli depicted Suvorov as a lighthearted old man. Byron's original, as we can see, is quite straightforward:

> Suwarrow, who was standing in his shirt
> Before a company of Calmucks, drilling,
> Exclaiming, fooling, swearing at the inert,
> And lecturing on the noble art of killing,—
> For deeming human clay but common dirt,
> This great philosopher was thus instilling
> His maxims, which to martial comprehension
> Proved death in battle equal to a pension.[22]

Shengeli's translation follows the original in form and content:

> Suvorov at that hour was commanding a platoon
> In his shirt, his coat off, teaching Calmucks,
> Perfecting them in the noble art
> Of killing. He was making jokes, fooling, swearing
> At the absent-minded and the inert. A born philosopher,
> From dirt—he did not tell human clay
> And declared the maxim that death in a battle
> Must be as tempting to a hero as a pension.[23]

As one can see, Shengeli preserves Byron's irony in the fourth and sixth line, the description of Suvorov's temperament in the fourth line, and the joke about the monetary value of death in battle, which sounds blasphemous to the Russian ear even in the twenty-first century. However inappropriate this comment of Byron sounds culturally, especially in relation to the national hero, Shengeli preserves the vision of the historic context described in the original.[24] Such daring decisions resulted in the almost unanimous condemnation of the translator.

"The readers would probably ask me," wrote Kashkin, "if probably it is what Byron has in the original. No, even if it looks like that, it is not like that at all!"[25] This ridiculing argumentation resulted in labeling Shengeli a formalist, which damaged his literary reputation and hurried his death in 1956.

> EVGENII WITKOWSKY: The vilification of Shengeli was a crime. Kashkin wanted to get rid of rivals, and writing an article about Shengeli, Byron, and the Suvorov case was sheer whistle-blowing, because Kashkin knew that Stalin worshipped Suvorov.
>
> Shengeli should not have experimented with the iambic meter in *Don Juan*. Had he stuck to the iambic pentameter instead of switching to iambic hexameter, the translation would have turned out better, and he would have protected himself easier.

An alternative to Shengeli's translation was offered by Tat'iana Gnedich whose Russian rendering of *Don Juan* was much more closely coordinated with the guidelines of the existing translation philosophy. It must be noted, however, that Gnedich's translation was created in extraordinary circumstances. Gnedich translated *Don Juan* in prison where she was put for her friendship with a foreign pilot. The most remarkable moment here is that Gnedich knew *Don Juan* by heart and translated the poem from her memory.

The translation of Gnedich received a cordial welcome from critics and fellow translators. In rendering the text, Gnedich exercised more freedom and independence from the formal features of the original, which, as mentioned above, was a general tendency of poetic translation in the Soviet Union. For example, in the translation of the aforementioned stanza Gnedich mitigated the image of war as *killing*, turning it into *killing with a bayonet or sabre* and left out the sarcastic joke about death or pension, which did not fit in with the noble image of the

Russian hero. Thus, the focus of the translation was shifted: Suvorov no longer looked like a cog in the war machine of the Russian Empire, but a brilliant general and a leader with better poise than described in the original.

> Suvorov, his coat off, in his shirt,
> Was training a battalion of Calmucks,
> And swore if someone, poor chap,
> Was clumsy or tired.
> The art of killing with a bayonet or sabre
> He taught skillfully; he believed
> That a human body, no doubt,
>   Is only a material suitable for a battle![26]

The translation of *Don Juan* made by Shengeli rendered Gnedich a service despite Shengeli's ruined reputation. Gnedich is known to have consulted Shengeli's translation in the process of editing her own translation; it is also quite clear that she was aware of the reasons for Shengeli's criticism and therefore was able to bring her translation in line of the expectations of critics.[27]

Kashkin was not the only one whose severe criticism contributed to the prejudice of the Russian readership against Shengeli's translation. The famous critic, poet, and translator Kornei Chukovskii dedicated a chapter of his book *Vysokoe iskusstvo* (A high art) to Gnedich's translation of *Don Juan* where he also criticized Shengeli for "mechanic preciseness" and "ponderosity."[28] The criticism poured onto Shengeli by universally recognized people of letters had a serious impact on Shengeli's reputation and encouraged the next generations of critics and translators to continue the vilification of his work.[29] Disapproval of Shengeli's translations was also expressed by Gnedich and some members of her translation seminar whose opinion on literary translation still count.[30] One of the few voices in the defense of Shengeli's translation was that of the famous translator and professor of linguistics Efim Etkind. In his book *Russkie poety-perevodchiki ot Trediakovskogo do Pushkina* (Russian poet-translators from Trediakovskii to Pushkin), Etkind intentionally diverted from nineteenth-century subjects in order to make a poignant comment, stating that "from the point of view of the 1930s, the translation of Gnedich is free; it is this particular type of translation that was perceived as translation in the 1960s, whereas the 'real translation' was denied any literary value at all."[31]

One can clearly see that the opposition *form-content*, which became one of the focal points in the dispute over Shengeli's translation, is far from being a purely literary controversy. Experiments with literary form, including translation experiments, were at their peak when the revolution of 1917 broke out. As we have seen above, many literary experimenters supported the Russian Revolution by getting actively involved in literary projects. Nonetheless, literary experimenting, encouraged at the initial stages, was gradually replaced by a more centralized approach. This gradual change in attitude toward experiments affected such major figures of the early Soviet literature as Vladimir Mayakovskii, whose major experimentation with form eventually gave him the reputation of a "fellow traveler" and "not a proletarian poet." This mutual disappointment of Mayakovskii and the Soviet authorities with each other eventually led to the poet's tragic death in 1930. It was also in 1930 that the Literary Center of Constructivists dissolved itself, thus giving way to the systematized approach of socialist realism, which was officially proclaimed in literature in 1934.

Two great translations of Shakespeare's *Hamlet* also became involved in the disputes of critics and translators over the form and content of the originals and translations, as well as their conformity to the Soviet standards. The two translations arrived almost at the same time. One of them was produced by Mikhail Lozinskii (1886–1955). One of the most distinguished Russian translators of the twentieth century, Lozinskii was known as the translator of Molière, Félix Lope de Vega, Prosper Mérimée, Victor Hugo, and Romain Rolland, and would later gain fame for his translation of Dante's *Divine Comedy*. Lozinskii's translation of *Hamlet* was first published in 1933.[32] It was soon followed by the translation made by the poet, writer, and future Nobel Prize winner Boris Pasternak.[33] Pasternak admitted later that he would not have started working on the translation of *Hamlet* in the first place had he known that the great Lozinskii was working on a translation already.[34] Later Pasternak would describe Lozinskii's translation of *Hamlet* as ideal.[35] Both translations are still recognized as masterpieces of literary translation.

However, the translations differed in their approach to the form and content of the Shakespearean play.

Lozinskii considered the form to be an invariant feature of any literary work, which had to be represented in translation at all events. "It is quite inevitable in poetic translation," wrote Lozinskii, "that

1) part of the material is not reconstructed at all, discarded, sacrificed;
2) part of the material is reshaped and represented in the form of substitutions and equivalents;
3) the material, which is not present in the original, is introduced into the translation.

The reasons for these deviations are multiple.

There are deviations called for by language differences, as it also happens in translations of prose.

But there are deviations that are typical only for poetic translation. These are deviations called for by the form. The form is tyrannical, and it has a right to be tyrannical, because without it the harmonious structure of poetry collapses. And it demands sacrifice.[36]

The philological approach of Lozinskii and his faith in rendering the form of the translated work was actively criticized in the publications of the 1960s. Among his critics was Chukovskii, who reproached Lozinskii for excessive equilinearity of his translations, which Chukovskii found unnecessary.[37] This criticism was actively taken up by other critics and writers; for instance, Iurii Gavruk dedicated several pages of his essay to the problems of equilinearity in Lozinskii's translation.[38] In the same book of essays, another translator and literary critic Wilhelm Levik sarcastically compares Lozinskii to a weight lifter. "When I think of Lozinskii's *Hamlet*, I, for some reason, think of the specialists in a completely different field—Zhabotinskii and Vlasov.[39] True, Lozinskii lifted a monstrously heavy weight, but what did this gigantic effort lead to, what is its performance coefficient?"[40] Levik insists that the way the characters speak in Lozinskii's translation "does not sound like normal free human speech."[41] This accusation is particularly noteworthy: while Lozinskii was criticized for making the characters in *Hamlet* speak in an unnatural manner, Pasternak's translation was conversely criticized for the naturalness of the characters' speech. In the same essay on translation, three pages after having criticized Lozinskii's translation, Levik characterizes the translation of *Hamlet* by Boris Pasternak in the following way: ". . . the road taken by Pasternak cannot become our common way because Pasternak's Shakespeare is essentially poorer than its great prototype . . . In his pursuit of colloquiality, of the vernacular, he reduces Shakespeare's vocabulary and approximates the speech of different characters."[42]

This vocabulary reduction mentioned by Levik should rather be called modernization, which Pasternak chose for *Hamlet* and which he translated as a play for the contemporary theater. The "intentional liberty" advocated by Pasternak resulted in the high colloquiality of his translation.[43] This colloquiality drew the criticism of literature specialists, but, at the same time, it was this colloquiality that stage directors and filmmakers chose over the philologically straightened translation by Lozinskii. Publishers preferred Lozinskii's translation (compare twenty-seven Soviet editions in Pasternak's translation vs. forty-one in Lozinskii's); Pasternak's translation, however, dominated in the Soviet theaters. In case of publications, Lozinskii's translation was mainly published in the editions of his complete works, whereas Pasternak's translation was favored by school editions for its clarity.[44]

The reaction of Soviet critics to Pasternak's translation of *Hamlet* varied from high praise to stinging criticism.[45] Gavruk, in his article quoted above, criticized Pasternak by saying that some parts of his translation were "overly modernized or, probably, just unfinished;" he accused Pasternak's translation of a lack of clarity and even of making the protagonist close "to the modern desperate bourgeois intelligentsia."[46]

The imminent danger of being unjustly accused of bourgeois sentimentality, anticommunist feelings, or dissidence impended on everyone engaged in arts and literature in the Soviet Union. Despite these difficulties, the profession of a literary translator never lost its special allure in the Soviet Union. With the language education provided at Soviet schools insufficient to maintain a basic conversation and with access to foreign literature limited and state controlled, translators were looked up to as people possessing special powers. Across the country, hundreds of people dreamt of becoming literary translators, learned foreign languages, and tried to translate. Most of these endeavors, however, ended in "writing into the desk," as the Russian saying goes—that is, translating for the sake of translating, piling the translations diligently into a desk drawer without any hope of getting them published. The translation business in the Soviet Union was a stable mechanism, with a distinct hierarchy and a well-developed set of requirements to enter the field.

Becoming a literary translator was not a mere question of talent and personal effort—it was an issue of going through all the necessary stages of initiation. Choosing a literary work to one's own liking and bringing it to a publishing house for approval and potential publication was an event reserved for experienced translators. With all publishing houses being state owned and, naturally, state controlled, the chances for an unknown translator were exceptionally small. Nonetheless, the 1960s were marked by the advent of a large number of young skilled literary translators into the Soviet translation market. Young qualified translators continued to enter the literary translation field in the subsequent decades. This arrival of the "new blood" was a consequence of a state-initiated project, which soon lost its officiality. At the end of the 1950s, beginners in the field of literary translation began to unite into semiformal groups of fellow thinkers ready for new literary experiments and knowledge. This phenomenon of the Soviet literary culture became known under the name of *translation seminars*.

Translation seminars came into being as the result of a change of policy of the Soviet authorities, who in the 1950s came to realize the necessity of improving Soviet poetry, which had been seriously neglected under Stalin.[47] The beginning of the Khrushchev Thaw was shortly followed by an important literary event—the Second All-Union Congress of Soviet Writers, which took place in 1954. The revision of themes and approaches to poetry made during the congress created possibilities for the Soviet poets to move away from the traditional Stalinist styles and subjects. Such official encouragement gave rise to numerous LITOs[48]— literary associations of young writers organized by publishing houses, universities, and other cultural organizations, where young poets could meet and discuss literature with older colleagues. Translation seminars constituted a form of LITOs and had the same structure: each seminar had a chair who presided at the seminar meetings and a relatively stable circle of members who were interested in literary translations of prose or poetry from different languages.

The seminars were open to all listeners and gradually turned into circles of fellow thinkers sincerely devoted to literature and translation. The literary seminars consisted of active discussions of literary texts and their translations—the old ones and the new ones— created by the students attending the seminars. Every participant had a say and an opportunity to present his/her translation of the analyzed piece.

This is how, for instance, the great Leningrad school of translation came about. In the 1950s and 1960s, the Leningrad Union of Writers offered regular seminars on different literary forms and languages. These seminars were supervised and chaired by the best translators of the time, who after Stalin's death in 1953 got a chance to get back to open literary activity, returning from prisons, exiles, and labor camps. One of them, for instance, was Ivan Likhachev (1902–72), who knew Baudelaire's *Fleurs du mal* by heart and translated it from memory while imprisoned in a camp. A political prisoner, Likhachev spent eight years of his life in labor camps and was forced to work as a sweeper in the city of Vol'sk in the Saratov region after his discharge in 1945. He was arrested again in 1948 and spent another ten years in a labor camp, finally getting rehabilitated in 1957. Once permitted to return to Leningrad, he engaged in literary translation again and was appointed chair of the English prose seminar even before being accepted into the Union of Writers—a powerful professional organization that united writers, poets, playwrights, scriptwriters, publicists, critics, and translators of the Soviet Union. Likhachev took up this position after Lev Khvostenko, the renowned translator of Mark Twain and Theodore Dreiser, died in 1959. Likhachev entered Russian translation history as the translator of *Waverley* by Walter Scott, *Lavengro* by George Borrow, and poetry by Joachim Du Bellay, Jean-Antoine de Baïf, Philippe Desportes, Emily Dickinson, and Gerard Manley Hopkins.

Another great name amid those who chaired Leningrad translation seminars was El'ga Linetskaia (1909–97), who shared a long exile with her husband under a false accusation of counterrevolutionary activity. Linetskaia spent the years of exile translating French poetry, Blaise Pascal and François de La Rochefoucauld. These translations were published later in her life alongside her brilliant translations of Jean Racine, François-René de Chateaubriand, Alexandre Dumas, Guy de Maupassant, Jerome K. Jerome, Lion Feuchtwanger, and William Faulkner. Linetskaia chaired the Romance (predominantly French) poetry seminar, which later trans-formed itself into the European poetry seminar, which was live for over thirty-five years until her death in 1997. Linetskaia thus became the teacher and inspirer of several generations of Leningrad translators: Maiia Kviat-kovskaia, Aleksandra Koss, Vladimir Vasil'ev, Inna Chezhegova, Mikhail Yasnov, and Sergei Stepanov. Her students continue to cherish the mem-ory of their late teacher, recognizing Linetskaia as a key figure in their translation education and career.

Apart from her extraordinary translation and teaching gift, Linets-kaia possessed a great talent for recognizing the abilities of her students and their predilections for different genres and styles.

MAIIA KVIATKOVSKAIA: I joined the seminar of El'ga Linetskaia in 1962. At that time, Linetskaia's seminar was attended by extremely talented people: Gennadii Shmakov, Konstantin Azadovskii, Inna Chezhegova, Vladimir Vasil'ev. All of us were Linetskaia's students, and what is quite remarkable is that we were very different from each other and pos-sessed different characters and talents. No one was like the other, but Linetskaia had a great gift to recognize what text would suit each of her students. It was Linetskaia who asked me whether I would like to try my hand at Théophile de Viau. It was in the first half of the 1960s. And I did try translating him: at first, there were several poems, and it gradually turned into my life project. I translated both his poetry and his prose, which is very interesting and sounds very contemporary even now. I translated his play *Les Amours tragiques de Pyrame et Thisbé*, I translated his ten odes cycle, each ode being far over a hundred lines. Therefore, I have translated an almost complete collection of works of Théophile, and I say "almost" because Théophile can never be complete, because many of his works were lost after his death.

VIKTOR ANDREEV: Linetskaia was very strict and would always say what she thought about the translation, despite the personality of the translator, the translator's social position, and the relations of Linetskaia with this translator.

I came to Linetskaia's seminar with my favorites Antonio Machado, Rafael Alberti, and Juan Ramón Jiménez and withstood the onslaught of criticism, which was poured on me by the older students who attended the seminar. Having thus shown character, I stayed in the seminar, and remained a faithful admirer of Linetskaia. Later I myself criticized other translators, fellow students, and newcomers, and I was terribly mean in my critique.

The discussions at Linetskaia's seminars were very heated. We could discuss four lines for an hour trying to find the optimal translation. Our criticism of each other's translations was such that some people left the seminar, being unable to take so much criticism. We were very young and did not understand that idealism was very far from practice. Unlike us, El'ga L'vovna knew this—she was extremely experienced. In addition, of all of us she was the kindest. She understood that if sixty percent of the form and content is conveyed in a poetic translation, it is a success. If there is no more than thirty or forty percent of original features conveyed, the translation is a failure, which results from the lack of effort on the behalf of the translator. At this point Linetskaia would turn into a strict critic: she was merciless when she saw that the translation was below the high standards that she had in mind.

Linetskaia's approach to the education of future masters of Soviet translation did not reduce itself to teaching them translation techniques—her seminars provided general literary education. Linetskaia would start every seminar with a reading of Russian poetry—from classics to modern pieces. This, in her view, was crucially important for literary translators, because every new translation was entering the context of the Russian literature and culture that each translator was supposed to be aware of. Students of Linetskaia were gradually introduced to the prose and poetry that remained unpublished and virtually unknown in the Soviet Union.

VIKTOR ANDREEV: El'ga Linetskaia would introduce us to the books that were forbidden or disapproved of—Khodasevich, Kuz'min, Tsvetaeva, Pasternak. She would secretly bring us books from home and begged us not to tell her husband because she did not want to make him worried.

At the end of the seminar, the students of Linetskaia would follow their teacher to her room in a communal apartment, where discussions of literature would continue and where unpublished or forbidden works would be read aloud.[49] Given Linetskaia's status as a former exile, these gatherings at her place were a very risky enterprise. Nonetheless, Linetskaia continued on the course, setting an ideal example of courage, talent, diligence, and honesty for her students.

Linetskaia's influence over her students cannot be underestimated. For thirty-five years, her seminar always enjoyed popularity among young translators, as well as distinguished members of the Union of Writers. For several generations of Leningrad/St. Petersburg translators, the seminars of Linetskaia remained a source of inspiration. "This world was inhabited by texts and people," wrote Linetskaia's student, translator Valerii Dymshits, "the texts were to be respected like people, people were to be peered into and listened to like texts."[50]

VIKTOR ANDREEV: Linetskaia's seminar started in 1954 as a seminar of poetic translations from Romance languages. Then English translators joined in the seminar, and prose translators came, too. Once her students joined the Union of Writers, she would make them leave the seminar, because there were too many people who wanted to attend it. Nevertheless, her old students would sometimes attend her seminars as guests, especially if they were interested in the poet or the poem planned for discussion. El'ga L'vovna was always happy when her old students came to the seminar sessions. She had a special call for teaching. She stopped chairing seminars only when she broke her hip just before her eightieth birthday.

"We still consult El'ga L'vovna," said Viktor Andreev in the gathering devoted to the centenary anniversary of his teacher in 2009.[51] He repeated the same words in his interview to me, describing his feelings about his deceased teacher in the following way:

VIKTOR ANDREEV: Up to now when I translate something or write something I always ask myself what El'ga L'vovna would think of it.

Another distinguished translator Tat'iana Gnedich came to chair her English poetry seminars after a long imprisonment, during which she translated the whole text of Byron's *Don Juan* from memory in her one and a half years in solitary confinement. Gnedich wrote her translations on the tiniest pieces of paper to save space. It is extremely unusual that her investigating officer, obviously moved by Gnedich's devotion to literature, allowed her to keep her translation and take it out of the prison when the inquest was finished and Gnedich was sent to the labor camp for ten years. In his interview to me, Mikhail Yasnov described the feeling of awe that he felt when he saw these small scraps of paper covered with tiny dot-like letters one could barely read.

The literary feat of Gnedich became the symbol of devotion to one's call among translators, and there is no wonder that it provided the basis for legends. One of them goes that after a year and a half of working in solitary confinement Gnedich finally got a cellmate. The indignation of Gnedich was such that the wardens had to call for the prison administration, which duly sent a military person to resolve the situation. "Why did you put this woman into my cell?" inquired Gnedich indignantly. "But, Tat'iana Grigor'evna, no one can bear solitary confinement for more than a year and a half," replied the military. Gnedich shook her head and, as the legend goes, replied, "Byron and I do not need anyone."

Gnedich's seminar contained fewer people than Linetskaia's seminar; however, it also became a stepping-stone for many Leningrad/St. Petersburg translators like Georgii Ben, Vasilii Betaki, and Galina Usova. It was Usova, who would later commemorate Gnedich, her seminar, and her translation of *Don Juan* in the book *I Bairona v soavtory voz'mu* (And we coauthor: Byron and myself).[52]

The fate of Likhachev, Linetskaia, and Gnedich was shared by the chair of the Scandinavian translation seminar Sergei Petrov (1911–88), an outstanding figure of the Leningrad literary world: a writer, a poet, and a literary translator. Petrov was able to write and translate from twelve languages, and knew yet more languages. He started to translate in prison in 1933–43, clearly realizing that as a political prisoner he would never be able to publish his translations. Nonetheless, Petrov's extraordinary literary talent worked its way out, making him a well-known and widely published translator in his lifetime. Among his most famous translations were works of Walter Scott, George Byron, Robert Burns, Stéphane Mallarmé, Charles Leconte de Lisle, Théophile Gautier, Francisco de Quevedo, Heinrich Heine, Carl Bellman, and Mikołaj Sęp Szarzyński.

The famous professor of Herzen Pedagogical Institute (currently Herzen State Pedagogical University of Russia) Efim Etkind chaired the German translation seminar. His encyclopedic knowledge, wonderful sense of humor, and striking personality made him and his seminars the center of attention for translators and wider circles of intellectuals.

INNA STREBLOVA: Etkind's seminars were always crowded. Linetskaia and Gnedich worked with small groups of translators and made their students go once they joined the Union of Writers, so that other people could take their place in the seminars. Etkind had a different approach: he was eager to let everyone in. He was a passionate lecturer, amazingly knowledgeable, and he was working on his new book on poetry in those days,[⁵³] so he was full of new ideas. Sometimes people would come to his seminars just to see the great professor and hear him talk.

Apart from his active involvement in academic research, literary translation, university lecturing, and chairing the seminar, Etkind made another important contribution to the education of talented Leningrad youth by creating a regular public event, which he called in the journalistic manner "The Oral Almanac: First Time in the Russian Language." The almanac events were hosted by the Leningrad House of Writers. During almanac gatherings, translators of all ages were able to recite their new translations. The almanac turned into a unique literary phenomenon and always attracted the attention of hundreds of people. It was during one of these almanacs, for example, that Joseph Brodsky first read out his translations from John Donne. The almanac united poets and translators of different backgrounds and gave them an opportunity to share the results of their work, which had not yet been published or seen by anyone. It was a way of receiving an immediate response from a wide audience of well-educated peers, who shared the passion for literature.

Mikhail Yasnov, who was not only a student but also a private secretary of Etkind, speaks about Etkind as a fearless person, with composure and courage of such extent that these characteristics in many ways predetermined Etkind's fate.

MIKHAIL YASNOV: Efim Grigor'evich knew no fear, and this annoyed the official organs immensely. They certainly kept an eye on him. Yet he went on doing what he thought was right, and this was catching. I remember a story, which serves as a good example of this. Once, we had a very big gathering of the almanac *First Time in the Russian Language*. The program consisted of two parts: translations from the languages of the Soviet Union came first; translations from other languages were scheduled after the break. There were many people presenting their translations from the languages of the Soviet Union; however, everyone was looking forward to the foreign section. At some point, people from the audience requested Efim Grigor'evich who, of course, was in charge, to cut the first part short, have a break, and pass on to translations from the European languages. Efim Grigor'evich stood up and said in a loud voice, "No, we are not doing anything else until the Soviet Union is done away with."

The outstanding personality of Efim Etkind gives us a perfect example of translation activism as defined by Maria Tymoczko: an engaged translator visible as a subject, with his efforts not restricted to translation alone but targeted at social and political change.[54]

Etkind courageously witnessed for the defense in the famous trial of Joseph Brodsky in 1964, maintained a friendship with Aleksandr Solzhenitsyn even after the writer's exile from the Soviet Union, and kept the manuscript of the forbidden novel by Solzhenitsyn *The Gulag Archipelago* at home. On April 25, 1974, in the course of one day, Etkind was stripped of his professorship, deprived of all the academic titles, and expelled from the Union of Writers on the charges of dissident and anti-Soviet activity. Half a year later, Etkind was forced to emigrate and moved to France where he became a professor at Paris X Nanterre University.

The French prose translation seminar was chaired by Vladimir Shor (1917–71), who was a literature specialist and a translator from French, English, and German. Among his translations are novels by Walter Scott, Horace Walpole, and George Sand, tragedies by Jean Racine, and poems by Victor Hugo, Charles Baudelaire, Paul Verlaine, Jules Laforgue, and Emile Verhaeren.

The German poetry translation seminar was headed by Tamara Sil'man (1909–74), a writer and a distinguished Leningrad specialist in Germanic philology. As a translator, she was known for her Russian translations of the poetry of Rainer Maria Rilke.

The success of the translation seminars encouraged the Leningrad Union of Writers to create new language sections. This is how seminars in non-European languages came about. One of them was the Asian languages translation seminar chaired by Boris Vakhtin (1930–81), a researcher, a playwright, and renowned translator of Chinese poetry. A nonofficial seminar on translation from the languages of the Far North was conducted by the poet Natalia Grudinina (1918–99) in her own home. Grudinina was an experienced teacher and trainer who worked with both young specialists and youth. Grudinina chaired the famous poetry club for schoolchildren in the Leningrad House of Pioneers, which was attended by many successful literary translators-to-be. A poet and a translator, Grudinina was also a political activist. For her active participation in the defense of Joseph Brodsky during his trial for parasitism, she was later suspended from her work with youth and was not published for a long time.

It is notable that the tradition of translation seminars was first established in Leningrad and not in the Soviet capital, which dominated in all spheres of arts, including literature. In comparison with Moscow translation seminars, Leningrad seminars demonstrate greater stability: the same people chaired Leningrad seminars for dozens of years, thus creating steady professional groups. Emily Lygo mentions a special literary situation in Leningrad that contributed to the importance and popularity of poetry during the Thaw. This acute interest in poetry determined the profile of the translation seminars of the Leningrad Union of Writers: the number of poetic translation seminars equaled, if not at times exceeded, the number of seminars devoted to prose. To a degree, Lygo ascribes the interest of Leningraders in poetry to the tremendous losses of Leningrad during the siege of 1941–44. The human toll, in Lygo's view, made the orphaned generation search "for a sense of cultural continuity," seek to rediscover the literary trends of the first decades of the twentieth century, and turn to the surviving members of the old intelligentsia for guidance.[55] While I do not in the least dispute the effect the siege of Leningrad had on poetry and prose written in Leningrad/St. Petersburg, I would like to point out that the search for cultural continuity and tutorship never faded in Leningrad in the 1920s through the 1940s. There is much evidence of this. Lectures of Iurii Tynianov, a distinguished man of letters, writer, critic, and one of the theorists of formalism, were popular among his students of the State Institute of Arts History in the 1920s until he abandoned his academic

career for health reasons.[56] Anna Akhmatova attracted universal attention in the most dangerous years of the 1930s and remained a source
of inspiration for many young writers. Lidiia Chukovskaia, daughter of
Kornei Chukovskii, later wrote her memoirs of Akhmatova in three volumes, where she described their friendship in the 1930s and the evacu-
ation that they both were forced to undergo during the war.[57] Writers,
poets, and linguists regularly got together to exchange their ideas at each
other's apartments, like the apartment of Anna Beskina, who was later
arrested and labeled a public enemy for hosting "a literary salon."[58] Poet
Osip Mandelstam did public readings of his poetry in Leningrad in the
winter of 1932–33, that is, a year before his arrest. It was in these public readings that Mandelstam proclaimed his allegiance to Acmeism as
authentic poetry, his words, as linguist, translator, and critic Vladimir
Admoni would later recall, "full of pride and defiance . . . , the mere
intonation of pride and defiance meaning death in those days."[59]

If one were pressed to explain the rise of poetic activity in Leningrad in the 1950s, I would dare to suggest that it was not the longing for
a sense of cultural continuity but the prevalence of this cultural continuity as such that turned the revival of poetry in Leningrad into such
an important cultural phenomenon. The return of the survivors of the
purges to Leningrad in the 1950s was, as Lygo correctly points out, pro-
motive of the rise of poetry, but I would also add here that the tradition
of poetic circles and societies had existed in St. Petersburg throughout
the centuries, reaching its peak during the Silver Age. This tradition,
although suffering a decline during the second quarter of the twentieth
century, was yet well remembered and longed for, and it naturally came
to life at the instant the political situation loosened up to some degree.

Despite the fact that Leningrad translation seminars outnumbered
Moscow seminars in the period under study, the major Moscow translation seminar predated the Leningrad seminar as it came about in the
1930s. Its structure and purpose was slightly different from the seminars
that were organized in the postwar period. This first translation seminar
of the 1930s can rather be called a circle: this was a circle of translators
gathered around their teacher Ivan Kashkin, the famous translator and
literary critic of the time. The small circle of his followers called itself the
First Team of Translators (*pervyi perevodcheskii kollektiv*). The word *first*

was used in the chronological sense, as nothing comparable had existed before; however, the ordinal *first* gradually turned into an indication of supremacy in the minds of literature and translation specialists. By the middle of the century, the First Team became the dominant group of literary translators who were universally recognized as masters of prose translation. The group became extremely active and productive after World War II; their first publications, however, came to light in the 1930s when they first translated stories by Hemingway. During the hardest times of World War II, Vera Toper, Evgeniia Kalashnikova, Nina Daruzes, and Mariia Bogoslovskaia were actively translating plays by Bernard Shaw; in the beginning of 1945, the collection of Bernard Shaw plays translated by the group was signed into print.[60] Starting with the 1940s, the *kashkintsy*, as the group called themselves, along with their teacher, actively engaged in the translation of works of classical and modern literature, predominantly from the English language. The number of works translated by the Kashkin circle is astounding; the list below is far from being complete.

VERA TOPER: *The Sun Also Rises* by E. Hemingway, *Hard Times* by C. Dickens, *The Game* and *Burning Daylight* by J. London, *Afloat* (original title *Sur l'eau*) by G. Maupassant, stories by E. Hemingway, J. Joyce, O. Henry, F. Kafka.

OL'GA KHOLMSKAIA: *The Mystery of Edwin Drood* by C. Dickens, *The Return of the Native* and *The Trumpet-Major* by T. Hardy, *Rip Van Winkle* by W. Irving, *An Ideal Husband* by O. Wilde, stories by E. Hemingway, J. Joyce, O. Henry, H. James, E. A. Poe, J. Galsworthy, W. Faulkner, S. Maugham.

EVGENIIA KALASHNIKOVA: *A Farewell to Arms, For Whom the Bell Tolls, To Have and Have Not, The Fifth Column* by E. Hemingway, *Pygmalion* by B. Shaw, *The Great Gatsby* and *Tender Is the Night* by F. S. Fitzgerald, *Martin Eden* by J. London, *The Bridge of San Luis Rey* by T. Wilder, *The Sea Eagle* by J. Aldridge, *Of the Farm* by J. Updike, *Little Dorrit* by C. Dickens, *The History of Henry Esmond* by W. Thackeray, *The Stronghold* by T. Dreiser, stories by E. Hemingway, N. Hawthorne, A. Bierce, J. Joyce, O. Henry.

NATALIA VOLZHINA: *The Grapes of Wrath* and *The Pearl* by J. Steinbeck, *The Old Curiosity Shop* by C. Dickens, *The Gadfly* by E. Voynich, *The Hound of the Baskervilles* and *The Lost World* by A. Conan Doyle, *Swan Song* by J. Galsworthy, *Power and Glory* and *A Burnt-Out Case* by G. Greene, stories by E. Hemingway, B. Harte, M. Twain, R. Stevenson, J. Joyce, O. Henry, H. G. Wells, S. Anderson, S. Crane.

NINA DARUZES: *The Adventures of Tom Sawyer* and *The Adventures of Huckleberry Finn* by M. Twain, *The Life and Adventures of Martin Chuzzlewit* by Ch. Dickens, *The Book of Snobs* by W. Thackeray, *The Turn of the Screw* by H. James, *A Woman of No Importance* by O. Wilde, *Mrs. Warren's Profession* by B. Shaw, *The Jungle Book* by R. Kipling, stories by J. London, Bret Harte, M. Twain, O. Henry, J. Joyce, R. Wright, G. de Maupassant.

MARIIA LORIE: *Great Expectations* by C. Dickens, *The History of Pendennis* by W. Thackeray, *This Side of Paradise* by F. S. Fitzgerald, *To Let* and *Swan Song* by J. Galsworthy, *The Painted Veil* and *The Razor's Edge* by S. Maugham, *Vile Bodies* by E. Waugh, *The Dark Lady of the Sonnets* by B. Shaw, *Under the Net, An Unofficial Rose, The Red and the Green, The Sea, the Sea* by I. Murdoch, stories by H. Melville, O. Henry, J. London, S. Maugham, V. Woolf, J. Galsworthy, T. Hardy, E. Hemingway, K. Mansfield.

MARIIA BOGOSLOVSKAIA: *Far from the Madding Crowd* by T. Hardy, *The White Gauntlet* by M. Reid, *In Chancery* by J. Galsworthy, *Byron* (original title *Don Juan ou la vie de Byron*) by A. Maurois, *The Bulpington of Blup* by H. G. Wells, *Intruder in the Dust* by W. Faulkner, *Candida, Caesar and Cleopatra*, and *Heartbreak House* by B. Shaw, *Waiting for Godot* by S. Beckett, stories by C. Dickens, E. A. Poe, O. Henry, J. London.

TANDEM WORK: *Our Mutual Friend* by C. Dickens (Volzhina and Daruzes), *Vanity Fair* by W. Thackeray (Kalashnikova and Lorie), *Islands in the Stream* by E. Hemingway (Volzhina and Kalashnikova), *The Dangerous Summer* by E. Hemingway (Kalashnikova and Toper), *The Winter of Our Discontent* by J. Steinbeck (Volzhina and Kalashnikova),

The Crusaders by S. Heym (Volzhina, Kalashnikova, and Daruzes), *The Diplomat* by J. Aldridge (Toper, Kalashnikova, and Kashkin), *The Man of Property* by J. Galsworthy (Volzhina and Lorie).

This list includes only major translations made by the Kashkin circle. Kashkin actively promoted his students; it was the combination of talent, education, luck, and their influential teacher's patronage that gradually turned the translators of the circle into the monopolists of Soviet translation of that time. The tremendous success of the prolific circle attracted much attention of younger translators. Responding to this interest, Ivan Kashkin and Mariia Lorie organized a joint translation seminar in the 1950s. The seminar did not last for long; the death of Kashkin followed in 1963, and it was not until 1972 that Mariia Lorie and Evgeniia Kalashnikova opened up a new seminar, which lasted for ten years, even despite Kalashnikova's death in 1976. This was a seminar for active translators already engaged in translation, attended by even such accomplished translators of the time as Inna Bernstein, who had already translated Herman Melville's *Moby Dick*. Larisa Bespalova was one of those who attended these seminars for a long time.

LARISA BESPALOVA: The seminars were arranged in the following way. Lorie and Kalashnikova would arrange it so that a publishing house would allocate a book of short stories to their seminar. We would translate stories and discuss them. The stories were distributed among us. One participant translated the story, another acted as a reviewer, and the rest were involved in the discussion. Kalashnikova and Lorie also split the group between themselves, so that each of them worked with half of the seminar group. I was supervised by Mariia Lorie. The seminar met once a month for the discussion of one story. This way we translated several collections of stories: the first one was Flannery O'Connor, the second was William Faulkner, the third—Francis Scott Fitzgerald, the fourth—Victor Sawdon Pritchett, the fifth—Herbert Bates, the sixth— Angus Wilson. There were seven books in total, but I did not take part in the last one. This was an interesting experience, although sometimes the participants were very negative in their critical remarks, which was quite painful. Although, I guess, our seminar was no exception to the general rule. Evgeniia Kalashnikova once confessed that sometimes she would leave Kashkin's seminars in tears.

Apart from the Kashkin circle seminars, translation seminars of the Moscow Union of Writers were at their height in the 1980s, as Evgenii Witkowsky noted in his account of the translation seminars and translation schools in Moscow.

EVGENII WITKOWSKY: There is no Moscow translation school, because there were dozens of schools. The tradition of seminars conducted by the Union of Writers in Moscow came about in the beginning of the 1980s—much later than in Leningrad. In the 1980s, there existed the clearly discernable school of Wilhelm Levik. There was also the school of Arkadii Steinberg, which I belong to: it descends from the south Russian school of Mark Tarlovskii and Arsenii Tarkovskii. There was the school of Aleksandr Revich. There was the Spanish translation seminar of Pavel Grushko. All these people chaired seminars. The younger school that came about along with the school of Grushko was the school of Andrei Sergeev, who did not conduct any seminars, but he still taught people how to translate.

The translation seminars had a much greater role than purely the education of prospective literary translators. The seminars provided an opportunity for talented translators to show their worth and get initial approval from the most talented specialists of the time. However, even more than approval, the young translators needed a special literary atmosphere, which the literary seminars were able to provide. It was no coincidence that the literary translation section was considered the most "unreliable" in the Leningrad Union of Writers: knowledge of foreign languages automatically stood for the freedom of choice and expression.[61]

The seminars were the start of a literary life and literary cooperation: many fellow seminarists maintained professional relationships and recognized each other as colleagues throughout their lifetime. It is quite notable that although all translators who were members of the seminars described them as an important starting point in their literary career, no one saw the seminars as a launching pad into business. The seminars created a special literary space, a professional fraternity, almost a family for many young translators. The chairs of the seminars were demigods to their students: having gone through hardships and injustice, they preserved their passion and respect for literature. They gladly shared their knowledge and experience with students and were happy to provide the most talented ones with translation commissions. And even though Linetskaia, in Viktor Andreev's words, kept repeating that she would always be happy to teach her students but would not be able to help them in building up their literary careers, students kept coming to her seminars, as they were driven by their passion for literature.

Nonetheless, it was the seminars where many translators got commissions for translations for the first time; these small publications symbolized the start of new translation careers. The translators gradually made themselves known by editors and publishing houses, and if the quality of the translations was good, the young translator would enjoy the steady growth of commissions.

MAIIA KVIATKOVSKAIA: My first commission—the Spanish poet Rafael Alberti—arrived soon after I had joined the seminar of El'ga Linetskaia. I was new to the seminar, and people in it barely knew me. When the order arrived at the seminar, the best pieces were taken by the most talented and experienced students. Eventually there were a couple of poems left that no one wanted to take, because due to their political content they were too pretentious. Alberti was a communist, and communist poems lacked certain charm. This is when El'ga Linetskaia asked me doubtingly whether I wanted to try to translate those poems. So I did, and it worked out well. One of those translations would still be reprinted from time to time when Alberti is published in Russian.

VIKTOR ANDREEV: I got my first big order through the seminar, too, though I had published some poetic translations before. The most amazing thing is that at the time my translations were selected for publication, I was out of the Soviet Union: I was teaching Russian in Guinea. As the Russian saying goes, "I was not present at my wedding." When I returned to Leningrad in 1975 after two years of absence, I learned that Moscow publishers were looking for me. The Biblioteka vsemirnoi literatury series was planning to issue the volume of translations of Spanish poetry of the twentieth century: Machado, Jiménez, Lorca, Hernández, and Alberti. Inna Terterian, a Moscow philologist, specialist in Spanish literature, was appointed editor for this volume. She studied the existing translations, and liked some, but not all of them, and she was looking for other translations to include in the volume. Terterian called Linetskaia for help, and Linetskaia asked Maiia Kviatkovskaia who was monitor of the seminar at that time if she could find copies of my translations from Spanish. Kviatkovskaia found my translations of Machado, Jiménez, and Hernández, which I had typed on tiny pieces of paper to save paper and ink. We did those tiny copies to distribute among fellow seminarists for discussion during seminars. Terterian had every right to refuse to read such poor-quality copies, but she did read my translations. I was lucky: the first poem in my translation that she paid her attention to was the poem of Machado, which she was determined to include in the volume and was looking for a good translation of it. Moscow translators whom she asked to do the translation of this poem either failed to convey the form, or the content. Then suddenly she came across the unknown me and she liked my translation of this poem. This made her take a closer look at my translations, and this is how forty poems that I had translated entered this volume.[62]

As one can see from the examples above, translation seminars turned out to mean much more for the Russian Soviet culture that they had been initially meant. LITOs were first founded, as Lygo correctly observes, as "crucial meeting points for young poets and establishment."[63] This formula applied to a degree to translation seminars, which were organized and hosted by an official government institution. Having started their history alongside LITOs, many translation seminars, nonetheless, gradually became semiofficial. Some seminar sessions were conducted at chairpersons' homes, students and mentors thus gradually turning into friends and fellow thinkers.

The Soviet translation seminars of the 1960s through the 1980s became a unique alternative to the existing reality. Translation seminars offered their members what they could not enjoy in their daily life, at their workplaces, or at their universities: freedom of expression, which consisted in individual translation decisions, as well as in the ability to defend one's own translation from criticism and the chance to express one's own opinion of other people's work openly. It is especially notable that chairs of the seminars demonstrated lenience, letting younger members of seminars engage in sharp criticism of each other. The final comments the chairpersons made in the discussions of translations were the most valuable both in terms of the weight of these comments and in terms of learning the way strong criticism should be expressed. Chairpersons of seminars possessed unchallenged authority and were universally respected by members of seminars, this high respect being no imposed obligation, but the reward for knowledge, patience, and recognition of their young students as colleagues. In the general context of the forced unconditional respect for seniors and the inability of self-expression in the Soviet Union, translation seminars presented an alternative reality, a subculture, which formed creative and outspoken individuals. As translator Oleg Juriev wrote about his teacher El'ga Linetskaia, "In the darkness and slush of the endless Soviet winter, in its fish oil, in its suffocating cold, she was a dry and radiant dove from the sunny forest of the 'world culture.'"[64]

The creative atmosphere of seminars and the chairpersons who were perceived as living legends continued to attract talented youth, which is why translation seminars enjoyed an extremely long history. A special phenomenon in this regard was the seminar of El'ga Linetskaia. Of all the literary groups created for adults,[65] the translation seminar of Linetskaia was by far the most long-lived: it existed for thirty-five years until the death of its one and only chairperson in 1997—that is, long after the fall of the Soviet Union. After Linetskaia's death, the position of the chair was alternately taken by Linetskaia's adult students, who carried on the tradition for several more years. Linetskaia as a mentor of several generations of Soviet literary translators became a symbol of inspiration, knowledge, and patience.

Translation seminars enjoyed such wide popularity that some chairpersons like Linetskaia and Gnedich had to introduce the rule that students had to abandon their places in the seminars once they were accepted into the Union of Writers. By doing this, the chairpersons continued to engage new students, thus opening up the literary world to a wider circle of talented people. This decision now looks symbolic: having seen the freedom of expression and wisdom of experienced chairpersons, recent members of seminars entered the Union of Writers and the official world of literary translation, where they had to rely upon the knowledge and experience they had gained in the creative atmosphere of the seminars. The links of translators with former fellow members of the seminars remained exceptionally strong, and the awareness of the presence of their best friends and severe critics among their colleagues contributed to the high quality of literary translations produced by Soviet translators.

CHAPTER 5

LITERARY TRANSLATION AS A PROFESSION

Commissions, Earnings, and the Union of Writers

Promotion of publications in the Soviet Union was a difficult task for both translators and editors. The elaborate scheme of subordination that existed in Soviet publishing, as we have seen in previous chapters, required receiving multiple approvals at every stage of the publishing process. Apart from being subject to censorship and state control, which consisted in careful supervision of published texts, their authors, and translators, the work of publishing houses also had to conform to annual and long-term publishing plans, all of which with no exceptions were studied and approved by Glavlit. Depending on the publishing house, publishing plans could also include publications of translations. Specialized publishing houses had separate foreign literature sections, which compiled separate publishing plans to be later incorporated into the general plan of the publishing house. Glavlit reserved the right to dictate to publishing houses its own terms of work and to change publishing plans, either forbidding the texts included by publishing houses into their provisional plans or, contrarily, adding texts into publishing plans. Publishing houses had to resign themselves to Glavlit additions to publishing plans even if they strongly disagreed with imposed decisions and considered the subjects or quality of suggested works inadequate. This rule equally concerned all subjects and genres, and both original and translated literature. Being included into the final publishing plan for a writer or a translator meant being approved both by the publishing house administration and censoring organs.

A literary translator was able to get a commission by a publishing house in two ways. The first one can be called an initiative "from above." It consisted in the publishing house finding appropriately qualified translators for a book already included in the publishing plan and approved by Glavlit. The other initiative came "from below" and consisted in individual translators creating applications to publishing houses, where they described the merits and style of the literary work they wanted to translate. Such applications were considered by the publishing house, and, in the case of approval, the book would be included in the publishing plan and the author of the application would get commissioned to do the translation. Applications were welcomed by publishing houses: they were a source of knowledge about new books of which the publishers might be unaware. Personal applications provided a good chance of getting a translation job: the interviewed translators were unanimous in stating that being commissioned by a publishing house was possible with a correct approach to publishers and a certain bit of luck. Three of the interviewed translators were able to confirm this information as insiders, as at different times they were officially employed by publishing houses as editors: Irina Komarova worked in Leningrad, whereas Muscovites Larisa Bespalova and Evgenii Witkowsky were editors in the capital.

IRINA KOMAROVA: The choice of texts for translation did not solely depend on publishing houses, even though publishing houses had their say in the selection of foreign-language literature. However, many works were selected by publishing houses themselves, and some were offered by individual translators via applications. In the two latter cases, the works had to receive further approval.

In case the publishing house initiated the translation project, it was, albeit with few exceptions, entitled to choose the translators. Publishing houses preferred dealing with experienced translators—members of the Union of Writers with a good reputation and a substantial number of publications. There was no shortage of excellent literary translators in the Soviet Union, and it often happened that the newcomers into the field were rejected automatically, unless introduced and recommended by older colleagues. The translators themselves describe the situation in the following way.

IRINA KOMAROVA: I was working in Uchpedgiz publishing house—later it transformed into Prosveshchenie publishing house. It was located in the House of Books.[1] We shared the building with Goslitizdat [later known as Khudozhestvennaia Literatura] and Iskusstvo publishing houses. Their offices were upstairs, which is why all the employees knew each other personally. This gave me access to some translation jobs.[2] For example, when Natalia Tolstaia, who was working in Goslitizdat, learned of my colleagues' and mine translation skills, she started to give us translation jobs now and then.

Nonetheless, my first translation jobs came to me from Ivan Likhachev, who was chair of the English prose translation seminar at the Union of Writers. This was the seminar that I regularly attended.

Getting translation jobs from publishing houses was difficult. Each publishing house had its own favorite translators, and young translators were offered translations very seldom.

The choice of literary works by publishing houses was done in two ways. Texts were either selected by the publishing house, or a translator could place an application for the text he/she wanted to translate. These applications were often rejected at the level of the publishing house, but in any case, no matter whether the text was chosen by a publishing house or applied for by a translator, the final approval was granted in Moscow by Glavlit. It is quite clear that one needed to be a well-known translator and a member of the Union of Writers to apply to a publishing house for a literary translation. Literary translation was handled by a very close circle of people, and to get into it one needed an official introduction. Young translators would usually get a text to translate from their better-known older colleagues. Chairs of seminars tried to get big orders, so that they could split them between several talented students and give a chance to do literary translation to all of them. Tat'iana Gnedich once got a huge order for Langston Hughes for her seminar students. The chair of the seminar I attended, my teacher Ivan Likhachev wheedled out several Hawthorne stories for us. This is how I got to translate "Edward Randolph's Portrait" and "Lady Eleanore's Mantle."

Sometimes it happened that a translator of a big literary work could not meet the deadline and would have to share some parts of it with other translators he/she knew. This is how I got to translate Sinclair Lewis's *Ann Vickers* together with Meri Bekker and Natalia Rakhmanova.

To sum it up, there were three sources of commissions for young translators:

1. assistance of older colleagues (my first translation of Hawthorne);
2. a streak of luck (in my case, Lewis and Fowles);
3. through friendship.

One thing is certain: had I not been working in Uchpedgiz publishing house, I would not have become a translator. There were talented people who attended the seminar of Likhachev, who never managed to gain proper access to literary circles.

SERGEI STEPANOV: To get into the translation business one needed to be known and recognized by publishing houses. It was not so easy, because the personal history of the translator was extremely important for publishing houses. A member of the Union of Writers was naturally preferred. Once the publishing house commissioned a translator to a job, it was almost certain that the translation would be published. Yet to get commissioned, one had to be known to publishers, so there had to be someone who would take you by the hand and introduce you to people. El'ga Linetskaia would get jobs for her students now and then. She gave us Herman Melville, for instance. Viktor Toporov helped me a lot: when he understood I was capable of translating, he sent me to Moscow to meet his friends, who were known in the literary circles. Natalia Grudinina also got me commissioned from time to time. The translators knew each other and recommended each other for different jobs. Sometimes famous translators had no time to cope with a big translation job, and they would offer parts of their big order to the translators they trusted. As newcomers, however, young translators could barely get any orders at all. The situation remained at a deadlock until translators finally got themselves introduced to the right people and met everyone who was important, until people started to say hello to them at the publishers'.

Getting oneself commissioned to a translation and coping with the job successfully once did not guarantee another commission. Permanent establishment within the field of literary translation was possible only for the officially recognized people of letters, namely, members of the Union of Writers—the most influential professional union of those who dedicated themselves to literature.

The Union of Writers of the USSR (*Soiuz Pisatelei SSSR*) was founded in 1934 at the First Congress of Soviet Writers to be a professional ideological union that would ensure ideological correspondence of literary works to the requirements of socialist realism.[3] Before 1934, Soviet writers were able to choose from a variety of literary organizations (Russian Association of Proletarian Writers—or RAPP, Left Front of Art—or LEF, Pereval, Union of Peasant Writers, etc.). Nonetheless, in its resolution of April 23, 1932, the Central Committee of the Communist Party branded the existing literary organizations as "narrow, impeding the serious spread of artistic creativity."[4] In the same resolution, the Central Committee of the Communist Party therefore called for uniting "all writers, who support the platform of Soviet power and strive to participate in the construction of socialism, into a joint union of Soviet writers that would have a Communist Party faction within it."[5] By doing so, the Central Committee was breaking its own regulation of June 18, 1925, *O politike partii v oblasti khudozhestvennoi literatury* (On the party policy in the sphere of literature), according to which any possible monopoly on literary activity granted by a decree or regulation was described as impermissible.[6] "The party cannot provide the monopoly to any of the groups, even to the most proletariat in its ideological content," stated the regulation of 1925, "this would mean to ruin the proletariat literature itself."[7]

However obvious the incoherence of the regulations of 1925 and 1932 might have seemed, the First Congress of Soviet Writers of August 1934 readily followed the regulation of 1932. The congress answered the call of the Communist Party by adopting the charter of the new union where socialist realism was defined as the main method of the Soviet literature and literary criticism.[8] The newly established Union of Writers was to stand guard for the principles of socialist realism and therefore the interests of the Communist Party, thus becoming a powerful tool of state control over literature and literary activity in the country. A reluctance or failure to join the union resulted in suspension from work: the writer or translator would get fewer orders, the publications would get scarce, and the rejected candidate would be gradually removed from the literary scene.

The Union of Writers had its board and secretariat located in Moscow; regional sections of the union were scattered throughout the country. There were Unions of Writers of the Soviet Socialist republics and of the autonomous republics of the Soviet Union, regional unions, and the separate sections of the Union of Writers in Moscow and Leningrad.[9] Structurally, they were replicas of the central organization and had a right to accept new members and supervise literary activity in the assigned regions.

Joining the Union of Writers was an important goal for people working in the area of literature and translation. Membership in the Union of Writers facilitated one's literary career and secured regular orders for translations and respect of fellow members. Many translators point out that they started to feel more independent once their literary occupation was confirmed by their membership in the Union of Writers. The Union of Writers provided its members with one more important advantage: the opportunity to remain officially unemployed. Under the Soviet requirements for universal employment, members of the Union of Writers enjoyed a precious privilege to stay at home during working hours and engage in literary activity. The labor documents would be kept by the personnel department of the Union of Writers, and members of the Union were able to work on the translations at home instead of combining their literary activity with a regular job.[10] Members of the Union of Writers were thus officially recognized as accomplished people of letters, which gave them a sense of security and acknowledgment. Maiia Kviatkovskaia describes this feeling in one sentence.

MAIIA KVIATKOVSKAIA: I joined the Union of Writers in 1979. This finally made me feel in my own right: officially recognized as translator, I could no longer blame myself for being a graphomaniac.

Apart from the status, regular orders, and the feeling of security, the Union of Writers created a comfortable and enviable atmosphere for its members. According to the Regulations of the Union of Writers, each regional organization had its literary fund that provided material support to its members.[11] Depending on the rank and importance of the writer, this material support could consist in providing members of the Union with apartments, holiday summer cottages (the so-called writers' dachas in writers' villages), vouchers for vacation centers or for Creativity Homes—vacation centers in attractive suburban areas where writers could enjoy comfort and quiet when working. Members of the Union of Writers also had better access to regulated items of supply and foods, to which most Soviet citizens had no access. Irina Komarova described this situation with a slight tinge of irony:

> IRINA KOMAROVA: Everyone had the same dream—to be accepted into the Union of Writers, which meant big orders and access to numerous privileges like the ability to receive subsidized vouchers for Creativity Homes, or the right to use Litfond dachas at Komarovo. But I joined the Union of Writers in December 1990, which was too late to use all those wonders.[12]

Admission into the Union of Writers was granted with great difficulties. To be admitted, one had to be a published writer or translator and to be recommended for admission by three members of the Union of Writers.[13] The application for admittance was first studied by the local section of the Union of Writers and subjected to a vote in which the applicant needed to poll two-thirds of all votes. Having been approved by the local Union of Writers, the candidature was considered by the board or the secretariat of the Union of Writers where the applicant needed to poll 50 percent of vote to be admitted.

> IGNATII IVANOVSKII: When the time came for me to join the Union of Writers in 1961, Anna Akhmatova made sure I got a solid recommendation. During one of her trips to Moscow, she convinced Samuil Marshak to give a recommendation to me. Marshak was busy and did not have time, and he told Akhmatova to write a recommendation herself so that he would sign it. Assisted by Marshak's relatives, Akhmatova wrote the recommendation while sitting in the next room, and then Marshak, indeed, signed it.

Another recommendation to Ivanovskii was given by Akhmatova herself.[14] Recommendations of reputed writers or poets along with a substantial record of published translations ensured a pass into the

Union of Writers. Submission of publications along with an application was obligatory, but the number of publications varied depending on the section of the union the applicant was seeking to join. Whereas original creative writers were supposed to have published two or more books, requirements for translators were less strict, especially for those engaged in the translation of poetry.

MAIIA KVIATKOVSKAIA: When I was joining the Union of Writers, I did not have a published book of translations, but only translations included in different volumes. The requirement of the Union of Writers to have two published books was lifted for translators because publishing a volume of your own translations equaled being awarded with a medal—that is, it was extremely difficult and honorary. Only distinguished translators like El'ga Linetskaia, Iurii Korneyev, or Mikhail Donskoi would get their translations published in a separate volume. Other translators could only dream of this. Therefore, to give translators a chance to join the Union of Writers the requirement was changed: the translator was required to have published a certain number of poetic lines to apply for membership. The recommendations were given to me by editor and translator Valerii Stolbov, and it was very important because he was a Muscovite. The other referee was Gleb Semenov whom I had known since 1938 when he chaired the seminar for schoolchildren in the Palace of Pioneers, which I attended when I was in junior school.

In general, publications were a very difficult requirement to meet. Young writers and translators found themselves in a vicious circle: they needed to publish to be accepted into the Union of Writers but had a hard time getting themselves commissioned and published because they were not yet members of the Union of Writers. The task was even more complicated because the amount of literature translated by the candidate was supposed to be substantial. Newcomers into the field of translation could not hope for a big commission for a translation. Seeking to get engaged in translation projects, young translators readily translated from interlinear trots—prosaic word-for-word translations of original verse. Interlinear trots were widely used to create translated poetry by poet-translators, who were unfamiliar with the originals and their languages (for more detail, see chap. 6).

SERGEI STEPANOV: I was accepted into the Union of Writers for my translations of several thousand lines of the locally important Mansyan poet Iuvan Shestalov. I submitted these publications to the Union of Writers along with my several translations from Thomas Moore.

Even a substantial number of publications and solid recommendations were not always enough to ensure automatic admittance into the Union of Writers. This happened to the Leningrad translator Viktor Andreev, who voluntarily gave up his place in the line for those who were waiting to join the union.

VIKTOR ANDREEV: To join the Union of Writers, I presented two books that I had published by then. One was *Chudesnye istorii pro zaitsa po imeni Lek* (Wonderful stories of Lek the bunny) translated together with Ol'ga Kustova. This was a collection of Guinean fairy tales, which I brought from Guinea and later translated from French. The second book was French children folklore *Malysh Russel' i drugie* (Cadet Roussell and others). Joining the Union of Writers for a translator was not that easy in the 1980s, because in those days the Union of Writers did not provide membership to more than one translator a year.

I had solid recommendations from the distinguished Moscow philologist Inna Terterian and the brilliant translator of Spanish literature Aleksandra Koss. Nonetheless, it took me a while to join the Union of Writers. The situation in Moscow was very anti-Semitic; most Jewish candidates were rejected. These rejections concerned only translators, and not writers and poets. This did not affect me directly because I am an ethnic Russian with a very common Russian name. Yet this affected me indirectly. Joining the Union of Writers was made in two stages: at first, the candidature would be put to vote in the Leningrad department of the Union of Writers and then the candidate was considered by the secretariat in Moscow. Thus, Jewish translators would get an approval in Leningrad, which would be then followed by a rejection in Moscow. In the middle of the 1980s, the Leningrad department asked for autonomy from Moscow, which was granted. This meant that the vote in the Leningrad department became sufficient for writers and translators to be accepted into the Union of Writers. Once autonomy was granted, the Leningrad Union of Writers started to accept the translators who had been rejected by the Moscow secretariat before. Since it was quite a long list of people, I joined the queue and had to wait. In fact, I was even asked if I could wait because I was just about to join. I did not mind waiting. So, I waited till 1988 and got accepted by the Leningrad department then; and I was also accepted into the main Union of Soviet Writers. Now I am a member of the Board of the Union of Writers.

All that time, I kept working, because the orders kept coming. There was a big demand for Spanish-speaking writers—Gabriel García Márquez, Jorge Luis Borges, Julio Cortázar. Thus, translations gave us income, which they do not do nowadays.

Membership in the Union of Writers was universally desired: the privileges and advantages it provided were extremely attractive for a Soviet citizen. The other side of the envied privileges, however, was the necessity to conform to the strict requirements set by the Union of Writers in the furtherance of the policy of the Communist Party of the Soviet Union. The Union of Writers was charged with an obligation "to teach people of letters the feeling of high responsibility for their creative work" and to carry out "active ideological struggle for the principles of socialist realism against bourgeois and revisionist influence, against false, pseudoscientific theories that render literature innocuous of its class content, against dogmatism and vulgarization in culture and arts."[15] A writer or a translator could be publicly condemned for "the conduct demeaning the Soviet literary person," or even expelled from the Union of Writers for "deviation from the principles and goals formulated in the Charter of the Union of Writers of the USSR."[16] A writer or a translator could also discredit his/her reputation by focusing on officially unwelcome subjects. Thus, in 1946 the poet Anna Akhmatova was expelled from the Union of Writers for "mystical experiences mixed with eroticism" and writer Mikhail Zoshchenko—for "depicting Soviet people as idlers and freaks, stupid and primitive people."[17] A serious reason for expulsion from the Union of Writers was foreign publications of works yet unpublished in the Soviet Union. The most famous case in this regard was the expulsion of Boris Pasternak for his publication of *Doctor Zhivago* in Italy in 1958. Later in the same year, Pasternak was threatened with deportation from the Soviet Union and forced to decline the Nobel Prize for literature.

Another reason for expulsion was allegedly anti-Soviet content of writing, for which the poet Aleksandr Galich was expelled from the Union of Writers in 1971. Accusations of anti-Soviet activity also gave substantial grounds for expulsion; thus, the writer Vladimir Voinovich was expelled in 1974 for his satirical writings and human rights activities. Voinovich was also incriminated by his samizdat publications, which were a reason for expulsion alone. It was for samizdat activity that writers Mikhail Kheifets and Vladimir Maramzin, who attempted to arrange an underground publication of Joseph Brodsky's poems, were tried in 1974. Finally, expulsion was inevitable in cases where members of the Union supported dissidents and took part in public protests, like the writer Lidiia Chukovskaia, who was expelled in 1974, or the critic Lev Kopelev in 1980. Expulsion from the Union of Writers meant loss of literary status, deprivation of opportunities to publish, poverty, and public bullying. The life of an outcast was experienced by Larisa Bespalova, whose husband, distinguished poet Vladimir Kornilov, was expelled from the Union of Writers in 1977.

LARISA BESPALOVA: My husband was officially expelled from the Union of Writers for signing the letter in the defense of Andrei Sakharov.[18] But, in fact, he started signing open letters back in 1966 in the defense of Siniavskii and Daniel'. Apart from that, in 1974 he started to publish abroad in *Kontinent* journal in Paris, *Grani* in Frankfurt, and other places. Some of his works were translated into foreign languages, too.

Larisa Bespalova demonstrated courage in her resolution to build up a career as a literary translator without joining the Union of Writers. After the expulsion of her husband, Bespalova made a voluntary choice not to apply for the Union of Writers membership. As she stated herself,

LARISA BESPALOVA: It would have even looked strange if I decided to join the Union of Writers while my husband was expelled. Of course, I did not even try to join it at that time.

Bespalova eventually joined the Union of Writers only in 1991, after Kornilov had been restored to his membership in 1988. Yet even as a nonmember of the Union of Writers Bespalova was able to publish her translations of *A Handful of Dust* by Evelyn Waugh and stories by Flannery O'Connor, William Faulkner, F. Scott Fitzgerald, and Angus Wilson. It must be noted, however, that Bespalova was an employee of an influential publishing house Molodaia Gvardiia. It was Molodaia Gvardiia that published her translation of *A Handful of Dust* in 1971. Other publications were possible due to Bespalova's membership in the translation seminar conducted by two distinguished translators of Ivan Kashkin's school, Mariia Lorie and Evgeniia Kalashnikova. The active engagement of Larisa Bespalova in the literary life of Moscow as well as her literary talent made her visible as a translator.

Officially recognized by the Soviet literary world, members of the Union of Writers were regularly commissioned to translations. Literary translation paid well, and with a bit of luck it could become a steady source of income.

INNA STREBLOVA: Literary translations paid very well. I remember the rates for prose quite well. In the 1960s and 1970s, one printer's sheet cost one hundred rubles in case of a small run, and when the number of ordered copies was big, the price of one printer's sheet amounted to two hundred rubles. This was a lot of money: my salary as a university professor was 120 rubles a month. When I translated *The Life of Count Federigo Confalonieri* by Ricarda Huch and got paid, I felt fabulously rich.

SERGEI STEPANOV: Literary translation could sufficiently provide for a living, especially if the translator was good at it. Poetic translations were paid by the line. For example, in 1970s and 1980s, a poetic line cost no less than one ruble, or even more. A reputed translator was able to get five rubles for a line. This means if one was commissioned to a translation, one could make a thousand rubles a day.

Despite the big earnings occasionally provided by translation, literary translators, including very successful ones, mainly preferred to remain officially employed by various state organizations in order to have a steady source of income. Most of the interviewed translators were employed: Irina Komarova was an editor in the Uchpedgiz publishing house, Evgenii Witkowsky, in the Molodaia Gvardiia publishing house, Larisa Bespalova, in the Molodaia Gvardiia publishing house and later in *Novyi mir* journal; Viktor Golyshev started his career as an engineer, and Inna Streblova and Sergei Stepanov were university professors. Literary translation commissions were difficult to obtain, and even members of the Union of Writers were not protected from lengthy periods of inactivity and literary unemployment. This sometimes led to tragic outcomes.

INNA STREBLOVA: The decision to earn one's living by literary translation was very risky. Some people, indeed, succeeded in doing it; however, most translators were officially employed elsewhere, thus combining their jobs with literary translation. Sergei Petrov, who was an extremely qualified translator, once noted that a big translation order was invariably followed by a long lack of orders or no orders at all. And this was true in my case, too: after I had translated *The Life of Count Federigo Confalonieri,* I did not receive any translation orders for several years.

Cases of literary translators leaving their official jobs, however, were not infrequent in the Soviet Union, especially when translators became aware of their talent and ability. One of the stories of success was that of Viktor Golyshev, an engineer by profession, who decided to give up engineering in 1964 for the sake of his true vocation.

VIKTOR GOLYSHEV: I first quit engineering in 1964. My freedom lasted for nine months, and then I ran out of money and returned to engineering. I told myself that I would quit once I had made a thousand rubles, which I did: once I realized I had 1,100 rubles, I left my job again. I have been teaching translation at the Literary Institute in recent years, but I never got back to engineering again.

Apart from talent, the successful career of Viktor Golyshev owed a lot to his acute sense of literary trends. The novels that he selected for translation were cutting-edge, and this definitely attracted the attention of editors, however apprehensive of novelty the publishers were forced to be. This ability to respond to changes in the literary situation was pointed out by Maiia Kviatkovskaia and Viktor Andreev as one of the most important, along with a knowledge of foreign languages and a passion for literature.

MAIIA KVIATKOVSKAIA: To be getting orders from time to time, the translator had to know about the major literary events. For example, when the quarter centenary jubilee of Shakespeare was celebrated in 1964, translations of Shakespeare's works were in high demand and were actively published.

VIKTOR ANDREEV: I entered Leningrad State University in 1966, and the Latin American literature boom followed shortly in 1970, when Márquez's *One Hundred Years of Solitude* was first published in Russian translation. The interest in Latin American literature was very high, which is why publishers needed people who were able to translate from Spanish. This is how I entered the profession. In 1969, my translations of poetry were published for the first time: Aleksandra Koss was translating a novel by Ramón María del Valle-Inclán and for some reason did not want to translate the poems that were used in the novel, and she gave them to me to translate. This was after the centenary anniversary of Valle-Inclán, and some of his works were translated on this occasion. This is how I got myself properly introduced to the Khudozhestvennaia Literatura publishing house.

Another proof of the importance of good timing and the translator's ability to react to the continuously changing situation of the translation market was given by Ignatii Ivanovskii in his book *Pochtovaia loshad'* (Stage horse). This is how Ivanovskii describes his first literary and financial success.

And the miracle happened. It called me on the phone and spoke in the voice of Daniil Mikhailovich Gorfinkel'. Daniil Mikhailovich had long ago compiled a volume of Longfellow translations, submitted it to a publishing house—and forgotten about it. It was the publishing house itself that reminded him of the volume: the President of the United States was planning to visit the Soviet Union for the first time after World War II, and anything suitable for the occasion was to be quickly published, Longfellow definitely met the requirements . . .

I, however, did not believe in the miracle and wanted to ignore it. But then the publishing house called. They asked me to come at once and sign the contract.

So I came. I signed it, without reading and without believing what was happening to me. Since the commission looked completely unreal, I did not even ask how much money I was going to get. Yet the people in the publishing house started asking questions:

"What is your bank account number? You do not have a bank account? Then the number of your bank book? Oh, you do not have one? Get one today. No money? But all you need to get it is five rubles. Borrow them somewhere."

The only person I could borrow some money from was my mother. On hearing my request to lend me some money so I could get big money from the publishing house, mother sighed and said,

"Well, I know you barely survive till your payday. But why tell me these lies? Money! From a publishing house! I prefer you told me the truth."

Two weeks passed. Indeed, I ran out of money before the payday. When it got really bad, I remembered my trip to the publishing house, and dropped by the bank just to make sure.

The cashier, a girl of my age, found the card, looked at it, and her face changed. Another girl came by, and she also looked at the card, but keeping silent was beyond her. She commented,

"Such earnings for such a young man!"

I took a look into my bankbook. The sum of money in it testified to the complete unreality of the situation—three thousand rubles. My monthly income in those days was forty-five rubles.

Pausing, I asked,

"May I take at least a hundred? I really need it, you know."

The girl blushed. The rich young man was definitely mocking her. But he looked so innocent and spoke so sincerely that she was confused. Shrugging her shoulders, she said,

"Take it all, if you like."

I took half and went to see my mother.[19]

Commissions from publishing houses varied in scope and type of literary texts to be translated. Editors distributed translation orders between translators who they thought were best suited, and therefore translators had no say in the choice of texts. To get themselves engaged in a translation project to their liking, translators needed to file individual applications. To make sure their individual applications were approved by the publishing house or journal, translators had to provide a convincing description of the prospective literary work and its merits. The application was then closely considered either by the editorial board of the publishing house, or by the specially appointed editors. The applying translator could also be requested to present a sample translation of the work he/she was applying for. If the final decision of the publishing house was positive, the publishers would sign an official contract with the translator, after which the translator settled down to the translation.

The application process, although complicated and regularly resulting in denials, offered good possibilities of getting oneself commissioned to the translate a literary work one truly enjoyed. Translator Larisa Bespalova, who also worked as an editor for thirty-one years of her life, confirms that Soviet publishers were eager to consider individual applications and reacted well to new names and titles.

LARISA BESPALOVA: It is true that publishing houses sometimes initiated the translation process, but access to foreign literature was limited. At first there was only one publishing house which received foreign literature on the regular basis—this was Progress, and then Raduga publishing house split from Progress 1982.[20] Other publishing houses were not provided with foreign books and mainly had to choose from individual applications. Active translators were usually interested in contemporary literature; some of them got books from abroad through acquaintances. This is why publishing plans for modern literature were mainly compiled on the basis of individual applications.

Leningrader Irina Komarova echoes the words of Muscovite Larisa Bespalova.

IRINA KOMAROVA: Publishing houses eagerly considered applications from translators: this was a good way to find new authors who would be of interest to the readers. Yet the number of rejections was huge. I remember how I decided I should translate Daphne du Maurier, made an application to the Goslitizdat publishing house, and was rejected.

Applications were rejected for different reasons. Ideology and fear played an important role in the selection of texts for translation, but editors and publishing houses were also guided by their personal preferences and prejudices for texts or translators themselves. Many translators mention that publishing houses had their favorite translators whom they felt comfortable and safe working with. Canonicity of translations was another important factor that affected decisions regarding applications. This means that there were translations that were considered exceptionally good, timely, or artistically valuable and that had a wide circle of readers. Applications for texts, translations of which already enjoyed success, were looked upon unfavorably. Competition with accomplished influential translators or canonical translations meant a hard struggle in which the prospects of success were very small.

> IGNATII IVANOVSKII: Aleksandr Anikst was obsessed with Marshak and his translations of Shakespeare; he saw to it that the potential competitors stayed away. Once he arranged an evening of Shakespeare's sonnets. I got an invitation to this meeting. The translators were supposed to be sitting on the stage, the chairs on the stage were arranged in three rows, and even though I was a translator of the sonnets, I was put into the back row, so that I knew my place.

> SERGEI STEPANOV: After I had translated T. S. Eliot in the 1980s, I took the translation to Moscow to show it to a publishing house. I was rejected on the spot: the publishing house said they did not want it, because the translations by Sergeev already existed and everyone was happy with them. I insisted I should leave them my translations for consideration, but there was no hope for success from the very beginning.

Dependence of publishing houses on state decisions and plans was another important aspect that created obstacles in promoting new authors and titles. Inna Streblova was emphatic in her statement that publishing houses were very limited in their freedom of choice of foreign literature and very far from being able to include anything they wanted into their publishing plans.

> INNA STREBLOVA: It would be completely wrong to say that everything in translation was determined by politics and censorship. Literary translation in the Soviet Union was also driven by economic and organizational factors. Publishing houses had fixed annual publishing plans approved in Moscow, and they had to stick to these plans. This necessity naturally limited the number of translators who could get involved in translation projects. This number was even more limited by the fact that two publishing houses were not allowed to translate and publish the same novel at the same time. This means there were more translators out there than translation projects available.[21]

This situation, however, did not discourage some translators from doing translations of lengthy literary works at their own risk and then offering their translations to editors. This was the strategy adopted by

Viktor Golyshev, who translated contemporary American literature, which evoked apprehension just by the country of its origin.

VIKTOR GOLYSHEV: With a couple of exceptions, everything that I translated in the Soviet times I translated by my own decision. I either had a verbal arrangement with a publisher, or offered my translations to journals, or—more rarely—to publishing houses. Even *Light in August* I translated without signing an official contract. I first offered my translation of *Light in August* to a publishing house and it was rejected; then I offered it to the journal *Novyi mir* in 1975, and they accepted it. Later the novel was published by the Khudozhestvennaia Literatura publishing house. The novel was never censored at all.

In fact, many translations were first accepted by *Novyi mir* journal before being published as a separate book.

LARISA BESPALOVA: Many books were published thanks to their translators. Lots of wonderful books were published after the applications of Elena Golysheva, Viktor Govyshev, Elena Surits, Rita Rait-Kovaleva.

As one can see, promotion of translation projects was difficult, but some translators and anthologists were able to succeed in their endeavors. Despite the complexity and challenges of the process of approval and commissioning, once the translator signed the contract with the publishing house, he/she could enjoy time and ample opportunity to produce a high-quality translation.

MIKHAIL YASNOV: The translator in those days could take time translating a text. Once the publishing house commissioned the translator to do a translation of a novel, the translator knew he/she had two years to get the translation ready. The editor would inform the translator of the deadline, and the translator would work without haste. He/she would go to a Creativity Home for several long stays to work there quietly and consult with colleagues on complicated matters. Once the translation was ready, the publishing house would start the editing process, which also took a lot of time. Then the publishing house would find a specialist to write a preface and commentaries to the text—the translator was not allowed to do this, as it was important that the preface and commentaries be written by a distinguished professor. After this, the book was studied by the publishing house's editor-in-chief, and it was a crucial point, because once the book was approved by the editor-in-chief, the book was secure in the publishing plan. It could happen, though, that the editor-in-chief would reject the translation. This mainly happened when the translator, who had been carefully chosen for the translation, managed to impair his/her reputation while translating the text—for example, if he/she signed a letter in support of dissidents.

It is notable that Yasnov indicates that prefaces and commentaries to the translated texts were not seen as a part of the translator's task. Muscovite Larisa Bespalova denies this point. As an editor of a publishing house and later a literary periodical, she saw multiple cases of translators writing prefaces and commentaries to their own literary translations. She points out that not every translator liked writing prefaces, but those who did and wanted to do so were usually permitted to perform the role of a commentator.

This discrepancy between the experience of Bespalova and Yasnov might be explained by their location in different cities. Moscow as the capital enjoyed more freedom, whereas Leningrad offered fewer publishing opportunities. Since the competition in Leningrad was extremely high and opportunities much smaller, translators were not able to compete with professional literary critics who were specially trained to write prefaces and commentaries and who also fought for being published for the same reasons as writers and translators: namely, for earnings, status, and membership in the Union of Writers.

Therefore, differences between the Moscow and Leningrad approaches to translation and publishing did not consist purely in the way the publishing process was organized. The differences lay in professional opportunities, as well as in the social and literary history of the two cities, which resulted in their never-ending competition, which to a certain degree continues to exist even now in the twenty-first century.

The cities of Moscow and St. Petersburg/Leningrad have been seen as bitter rivals ever since St. Petersburg was founded by Peter the Great in 1703 and soon made the capital, thus partially depriving the old capital of Moscow of its former glory. Built to rival European capitals, St. Petersburg flourished for two centuries. Yet when the danger of intervention and the proximity to the national border forced the Soviet government to move the capital from Petrograd[22] back to Moscow in 1918, career opportunities moved together with the capital, leaving Petrograd to settle for the reputation of the second city of the country.

In her description of the cultural situation in the Soviet Union in the 1920s and 1930s, Katerina Clark speaks of the tremendous rise of the status of Moscow as a political and cultural center as "a matter not of a historical accident, but of necessity."[23] Speaking of the strategically developed cult of Moscow, Clark observes,

> Moscow culture became Soviet culture in two senses. First, in that the absolute majority of the commissions and publication outlets and the most privileged housing and living conditions for intellectuals were established there, Moscow became the place where culture was "happening." A steady stream of intellectuals relocated to the capital. Second, culture spread centripetally. Exempla from Moscow (architectural styles, theatrical repertoires, etc.) were mandated for everywhere else. Leningrad, the former capital . . . and rival, remained an equal really only in film and ballet; even the edicts, journals, and critics that set the cannon came largely from Moscow.[24]

This administrative and social allocation of Leningrad to second place, however, did not extinguish the fire of rivalry. Different schools in different spheres of science and research continued to emerge in the two cities, deepening the rift between the two capitals. Moscow and Leningrad phonological schools, schools of clinical psychology, finance, and even ballet and figure skating—these are but a few examples of the invisible opposition of the two cities. Literary translation practice in the Soviet Union made its contribution to the distinction between Moscow and Leningrad.

In the beginning of the 1960s, both the Moscow and Leningrad departments of the Union of Writers conducted literary translation seminars, and both cities possessed a vast number of universities to produce highly educated language specialists; they both had publishing houses to publish books on different subjects including literary translations. Despite these seeming similarities, Moscow translators enjoyed more freedom and wider opportunities to get themselves published. The location in the capital ensured career promotion for Moscow translators over Leningrad translators, and the difference between the schools "was not determined by creative, but rather by near-creative reasons called into being by strict centralism and culture control" in the USSR.[25]

A representative of the Leningrad translation school, Mikhail Yasnov elaborates on the differences between the two translation schools in his article "Khranitel' chuzhogo nasledstva" ("The keeper of foreign possessions"). Ascribing the phenomenon of the two translation schools of the Soviet Union to economic and political factors, he points out that wider publication opportunities in Moscow resulted in a higher percentage of literary flaws, which in their turn resulted in the reputation of Moscow translators as less organized, more permissive, and more self-indulgent. In Leningrad, Yasnov writes, "it was much harder to get commissioned to translate the poet one wanted to translate. This is why Leningrad translators assumed more difficult and more refined tasks which Muscovites had rejected for this or that reason."[26] Readiness to take up complex tasks under conditions of work deficiency created the reputation of Leningrad translators as precise, careful, and reserved in their creative work.

IRINA KOMAROVA: Big projects mainly took place in Moscow: Leningrad translators would get mere leftovers from their Moscow colleagues. We were mostly getting "crumbs" until the blessed 1990s, when I eventually retired from the publishing house.

MAIIA KVIATKOVSKAIA: There was a hierarchy in the distribution of orders. Moscow would send to Leningrad anything that for this or that reason had not been taken by Muscovites. In Leningrad, the best pieces were rightfully given to older and more experienced translators. The remaining pieces were offered to students of seminars.

MIKHAIL YASNOV: In Khudozhestvennaia Literatura in Leningrad, there was a wonderful editor Nina Snetkova, who was very reluctant to let young translators anywhere close to the publishing house. It was quite clear why she did that: there was not much work available. It is true that there was no difference between Moscow and Leningrad schools of translation, but there were more publishing opportunities in Moscow. It was easier to promote translations in Moscow. And what one could not get published in Moscow would be heaped down on Leningrad. This is why Leningrad had a strong circle of poetic translators, who did what the Muscovites could not finish. This is why the requirements for the quality of translations in Leningrad were higher than in Moscow.

Despite this rivalry between Moscow and Leningrad, I was much more friends with the Moscow department of the Khudozhestvennaia Literatura publishing house rather than the Leningrad department, even though I was from Leningrad. It so happened that Maurice Wachsmacher worked as an editor in the Moscow department of Khudozhestvennaia Literatura. I was friends with him: he was the one to whom I first showed my translations as a young translator, and he was very kind to me.

This border between the Moscow and Leningrad translation schools was purely artificial, it was a type of social differentiation: the life of Muscovites was easier, the life of Leningraders—more difficult. In the personal archive of Efim Etkind, one can find his correspondence with Oleg Lozovetskii regarding the book of Verlaine translations that was being prepared in Moscow at that time and was finally published in 1969. Lozovetskii was appointed editor for his book. This was the first book of Verlaine translations compiled by Etkind, which included translations by such great translators of our time as Anatolii Geleskul, Maia Kviat-kovskaia, Vladimir Vasil'ev, Ariadna Efron. Lozovetskii, as the correspondence clearly shows, opposed Etkind who kept sending him translations of Leningrad translators, such as Maiia Kviatkovskaia and Sergei Petrov, whereas Lozovetskii was determined to publish only Muscovites. Indeed, sometimes it looked as if some Moscow editors were determined to make Leningrad look a province, and Moscow—the only center.

VIKTOR ANDREEV: Most great works of literature were taken by Moscow translators. And it is too bad that Moscow translators produced a lot of low-quality translations. Nonetheless, Boris Pasternak, Marina Tsvetaeva, and Samuil Marshak, who were devoted to translation and created masterpieces, were from Moscow. Yet, Muscovites were used to earning money by translating. It was not quite the same in Leningrad. There was not that much to translate, and what there was mainly consisted of very difficult writers like Francisco de Quevedo or Miguel de Unamuno whom Muscovites did not want to translate because translating them required much effort. Moscow translators were after money, and Leningraders did not have much choice and were used to hard and meticulous work. Leningrad translators were ready to take smaller orders and work for less money.

Leningrad translators would also get less exciting pieces for translation. If, for instance, Rafael Alberti was published in Moscow, his communist and political poems that had to be included into the volume for political reasons would be sent to Leningrad because Muscovites could afford to be picky. Leningrad translators were eager to compromise and take less important pieces because there were fewer orders for translation here in Leningrad than in Moscow.

Larisa Bespalova gave a straightforward analysis of the Moscow-Leningrad rivalry from the point of view of an experienced editor. She insists that Leningrad translators filed fewer applications and had a different translation approach.

LARISA BESPALOVA: As an editor for Molodaia Gvardiia, I did not receive any applications from Leningrad translators. In fact, it did not matter where the translator lived. It mattered whether he was a good translator or not. The only complication in the precomputer era was the editing process, which would be more difficult in such cases. For instance, when I worked at *Novyi mir*, I was the editor for the translation of Faulkner[27] made by the Leningrad translator Meri Bekker. I know that Bekker received many orders from the Goslitizdat publishing house, which mainly published classics of foreign literature. Goslitizdat therefore did not need individual applications and decided upon the distribution of orders itself.

Leningrad translators were usually more reserved, although there were exceptions. The Leningrad school is different.

Admitting the lack of balance in the distribution of translations and opportunities, Muscovite Evgenii Witkowsky, who worked as an editor in the publishing house Molodaia Gvardiia in the 1970s and 1980s, notes that the animosity between Moscow and Leningrad was reciprocal and Leningrad publishing houses also published Moscow translators with great reluctance.

EVGENII WITKOWSKY: It is true that some translations were sent to Leningrad purely because Moscow editors did not like the text or did not want to deal with it. Nonetheless, Moscow publishing houses readily published Leningrad translators, whereas Leningrad publishing houses never published Moscow translators. The thing is that Leningrad is smaller, and there was not enough space for everyone in Leningrad.

The domination of Moscow over Leningrad affected both the distribution of commissions and the application process as such. Leningrad applications for new titles and authors were sometimes lost to Moscow translators and publishing houses.

INNA STREBLOVA: Another difficulty for Leningrad translators was that most of the publishing houses here in Leningrad were branches of Moscow publishing houses. This meant that all applications needed to receive approval from the Moscow headquarters of the publishing house. This is how our applications got "taken over" by Muscovites. That is, applications of Leningrad translators were first rejected for this or that reason, and then all of a sudden the novel that had been applied for by a Leningrader would come out in a translation done by a Muscovite.

Echoes of the old grievances still smart in some comments of the translators who dreamt their potential would be fulfilled to a maximum. Viktor Golyshev summed up the situation by expressing the opinion that Leningrad translators experienced the shortage of orders due to their distance from Moscow as the center of publishing activity.

VIKTOR GOLYSHEV: The truth is one had to be at hand to get oneself commissioned and to get orders. When my mother [Elena Golysheva] moved to Tarusa, which is 130 kilometers away from Moscow, her earnings became smaller. Even though she had a phone and publishers could contact her, there was only one editor she kept working with—an old friend, who liked her. People get quickly forgotten.

As one can see, the rivalry between Moscow and Leningrad translators consisted in the economic and sociopolitical differences between the two cities. Occasional presumptions of the existence of two separate translation schools with different approaches to translation and creative writing, as well as alienation of the two publishing circles, seem to be lacking substantial proof. Moscow and Leningrad translators admit the difference in the number of opportunities, but they mutually compliment translations produced in the other city. Thus, Leningraders speak about the boldness and brightness of literary translations made by Moscow translators, as well as the courage of Muscovites in their selection of controversial and politically inconvenient works. Muscovites mention the diligence of Leningrad translators, their commitment to translation tasks, and attention to detail. Mutual respect of translators and editors was formed, as we have seen, despite a highly competitive working environment, unequal allocation of translation orders, and highly politicized context of their activities. What is now quite clear is that translators saw themselves as a single community of fellow thinkers, with its members living in different cities of the Soviet Union, yet united by a common passion.

CHAPTER 6

POETRY IN TRANSLATION

To Match or Not to Match

Poetry has traditionally played an important role in Russian culture. The image of the poet as a national hero, a fighter, or even a martyr dominated the Russian literary vision for centuries. The aphoristic beginning of the poem by Evgenii Evtushenko saying that a poet in Russia is more than a poet became the manifesto of poetic creativity in Russia and the Soviet Union.[1]

The nineteenth century in Russia closely linked poetry with the notion of civic consciousness and engagement in social activity. Poetry was ascribed special powers; poets themselves defined the role of poetry as missionary (Aleksandr Pushkin), exemplary (Mikhail Lermontov), social (Nikolai Nekrasov), and prophetic (Fedor Tiutchev). Special functions of poetry were gradually transferred onto poetic translation, which Russian poets eagerly engaged in. Active experimenting of poet-translators with the form and content of translated originals stirred up heated discussions of approaches to translation, which took place in the eighteenth and especially in the nineteenth centuries.[2] The interest in original and translated poetry remained alive throughout the decades and gradually shifted into the twentieth century and the Soviet era.

Having experienced a decline in the 1920s through the 1940s, the interest in poetry revived in the 1950s after the death of Stalin. State-initiated projects gave Soviet citizens ample opportunities to engage into literary activity by joining literary associations (chap. 4). By the 1960s, poetry and poetic translation became the point of intersection of interests of different social groups of Soviet society. The state investment in poetry in the 1950s was targeted at turning it into an ideological mouthpiece. Poetry, however, took a different course, gradually redeeming its status as the voice of dissenters, as the historically formed demand of the general reader by far exceeded the demand dictated by the state policy. People took part in semilegal open-air poetry sessions, circulated poetry in underground publications or handwritten copies, and sang along with singer-songwriters, the advent of whom in the 1960s became a distinct trend in Soviet culture.[3] In the subsequent years, the state continued to favor poetry and poetic translations, and Soviet citizens remained its avid readers, albeit for different reasons. Engagement in poetic translation thus acquired a new role: directed and controlled by the state, poetic translation was a response to the emotional and social needs of readers mixed with genuine curiosity and interest in the forms poetry took beyond the Iron Curtain.

Yet it was not purely translations from European languages that Soviet translators of poetry engaged in. Poetic translation was put to use by the Soviet state and made to perform social and political tasks. Such events as the suppression of the Hungarian Uprising (1956), the Cuban Missile Crisis (1962), and the invasion of Czechoslovakia (1968) in the general context of the Cold War required a natural counterbalance in order to assure Soviet citizens of the state's peaceful intentions.[4] Promotion of the federative principle of multinationalism was extremely important at that time: it contributed to national unity and served as a firewall from accusations of aggression. The federative principle of multinationalism manifested itself specifically in the state multilingualism, which was officially stipulated by the Soviet constitution and therefore had to be conformed to on all levels of social life including original literature and literary translation, despite the fact that the Russian language was politically maintained as the language of the dominant majority and the lingua franca of the USSR.[5] A well-cultivated domestic image of a friendly multinational state did not comport with the militant international image, which made many Soviet citizens discard information on militaristic aggression of the Soviet Union as false.

It is striking that the propagated multinationalism and the strict control over publishing coexisted despite their being mutually exclusive. As a feature of an open society, the principle of multinationalism is variety oriented: it proclaims equality and sustains mutual respect and interest of society members in nonnative languages and cultures. On the other hand, a well-developed system of control and bans is a feature of a closed society; it is a measure taken against variety, including language, cultural, and creative variety of nations and individuals. Multinationalism and multilingualism were legally proclaimed and overtly propagated in the Soviet Union, even though the observance of language freedoms in the country was very far from being consistent. At the same time, censorship and close control of social activities of Soviet citizens, although absolutely real and omnipresent, were covert, barely mentioned officially and seldom spoken about in everyday life. This opposition of visible and invisible powers and philosophies determined the course that Soviet publishers, writers, and translators had to steer in their work.

The widely propagated friendship of nations, which implied friendly relations of the peoples of the Soviet Union and the countries of the Communist bloc, was expected to manifest itself in different spheres of social life, including publishing. Publishers were thus required to produce substantial amounts of literature translated from the languages of the Soviet Union and the languages of the allies of the Soviet bloc. The interest of the general reader, however, was centered on world classics and modern works translated from major European languages (English, French, German, Spanish, etc.). To ensure the interest of readers, translations from languages of limited circulation therefore had to be as high quality as those from widely spoken languages. The high quality was hard to achieve in this regard due to the fact that a very limited circle of specialists knew languages of limited circulation and not all these specialists were capable or willing to engage in literary activity. This necessity of representing the variety of Soviet national literatures in publishing substantiated the social and literary utility of interlinear trots. As mentioned in chapter 5, by interlinear trots I understand word-for-word prosaic translations of original poetry, which function as intermediate links between original texts and poet-translators, who are unfamiliar with the source language. Poems in the target language are therefore recreated indirectly, because the translator does not deal with the original, but with its prosaic translation into the translator's native language or, in historically more distant cases, into a third language.

The use of interlinear trots in poetic translation was a well-known practice, which was actively employed in Russia long before the revolution of 1917. One of the popular translations from interlinear trots of the nineteenth century was the translation of Homer's *Odyssey*, which the celebrated Russian poet, writer, and educator Vasilii Zhukovskii made from a German interlinear trot. Zhukovskii's translation was highly praised by Nikolai Gogol for its ability to communicate the qualities of the original better than the original itself. Seen as a form of cultural appropriation, translation was thus permitted, if not expected, to use interlinear trots, which, among other things, became an important nineteenth-century contribution to the shaping of concepts of adequacy and creativity in the Russian translation philosophy.[6] An interlinear trot was looked upon as a necessary tool and a common means of poetic translation. For example, in 1910–16 the Russian poet and translator Valerii Briusov edited the unique anthology of Armenian poetry translated from interlinear trots by the most progressive contemporary poets and writers, among whom were Aleksandr Blok, Fedor Sologub, Viacheslav Ivanov, and Konstantin Bal'mont.[7]

The use of interlinear trots in translating poetry was therefore a practice well familiar to translators and publishers when the Soviet Union came into being. The heightening of interest in interlinear trots in the Soviet Union was determined by the shift in the role of literature, which was supposed to serve public purposes, including education. Literary translation became a secure source of high-quality literary texts required for education, especially in those languages of the Soviet Union that had either undergone script reforms or were starting to introduce scripts for the first time.

In context of the high demand for new literary texts, interlinear trots were considered useful for introducing readers to the variety of national literatures and for educating a new generation of well-qualified literary translators who, upon learning the language while translating from the

interlinear trot, would later be able to translate from the original too.[8]
This strategy was initially justified because, whereas publishing houses
could choose from a large number of poet-translators from major European languages, the number of poet-translators from Slavic languages,
Asian languages, and the national languages of the Soviet Union was
limited. The term *interlinear trot* is mainly associated with poetry,
although interlinear translations of prose also existed in the Soviet literary practice in translations from the languages of the Soviet Union
into Russian.[9] Interlinear trots of prose were gradually replaced by direct
translations from originals by the middle of the twentieth century, but
interlinear trots of poetry took root in the Russian translation tradition,
however temporary the measure might have initially looked. Interlinear
trots of poetry were found to be convenient, and translations of poetry
were often done via interlinear trots, at times even from the most popular and widely spoken European languages.

Interlinear trots varied in the degree of detail they provided; they
could be very detailed or very sketchy, depending on who prepared
the interlinear trot and who was supposed to translate from it. In some
cases, interlinear trots included information on phraseology, implications, and allusions or described in closer detail the prosodic features,
stylistic devices, or imagery, which is why a good interlinear translation
was highly valued by poet-translators. Evgenii Witkowsky mentioned
that there even existed a term, *Stalin's interlinear trot (stalinskii pod-
strochnik).*[10] The term was used to define a set of interlinear trots of one
poem, each focusing on a different aspect of the poem; such a set of
interlinear trots also included the complete transliteration of the original with Cyrillic letters.

Therefore the use of interlinear trots was a completely acceptable
translation practice that was employed both by beginners in the field and
reputable poet-translators. Marina Tsvetaeva, who spoke French, German, English, and Spanish, also translated from Czech, Serbian, Croatian, Bulgarian, Georgian, Polish, and Yiddish. Samuil Marshak, the celebrated translator of Shakespeare, Keats, Burns, and Blake, is also known
for his translations of the poems of Mao Tse-tung from interlinear trots.
Another example is poet Anna Akhmatova, who knew French, Italian,
German, and English and translated from Serbian, Czech, Bulgarian,

Romanian, and Korean. It was Akhmatova who translated a big collection of Rabindranath Tagore into Russian—also via interlinear trots. Akhmatova found the employment of interlinear trots in translation quite natural and justified their use, saying, "We all translate from an interlinear: the one who knows the language of the original sooner or later gets to see the interlinear translation in front of him."[11] Joseph Brodsky also actively translated from many languages including Greek, Polish, Czech, Dutch, Lithuanian, Estonian, and German.

Due to the existence of interlinear trots, poetic translation gradually turned into a steady source of income for many Soviet poets. Some of them, like Akhmatova, Tsvetaeva, and later Brodsky, did it to provide for their living and to stay involved in literary activity that could result in publications. Unable to publish their original poetry, poets voluntarily dedicated themselves to translating poetry written by others, thus keeping their status as published poets. Other poets saw translation of poetry as easy earning—and, indeed, as we have seen above, translation of poetry paid very well (see chap. 5). Influential poets who had worked their way up to recognition and approval of officials of different ranks exercised their right to select poetic pieces for translation and were usually able to find someone to create an interlinear trot for them, if such a necessity arose. For several decades, there even existed an unofficial profession called *interlinear trotter (podstrochnikist)*, which gradually ceased to exist, as interlinear trots continued to be produced by fellow translators, editors, and anthologists.

A literary translator in the Soviet Union was permitted to remain monolingual, however contradictory to the professional requirements this may sound. As Valentin Uvarov noted in his article in 1981, "the main quality of the translator is not the knowledge of two or more languages (the translator may not know languages and yet remain a translator), but the knowledge of his/her role. Rather than the one who knows languages, the translator is the one who behaves like a translator."[12] The quoted passage from Uvarov clearly outlines the literary appropriation tendency. The awareness of one's mission is defined here as more important than the knowledge of the source language, which makes the mission here lopsided and focused purely on the target language, culture, and social context.

Translators who did not know foreign languages were nonetheless actively resented by many editors and anthologists. For example, Evgenii Witkowsky describes his experience of fighting low-quality translations and underqualified translators in the following way:

EVGENII WITKOWSKY: I am convinced that interlinear trots are harmful, but not absolutely harmful. Interlinear trots make sense when they go about translating from the language that very few people know. This is why I once used a Danish interlinear trot when I translated from the Inuit language. The original was read out aloud to me, so that I could grasp the rhythm.

It is not surprising that interlinear trots were actively used in poetic translations from the languages of the USSR and socialist countries. Yet translations from interlinear trots from widely spoken European languages were usually a fake done for the sake of easy money. I used to prepare interlinear trots for the so-called distinguished Soviet poets. They all had someone to prepare interlinear trots so that they could rhyme the translation. And as an anthologist, I needed to fight this situation because sometimes the so-called great Soviet poets were literally imposed on me as translators, even though everyone knew they could not speak foreign languages. I learned to resist them silently. When I was commanded to take on a translator I did not want, I agreed and readily provided the person imposed on me with interlinear trots. Yet, as an editor and anthologist, I could distribute texts for translations the way I wanted. This was my loophole: I would arrange it so that half of the poems given to this translator would be very easy to work with, and the other half would be extremely difficult. Translators imposed on me failed to cope with the difficult part, because it required knowing the language, be it with or without an interlinear trot. Once they failed, they refused to take up the job themselves, and having them out of my way I was able to employ people who were qualified for the job.

Literary translation in the Soviet Union was able to provide translators with steady income. Unlike long prosaic texts, which would mainly be given to members of the Union of Writers, poetry as a small-scale literary form gave young translators a chance of getting at least a small commission. In this regard poetic translation from languages of the Soviet Union was a job that was on hand. Apart from being a source of income, poetic translations from languages of the Soviet Union had a good chance of publication, which is why young translators readily translated from interlinear trots. The translator's personal preferences were irrelevant in these cases, as translators could not afford to be picky and therefore took every opportunity available.

MIKHAIL YASNOV: I produced most of my translations in the post-Soviet times, for in the Soviet times all I could do is translate the works of the Soviet non–Russian language poets just in order to survive. In those days, I was not published very often, because I had been the personal secretary of Efim Etkind. This is why the whole lengthy period of twelve years starting with 1974 when Etkind was forced to emigrate could be called a dead season for me. [13] It lasted till 1986–87 when I had my first book published.

Etkind introduced me to Moldavian poetry, and because by that time I had already learned French, I quickly realized that all Romance languages were similar. This is how I started going to Moldavia and translating Moldavian poets. I did it for a living, to tell you the truth. This lasted for quite a while till there came up other translation opportunities.

Translation from interlinear trots could not in any way be called translation. This was a stretch: an interlinear trot was a linear word-for-word translation, based on which the literary translator would create a poetic text in Russian, the quality of the produced text largely depending on the talent and sympathies of its translator.

In the case of poetic translations from languages of the Soviet Union, translators had an important advantage, since a lot of the translated poets were living at the moment the translation was made. Most of them had a decent command of the Russian language, and their personal wish to get their works translated into the politically dominant language of the country made them very cooperative with their translators. Poet-translators into Russian were able to contact the authors to be advised on the style, prosody, or the message of the poem.

SERGEI STEPANOV: My first translation was made from the Altai language via an interlinear trot. Such things as the meter, for instance, could be agreed upon with the author of the poem. If the author was not available, I had to decide on the prosody myself.

VIKTOR ANDREEV: In the 1980s, I translated the poetry of Khaim Beider via interlinear trots. Beider was one of the leading Soviet specialists in the Yiddish culture. He wrote poetry in Yiddish too. Beider spoke perfect Russian, of course, but did not want to do his own poetic translations. Beider would provide me with interlinear trots and explain to me his poetry, the context in which it had been written, the feelings he had experienced at that time. He also read his poems aloud to me, so that I could get the feel of the prosody. I was not the only translator who worked with Beider; he would compare translations made by different translators and then decide which one he liked best.

MIKHAIL YASNOV: The choice of approaches to translating poetry was made differently with each poet. For instance, there was a wonderful Moldavian poet Paul Mihnea who invited me over to his place in Chișinău for three weeks. Well, he talked my head off with his poems. He made me translate every poem hundreds of times, so that the translation would match his vision of his poetry. His Russian was good, and he had a clear idea of the way his poems were supposed to sound in Russian. His poems were wonderful, one cannot deny it. He had a deep philosophical nature; he was bright and extraordinary in every sense. He also was a good person, and we made very good friends.

Yasnov's optimistic description of his cooperation with Mihnea is very demonstrative of the general tendency. Despite the fact that many translators looked upon working with interlinear trots as a source of income or a stepping stone to making a literary name and getting commissions for translations from major European languages, many translators enjoyed translating from interlinear trots as well. Engagement in translation from languages of the Soviet Union gave a feeling of freedom; in many cases it also meant traveling. Since the Iron Curtain made traveling abroad complicated or almost impossible, traveling to other republics, getting introduced to new cultures, and meeting new people was an extremely exciting experience. Mikhail Yasnov describes this feeling in detail.

MIKHAIL YASNOV: I do not regret facing the challenges of translating the poetries of the Soviet Union; this was a good school. I met all kinds of poets, thus learning how to deal with people. For instance, there used to be a wonderful Nenets poet Leonid Laptsui. My mentor Natalia Grudinina translated quite a lot from the languages of the Extreme North, and she arranged some commissions for me, so that I could earn some money. I translated a lot of Northern poets. Cooperation with Laptsui was a long and fruitful one. It started when I once sent him a draft of my translation of one of his poems, and he liked it, and began to send me his interlinear trots in Russian. This was how our cooperation began.

In the case of the poets of the Extreme North one could not help modifying the original poetic form, because their poetry is arranged in akyn style, which consists in the spontaneous account of what is going on at the moment. Secondly, their poetry does not rhyme, which is very different from what we are used to.

But it was interesting learning a completely different world and different ethnography. Those fifteen years that I remained unpublished as a poet, I got myself acquainted with the life the people of the Extreme North, Moldavians, Estonians, Latvians, Georgians—I worked with all kinds of people and made friends with them.

As one can see from the examples, translations from interlinear trots facilitated close cooperation of the peoples of the Soviet Union and strengthened the friendly ties, as they were intended to do. Nonetheless, interlinear trots were by nature target language oriented, and apart from the cases of direct cooperation of poets and their translators, the use of interlinear trots in translation was by definition a domesticating practice. Interlinear trots facilitated cultural appropriation, because they performed mediating functions, turning foreign poetic texts into a semiproduct in the Russian language that translators had to work with. Even with due respect to the authors of originals, poet-translators faced the task of improvement rather than translation. Unlike originals, interlinear trots were almost no man's texts, with the authorship, original content, and style diluted by mechanical rendering. Interlinear trots as texts of indistinct authorship encouraged translators to be more daring in their literary experiments: with the feeling that the presence of the original author was blurred, translators sensed they had more right to place themselves in the position of the cocreator. This feeling was very well described by the poet Bella Akhmadulina, who at one time also earned her living by translation from interlinear trots.

A poem undergoing translation lives a complex threefold life. It exists full-bloodedly in its native language and then seemingly dies in the interlinear trot. Devoid of its former harmony and music, it looks numb, breathless. And this is the most dangerous, the most disquieting moment in the poem's fate. How will the translator handle it? Will he be able to resurrect it, to give it a new life, no less generous and sonorous, or will he leave it inanimate? . . . the translated poem must not become an obscure allusion to its original, but a fully fledged participant of another poetry, a feast of another language."[14]

The conviction that the translation should become a reality of the target culture clothed translators with great authority. Devoid of the structure and poetics of the original, interlinear trots were able to reduce the translated work to a limited context, which would then be able to fit in with the local norms and expectations. Akhmadulina herself confessed, "I never tried to conform to the external features of the poem: meter, rhyming scheme—as I held by the truth that the laws of sound are different in all languages. Full of love and sympathy towards the poems I was entrusted with I wished them only one thing—that they become contemporary Russian poems close to the contemporary Russian reader."[15]

This statement does not result purely from the feeling of seeming impunity that the translator was able to experience when working with interlinear trots; the approach described here was predetermined by the mediating function of the interlinear trot. Text mediation deprives the translator of the ability to make detached judgments regarding the form and content of the original text and, consequently, to decide independently upon the attachment of priorities and the translation strategy. This is vividly seen in translations done via interlinear trots by most celebrated and universally respected translators of the twentieth century. Let us, for example, take a look at the translation from Bulgarian made by Anna Akhmatova. Despite the close proximity of the Russian and Bulgarian languages which was in many respects able to assist in the interpretation of the interlinear trot, the poem of Elisaveta Bagriana "The Call" in Akhmatova's translation underwent substantial semantic and structural transformation.

Bulgarian original by Elisaveta Bagriana[16]	Russian translation by Anna Akhmatova[17]
Аз съм тук зад три врати заключена и прозореца ми е с решетка, а душата волна, волна птица в клетка, е на слънце и простор научена.	Здесь я замкнута, крепки засовы, И в окне решетки черной прутья, Ни запеть не в силах, ни вздохнуть я, Ни в родной простор умчаться снова.
Пролетни са ветровете полъхнали, чувам гласове призивно ясни. Моя плам непламнал ще угасне в здрача на покоето заглъхнали.	Как томятся в тесной клетке птицы, Зов весенний слышу сердцем ясно, Но огонь мой гаснет здесь напрасно В душном сумраке глухой темницы
Рзатроши ключалките ръждясали! Дай ми път през тъмни коридори! Не веднъж в огрените простори моите крила са ме понасяли.	Так разбей замки—пора настала Прочь уйти по темным коридорам. Много раз по солнечным просторам Я веселой птицей улетала.
И ще бликнат звукове ликуващи от сърцето трепетно тогава . . . –Но зад тези три врати, споделен, моя пламнал зов дали дочуваш ти?	Унесет меня поток певучий, Что из сердца трепетного льется, Если до тебя он донесется . . . –Слышишь из темницы зов мой жгучий?

Original by Bagriana, literal translation from Bulgarian:

> I am here locked behind three doors, / My window is barred, / And my soul is a free, free bird in a cage, / And it has been raised in the sun and open space.
>
> Spring winds have blown, / I hear voices invitingly clear. / My flame will go out unflamed, / Faded in the dusk of the quiet.
>
> Destroy the rusty locks! / Give me the way through dark corridors! / It was not once that to the lit up spaces / My wings took me.
>
> And joyous sounds will stream / Then from the thrilled heart. /—But from behind these three doors, stifled, / My fervent call will you hear?

Translation by Akhmatova, literal translation from Russian:

> I am locked here, heavy are the latches, / And in the window there are bars of the black railing, / I have no power to sing, nor to sigh, / Nor to fly away to the dear open space.

How birds pine in a narrow cage, / The spring call I hear with my heart clearly, / But my fire is going out here in vain / In the choky dusk of the blind cell.

So break the locks—it is time / To go away down the dark corridors. / Many times across sunlit spaces / I flew away a merry bird.

I will be taken away by the canorous flow, / That flows from a thrilled heart, / If it reaches you . . . / —Do you hear from the prison my burning call?

As we can clearly see here, in her translation, Akhmatova introduces imagery different from that of the original. In the original, the focus is on the image of the bird and the longing for freedom; in the Russian translation the focus is on the bird's sufferings in captivity. Whereas in the first stanza the first and the second lines are mere statements and the other two are devoted to the memories of free life, in Akhmatova's translation the first two lines include extra characteristics of the cage, and the other two give a detailed description of the feelings of the captive. The second stanza of the translation introduces the word *call,* which is also the title of the poem. The word *call* is used in the sense *the call of spring,* which preempts the ending and creates confusion: *the call* in the original is the call of the captive; the word itself is mentioned only in the last line of the poem. In the translation there are, in fact, two calls: that of the spring and that of the captive, that is, a call of freedom and the call of captivity. The final stanza of the translation differs from the original in its structure; the mention of three doors is omitted, which destroys the closed-in stylistic organization of the original that begins and ends with the reference to the obstacle on the way to freedom.

The third stanza of the translation sounds strikingly familiar to the Russian ear due to Akhmatova's accidental introduction of her own original imagery into translation. The phrase *the merry bird* is nowhere to be found in the original; however, it is known to have been used by Akhmatova in one of her most famous early works. Compare, for instance,

> And I buried my *merry* bird
> Beyond the round well, near the ancient alder tree.[18, 19]

The adjective *merry (веселый)* is one of the favorite adjectives used by Akhmatova to contrast sad and tragic contexts, comparable to the context of Bagriana's poem.[20] This preference is obvious enough to have been well sensed by Akhmatova's translators, who tend to observe the coherent usage of this adjective in their translations, like Judith Hemschemeyer did in the translation quoted above and the following translations:

> I am cold . . . Winged or wingless,
> The *merry* god will not come to call.[21]

> What fun to fan the *merry* wasps away
> From your green eyes.[22]

> Forgive me, my *merry* boy,
> For bringing you death.[23]

The view of translation as a means of cultural appropriation and the way to enrich the Russian literature with new forms and subjects remained deeply rooted in the Russian translation practice after the fall of the Soviet system. Despite changes in the Russian mentality and literary thinking, the domesticating approach remained welcome by a substantial number of readers and critics for many years. In 1999, the famous Russian translator and critic Viktor Toporov wrote, "To create something of interest in translation one has to make sure that there is an unoccupied place for it in the Russian treasury of poetry . . . One has to translate as if writing the text for the first time . . . If the temperature of the original makes thirty-seven, it has to soar up to thirty-nine in the translation, otherwise the reader [of the translation] won't feel anything."[24]

Opponents of interlinear trots, however, voiced their disagreements quite clearly already in the 1960s. In 1963, Efim Etkind wrote that interlinear trots impeded both the transfer of creative expressivity of the original and the employment of the creative abilities of the translator.[25] The result, in Etkind's view, was poor and unable to prove credible to the reader. "Can one fall in love through an intermediary, get inspired with the help of an interlinear trot? It is counter-natural and totally unfeasible," argued Etkind.[26]

Pointing out that interlinear trots can prove useful in cross-cultural communication, Andrei Fedorov called translation from interlinear trots "hybrid creativity," recognizing it as "individual creative work based on the impulse coming from the foreign source."[27] Fedorov thought it necessary that, when published, such translations should be marked as "free" or as "variations" in order to make the level of proximity to the original clear to the reader of the translation.[28]

Interlinear trots were used not only for translations from the languages of the Soviet Union, but also from other languages. Surprisingly enough, the initial idea of teaching translators rare languages by allowing them to translate via interlinear trots eventually bore fruit. The well-developed translation school of the Soviet Union led by the most talented and experienced people of letters of the time educated several generations of literary translators who double-checked every word in the trot through dictionaries and encyclopedias. Maiia Kviatkovskaia, a distinguished translator from Spanish, was one of those translators of poetry who learned a foreign language via interlinear trots.

MAIIA KVIATKOVSKAIA: I was a graduate of the French department of the Foreign Language Institute, and my second foreign language was English. I also learned German at the secondary school. When El'ga Linetskaia offered for me to take part in the translation of the poetry of Rafael Alberti, I did not know Spanish and used interlinear trots. After I had successfully coped with these translations, I became known in the publishing house Khudozhestvennaia Literatura and I would get commissions for translations from Spanish now and then. First I translated from the interlinear trots, but gradually I realized that I looked at the originals much more often than at the interlinear trots. This is how I gradually learned the Spanish language.

It is notable that Maiia Kviatkovskaia gained her first recognition as a poet-translator also due to her translation from an interlinear trot.

MAIIA KVIATKOVSKAIA: What also made me known as a translator was my victory in the all–Soviet Union contest for the best translation of one poem. This was the poem of the Lithuanian poet Salomeja Neris.[29] I shared my second place with Natalia Astafieva, and the first place was not given to anyone.

The practice of poetic translation via interlinear trots in the Soviet

Union gave contradictory results. On the one hand, the use of interlinear trots affected the reputation of poetic translation by making it seem like a leisure activity. It is no wonder, therefore, that in the course of Brodsky's trial for social parasitism—that is, for not working or serving the country—the court did not consider Brodsky's poetic translation activity as a substantial proof of his employment or engagement in productive labor. The ability to use interlinear trots also attracted random people who saw translation as a source of easy income. Despite these deplorable consequences, the use of interlinear trots in poetic translation cannot be denounced as an absolute evil. Interlinear trots became a source of creative opportunities and new knowledge. Translations from interlinear trots were a way to engage in literary activity, at times the only way to gain access to the world of literature and publishing for young translators. While translating from the languages of the Soviet Union, translators were given a precious chance to travel and to meet highly qualified literary professionals. Both travel and new acquaintances provided young translators with knowledge of other cultures, traditions, literatures, and approaches to creative work. Some young translators took interlinear trots as a special opportunity to learn new foreign languages, thus making themselves invaluable multilingual specialists. Under Soviet limitations on the freedom of residence and freedom of travel, young translators acquired their emotional education by absorbing cultures of translated literatures and by trying to understand the logic of the languages that they did not have a chance to speak in their everyday life.

CHAPTER 7

THE INVISIBLE HAND OF CENSORSHIP

It has often been noted that engagement with literary translation in the Soviet Union meant entering a highly politicized context. As Susanna Witt notes, translation was "far from being a neutral activity of fraternization; it was a process that could be analyzed in terms of power and subjection."[1] For the Soviet state apparatus, censorship of literature in the country was an activity of prime importance, which contributed to the maintenance of the existing balance of power. Apart from careful control of literature and personal biographies of published writers, censoring organizations had the right to dictate on the style and content of all literary works published in the country, thus channeling the official position of the party to all citizens of the country. In literary translation, severe control by censoring organs resulted in two opposite tendencies: silent assent and compliance on the one hand and, on the other hand, the unstinting perseverance in experimenting with literary forms and styles as opposed to the propagated conventionalism.

VIKTOR ANDREEV: Do you know the Russian metaphoric expression *Sauerkraut is made under pressure?* Well, this is what being a translator meant in those days. The original poets and writers were pressured—think of Akhmatova, Pasternak, Tsvetaeva. And because the original creative activity was impeded, people would go into literary translation.

And because great poets had to become translators, they set the highest standards of translation for others.

Active interference of censorship with the issues of creative writing and a high level of suspicion toward foreign works in the Soviet Union were not able to prevent translation of foreign literatures. Having opted for socialist orientation, the Soviet Union needed to maintain a reputation of a model state that showed respect toward the achievements of world civilization in all spheres of science and the arts, including literature. The Soviet readership was considered entitled to be acquainted with the best works of world literature, which required active development of translation practice in the country.

Under the system of control of the state over the process of selection of literary works, their translation, and publication, the activity of Soviet publishing organizations depended on the instructions issued by the Soviet government. As of the beginning of the 1920s, all the publishing houses in the Soviet Union belonged to the state and, therefore, fulfilled its political will and followed the policy set out from above. All books promoted for translation and publication were carefully screened. This control affected the complete translation and publication process from the selection of the original for translation and the translator to perform the task to proofreading, final editing, and selection of the cover of the published book. The fate of each publication was different and in many respects depended on the human factor, because editors and publishers involved in the decision-making process demonstrated different degrees of courage and took up different amounts of responsibility. Reasons for rejections were numerous and unpredictable. Selected subjects, casual observations, images employed in the literary work—anything could become the critical factor that would result in a publication ban. Arlen Blium notes, for instance, that the mere mention of Lev Trotsky was sufficient for the book to be withdrawn.[2] In making their decisions, censors were guided by the current political situation and instructions of the Communist Party, because lists of requirements for the content and style of literary works did not exist. Illustrating this phenomenon, Tat'iana Goriaeva quotes the discussion between the head of Ukrainian department of Glavlit Polonnik and the head of Glavlit Omel'chenko that took place in a meeting of Glavlit administration in 1946.

> COMRADE POLONNIK: We think the time is ripe for guidelines regarding literature. If we look back on our history, they used to issue instructions as to what kind of literature could be allowed.[3] There must be a code of requirements to literature. If the old censorship forbade writing anything besmirching women, tarnishing the sanctity of marriage, defaming the image of the officer, we do not have any guidance of this kind.
>
> COMRADE OMEL'CHENKO: You are asking for a general model for literature, a framework?
>
> COMRADE POLONNIK: So that a censor knows the criteria of literature assessment.
>
> COMRADE OMEL'CHENKO: A censor is no editor—he is a person who fulfills certain functions he was entrusted with. Your suggestion is not clear to me. Literature is not making shoes. It is not a shoe factory where one could advise on the cut. This is a scholastic question.
>
> COMRADE POLONNIK: I would like to get at least some instruction from you.
>
> COMRADE OMEL'CHENKO: I think this is nonsense. Take it as an instruction, if you like. What kind of regulations can one invent for literature?
>
> COMRADE POLONNIK: I mean the regulations of 1885. The regulations for literary censors.[4]

The quoted dialog is demonstrative of the reluctance of Glavlit senior administration to provide censors with basic guidelines for assessment of literary works. Lack of legal clarity was very useful in the context of continuous change of allies, preferences, and prejudices of the Soviet government. Some writers who initially appealed to the Soviet authorities, like André Gide, were later disfavored. Changes of attitude concerned not only individuals, but also particular books, which could be withdrawn from the general access. For example, Blium describes the perils of Lion Feuchtwanger's novel *Moscow 1937: My Visit Described for My Friends* which was eventually qualified as a restricted-access book. Written immediately after Feuchtwanger's visit to Moscow, the book was closely studied by competent organs of the Soviet Union and finally published by the end of 1937. Despite Feuchtwanger's support of the Soviet regime and his blind belief in the rightfulness of the second Trotskyist trial he attended in Moscow, the book was soon withdrawn from general access. This was motivated by regular doubts expressed by Feuchtwanger regarding Stalin's personality cult and the issue of the freedom of speech that was proclaimed by the Soviet constitution but barely granted in reality.[5] This withdrawal, however, did not affect the translations and publications of other books by Feuchtwanger, who remained one of the most widely read German-language novelists in the Soviet Union.

Bearing the name of the Main Administration for the Protection of Military and State Secrets in the Press under the USSR Council of Ministers, Glavlit created very detailed lists of state secrets. These lists, called "Reports of Important Cross-outs and Confiscations," were revised every five to six years and were required to be used by all censors of the Soviet Union, who nicknamed these lists Talmuds due to their extreme detail and length (up to three hundred pages).[6] Blium gives an account of his conversation with the high-ranking censor Solodin, who admitted that the main rule for censors was that no one "could publish any information containing state or military secrets or information, which misinformed the reader. It was the second part of the formula that did the trick," Solodin said.[7] The vague and ambiguous formula applied to any subject, style, or idea that could be duly accused of spreading misinformation.

On each of the stages of the censoring ladder described in the previous chapters the executives studied the text with a mixed feeling of power over the text and its author (translator) and dread of the opinion of the executive of the next higher rank. This mixture of power intoxication and dread of punishment was described by the brilliant scholar, translator, and political exile Efim Etkind as a feudal psychological complex, the bearer of which feels like a vassal and a tyrant at the same time.[8] The lack of guidelines for literary censorship led to unpredictable outcomes. Any book could be rejected at any level of the censoring ladder for any reason. The awareness of the imminent danger of rejection made translators extremely cautious: at times it was translators themselves who censored their own translations to make sure they were published. In his *Zapiski nezagovorshchika (Notes of a Non-Conspirator)*, Etkind made poignant observations about self-censorship in Russia, describing it as more harmful at times than all the other censoring stages taken all together.[9]

INNA STREBLOVA: Even though censorship was the responsibility of the whole pyramid of the Soviet publishing business, we, translators, self-censored ourselves quite well. We did that already on the level of our applications to publishing houses and the selection of books for translation. If, for instance, the author we were interested in was known to have said something negative about the Soviet Union, we just did not apply to translate him/her, because we knew the application would be rejected.

The desire of translators to make sure that their translations made their way to Russian-speaking readers, as well as the need of translators to maintain their good reputation and to provide for their living, in many ways determined the choice of literary works for translation. Since publishing houses were eager to consider new applications from practicing translators in order to be able to create effective publishing plans, translators tried to make sure that their applications and prospective translations would meet the expectations of the publishing house. Such promotion of the interests of the dominant group (here—the Communist Party) was in many ways involuntary; it was driven by faith that compliance with the governing ideology was the only way translations could reach the readers. Yet self-censorship was not always a conscious activity; in fact, two out of ten translators insisted they had never censored themselves. Others stated that self-censorship was present in various forms and, mainly, in the very selection of the book for translation. This is how the situation was described by Viktor Golyshev.

VIKTOR GOLYSHEV: Censorship does not start with the author, or editor, or censor, but with the translator. It is the translator who knows or assumes whether the book will be accepted to be published. Self-censorship takes place when you decide whether to translate the book or not. I wanted to translate John Steinbeck once, but it was just the moment at which Steinbeck had spoken in favor of the war in Vietnam, and I realized it was not the right time. *The Wayward Bus* was published later, in the 1980s. But whatever doubts there might have been, I never censored my own translations once the decision had been made. The translator always deals with the text, you know. If the translator wants to harm the text, better not translate it at all. And any mitigation or substitution means doing harm to the text, this I know for sure.

Golyshev points out the fact that an untimely choice of an author or a book disfavored by authorities meant that the translation would suffer multiple rejections and finally remain unpublished. Translators who worked under the Soviet regime had an acute sense of appropriateness: they were able to distinguish between the literature that could get through the approval and publication process and the literature that would be rejected by censors and in great probability harm the career of translators and their editors. Larisa Bespalova, translator and editor, proves this point.

> LARISA BESPALOVA: Of course, there were books we could not publish. For instance, we could not publish George Orwell's *1984* or *Animal Farm*. We knew it and did not even try to publish them.

What is also quite notable is that most translators state that they were barely aware of Glavlit or censors during their work. They mainly mention the fear of the opinion of the editor who was allocated to them. The pyramid of the Soviet publishing system was structured so that only the neighboring levels had direct contact with each other. Viktor Golyshev gave the following description of the situation.

> VIKTOR GOLYSHEV: I did not have any idea of censorship and never thought of it. For me everything depended on the people who published (or did not want to publish) my translations.
>
> I heard of Glavlit only from my mother who translated a lot of plays; therefore I had a very vague understanding of what Glavlit was. But in general it was no more than five times in those years that I heard this name spoken aloud. To put it shortly, I knew that Glavlit controlled the plays and stage productions, but I did not know what else it did.

Viktor Golyshev was not the only translator who was not aware of Glavlit's omnipresence. Larisa Bespalova, who as an editor had to take active part in the decision-making process regarding approvals of applications, describes her experience with Glavlit in the following way.

> LARISA BESPALOVA: I do not remember Glavlit finding fault with foreign prose. In the Molodaia Gvardiia publishing house, there was a permanent Glavlit employee, he had his own office, and I do not think I could remember him. I know that the Russian prose section of *Novyi*

mir had regular confrontations with Glavlit, but Glavlit did not have an office there.

As one can see, the pyramid of the Soviet publishing system ensured the mutual fear of individuals occupying neighboring levels of the pyramid of subordination. The fear of the rejection of a publication was inherent to everyone directly engaged in publishing. Translators, editors, editors-in-chief, editorial boards, and reviewers all felt their personal responsibility for passing the publication and reported to the next higher step of the ladder, making sure their job was approved of. The lack of clarity in Glavlit regulations and partial unawareness of individuals of Glavlit activities and functions made the process of passing the publication into print very complex and resulted in multiple bans and rejections of publications at different levels. In this book, the reasons for rejections of publications will be presented in three main groups: personal background of authors, content of literary works, and literary styles. This grouping, however, is done for convenience of presentation and is not based on any official instructions or prescriptions to publishing houses due to the fact that those prescriptions never received the form of an officially published document.

UNWANTED AUTHORS

In his analysis of the reasons for withdrawals of books from general access in the Soviet Union, Blium emphasizes the role of the so-called personified approach. This approach consisted in withdrawals and rejections of books on the grounds of the personal biographies of their authors. Symbolically, any withdrawal of books from general access means erasing names of their authors from the collective memory, causing their civil death. "If one stops to mention a name (or an event)," writes Blium, "it means neither of them actually exists in reality. Even more so: it *never* existed. The name had a magical meaning attached to it like in pagan times."[10]

Damnatio memoriae was applied not only to those writers who demonstrated their clear disapproval of the Soviet regime, but also to those who were initially enthusiastic when the Soviet Union originated as a state. To illustrate this, Blium gives a detailed account of the publishing history of André Gide, whose books enjoyed success in the Soviet Union in the 1920s and 1930s. In 1933, the portrait of Gide was published on a postcard alongside with quotation from his speech addressed to "the young constructors of the USSR," in which he expressed his gratitude "for that great hope that you put into our hearts and for your wonderful exploits."[11] The publication of four volumes of the works of Gide followed in 1935–36; the fifth volume, however, never saw the light of day. The reason for this sudden change was Gide's publication of his book *Retour de l'URSS* in 1936, in which he described his complete disillusionment with communism after his trip to the USSR. The book was soon translated into Russian and published in Zurich (1937) and Warsaw (1939) and became a sufficient reason for banishing Gide from the Soviet literary stage. The already existing books were moved to restricted-access collections of libraries, and new publications were banned.[12] The short article about Gide in the *Kratkaia literaturnaia entsiklopediia* (Brief literary encyclopedia) in 1964 described him as a bourgeois individualist who sympathized with socialism for a short time but pulled back after his visit to the USSR. Gide's literary style was identified as affected, and his position during his immigration in Tunis during the occupation of France was characterized as the "position of an indifferent observer."[13] Such descriptions erased all hope for further publications of Gide in the Soviet Union. Naturally, all the applications of translators and publishers regarding Gide were rejected automatically. Irina Komarova also mentions Gide's name among those whose works could never get approval in the Soviet Union.

IRINA KOMAROVA: Some authors would get a much faster approval for translation than others. Some would have a really difficult time to get approved. Among the most difficult ones were Aldous Huxley, Henry James, and Edith Wharton. Ezra Pound and André Gide were an absolute taboo—they were rejected automatically. Sartre and Simone de Beauvoir were also quite unwelcome. It looked like a real struggle between the two sides of the barricades, when individual translators and publishing houses would try to sneak through with new authors and new ideas. Yet many individual attempts enjoyed success. Thus, Nina D'iakonova, a prominent professor of literature and literary critic of that time, managed to get a collection of short stories of Huxley through all stages of approval. D'iakonova's opinion was respected and considered valuable, she was often invited to review translation applications, and her reputation was in many respects a deciding factor in the approval of Huxley's volume. But although D'iakonova managed to get the permission for translation and publication of Huxley and was appointed editor for the volume, she could not choose all translators herself, and some of the translators for this volume were appointed by the publishing house. I was the coeditor for the book, which was finally published in 1985.

Professor of Leningrad State University Nina D'iakonova also played an important role in promoting the prose and poetry by Rudyard Kipling in the last quarter of the twentieth century. Kipling was seen as a politically hostile and, hence, undesirable writer; a considerable number of his works were banned in the Soviet Union. Despite the fact that Kipling's poetry and its translations had indisputable influence over the Russian poetry of the twentieth century—from Nikolai Gumilev to Aleksandr Galich—Kipling's poems remained unpublished for the lengthy period of 1936–76. The forty-year-long ban and the active criticism of Kipling in the USSR was a furious reaction to Kipling's imperialistic and colonial views and his undisguised dislike of the Russian Empire and later the Soviet Union, which he particularly detested. Already in 1931, the entry *Kipling* in the *Literaturnaia entsiklopediia* (Literary encyclopedia) was full of criticism of Kipling's works: "The ideological baggage of Kipling is imperialistic, outright conservative, full of racial pride, and Anglo-Saxon chosenness. The political position of Kipling is primarily the destiny of the Empire; anyone who infringes on its integrity is a criminal."[14] This entry in the *Literaturnaia entsiklopediia* led to the almost total ban that was soon imposed on Kipling's works.[15] And although the ban on prose was soon partially lifted, publications of Kipling's poetry were suspended for almost fifty years. The ban on Kipling's poetry was broken only once, in 1936, when the Leningrad editor, anthologist, and translator Valentin Stenich published a small volume of selected poetry of Kipling in translations of the most talented contemporary poets.[16] To secure the publication, Stenich included in his volume a lengthy introduction of Rashel' Miller-Budnitskaia who actively criticized Kipling as an author whose poetry as "a great achievement of Western imperialism" personified "the moods and ideas of our enemy."[17] Despite the precaution, the boldness of Stenich, his literary engagement, and his eagerness to publish and translate unwanted and questionable literature resulted in his arrest; less than two years after the publication of the volume Stenich was shot for counterrevolutionary activity.

The poetry of Kipling was ignored until 1976; publications of his prose were limited to his *Jungle Book*, which was presented to readers as children's literature. The reason for such expulsion of Kipling from the Soviet translated literature was not purely his colonial and imperialistic moods, but mainly his undisguised dislike of the Russians and then the Soviets. As early as 1889, Kipling began his story *The Man Who Was* in the following way: "Let it be clearly understood that the Russian is a delightful person till he tucks his shirt in. As an Oriental he is charming. It is only when he insists upon being treated as the most easterly of Western peoples, instead of the most westerly of Easterns, that he becomes a racial anomaly extremely difficult to handle."[18] This statement was later metaphorically repeated by Kipling in his poem "Truce with the Bear," which up to today still remains very little known in Russia, even though its translation was first published in 1922 in the volume of the celebrated translator of Kipling Ada Onoshkovich-Iatsyna[19]; and then, as if by a miracle, it reappeared in the 1936 volume compiled by Stenich.

The metaphorical nature of the "Truce with the Bear" gives room for freedom of interpretation; however, another poem of Kipling written in 1918 is straightforward and does not leave the reader any reasons to doubt the political views of the poet. Devoted to the Russian Revolution of 1917 and its consequences, Kipling's poem "Russia to the Pacifists" sounds a requiem for a dangerous but yet respected rival:

> God rest you, peaceful gentlemen, but give us leave to pass.
> We go to dig a nation's grave as great as England was.
> For this Kingdom and this Glory and this Power and this Pride
> Three hundred years it flourished—in three hundred days it died.[20]

The translation of this apocalyptic description was politically unacceptable in the Soviet Union. The sole final stanza with the central phrase "So do we bury a nation dead" ruled out the possibility of publication of the poem in the Soviet Union. Thus, the translation of "Russia to the

Pacifists" by Vasilii Betaki was first published in the Russian translation only in 1986 in Paris.[21] Also in 1986, independently from Betaki, another translation of the poem was made by the Russian scholar Mikhail Gasparov. Gasparov fearlessly recited his translation in the official gathering in honor of his own jubilee, thus exposing himself to a great risk: the public recital made official organs extremely interested in Gasparov's biography and work.[22] Gasparov's translation of the poem was later published by Witkowsky twelve years after the described events.[23]

Political affiliations of authors were sometimes considered a much more important factor in the decision-making regarding publications of their works than the content of these works as such. Some writers were approved due to their communist activity or friendship with famous communist activists, despite the controversial subjects or styles of their works. For example, the communist leanings of many Latin American writers in 1960s and 1970s resulted in the Latin American boom and the universal excitement of Soviet readers about Latin American literature.

> VIKTOR ANDREEV: Latin American writers were actively translated into Russian. They were incredibly interesting and different from what we knew here. Another fine feature of them was that they were seen as progressive and mainly socialistic—apart from Jorge Luis Borges, of course. Although Borges was translated as well. In his youth, he wrote poems in honor of the Russian Revolution and Lenin, which definitely helped in getting him published in the Soviet Union. He was also highly valued by the Nobel Prize winner Pablo Neruda, who was a communist. Borges never made any negative remarks about communism. This is why Borges was translated into Russian during his lifetime.

Political views of original writers and poets were the determinative factor in the Soviet selection of texts for translation. The author's loyalty to communism or, at least, neutral political views were of crucial importance to Soviet publishers. Active opposition to the communist philosophy or especially a retreat from communism resulted in bans on the works of the rebel in the Soviet Union.

> MIKHAIL YASNOV: Louis Aragon was eagerly published in the Soviet Union because he was the main singer of communism in France. At the same time Aragon's contemporaries remained unpublished in the Soviet Union because they opposed Aragon and refused to join the Commu-

nist Party. The publication of Guillaume Apollinaire's poetry translated by Mikhail Kudinov also faced great difficulties in 1967.

EVGENII WITKOWSKY: Glavlit was oppressive. When we were planning the publication of the anthology of Western European poetry of the twentieth century in the Biblioteka vsemirnoi literatury series, we were very limited in our selection of poets. Out of French poets, for example, there was a chance we could include poems of a right-winger, but there was no chance of passing someone the party officials considered a renegade—that is, the person who had severed himself from the Communist Party. Such person, for example, was the French poet Pierre Emmanuel. It was hard to get Emmanuel into the book, especially because Emmanuel was alive at that time, but we finally did it. And it looks like it was the only time the living renegade got published in the Soviet Union.

There also was a difficulty with the selection of German authors. If an author emigrated from East Germany to West Germany, the USSR would stop publishing his/her works. For instance, the German poet Peter Huchel was presented to Soviet readers as a procommunist, although he conflicted with the authorities of East Germany and became the object of ideological criticism in his country. Huchel published his works in West Germany while living in GDR, and later emigrated first to Italy, and later to West Germany.

When the German poet Wolf Biermann moved from East Germany to West Germany, he was automatically denied publication in the Soviet Union. Sudden immigrations of seemingly procommunist authors to the West resulted in the strange incoherence of some anthologies. Indeed, some anthologies exist in two versions: in the first half of the edition there would be poems by one author, and in the second half of the edition his/her works would be substituted with someone else's.

The whole image of Heinrich Mann was distorted in the Soviet Union. Mann was presented to the reader as a procommunist. The same concerned Bertolt Brecht, despite the fact that he kept all his copyrights in West Germany and did not get on well with Johannes Becher, poet and minister of culture of East Germany. The works of Brecht were translated and published very selectively in the USSR: only those works by Brecht that could be linked with the communist ideology got into print.

A positive attitude from publishers could change overnight if the foreign writer did something that contradicted the policy of the Communist

Party of the Soviet Union, or, even worse, openly condemned the Soviet regime and values. Such situations were perceived as emergencies; books of the rebellious writer or poet were then urgently withdrawn from publishing plans or even from print with the subsequent destruction of the typeset pages.

LARISA BESPALOVA: It got difficult when the writer included would suddenly do something like signing an open letter. Thus, for instance, Graham Greene was banned in the Soviet Union for quite a long time because he signed a letter in the defense of Siniavskii and Daniel'.

I worked in *Novyi mir* when Robert Penn Warren's novel *Flood* translated by Elena Golysheva was about to be published by the journal. It was at that point when Warren said something incompatible with the Soviet reality (they did not find it important to tell us what it was). The editor-in-chief of *Novyi mir* Sergei Narovchatov then decided against the publication of the novel. To get the novel published, I asked the Foreign Commission of the Union of Writers for support. The Foreign Commission eagerly supported me, yet Narovchatov flatly refused to publish the novel. He soon died, though, and we published the novel in 1982.[24, 25]

For the maintenance and channeling of Soviet ideas to the general Soviet reader, publishing houses were also supposed to publish works of ideologically welcome writers. In their search for politically appropriate writers, publishers and translators discovered a lot of writers whose fame in the Soviet Union eventually surpassed their popularity in their home countries.

EVGENII WITKOWSKY: There existed convenient foreign writers like Gianni Rodari or Alex La Guma, whom no one knew in their native countries, but whose works were published in millions of copies in Russian translation in the USSR. Several generations of Russians grew up on Gianni Rodari's fairy tale *Cipollino*, which no one read in Italy. Luckily, Rodari was quite a good writer, and publishing him was worthwhile.

The fairy tale *Cipollino* Witkowsky is referring to has remained popular children's reading in Russia. The Italian writer, journalist, participant in the Resistance, and member of the Italian Communist Party Gianni Rodari created his fairy tale on the basis of a clear social problematic, putting the opposition of the rich and the poor into the focus of the plot. This seeming complexity is balanced out by the captivating characters of the fairy tale who appeal to children of all ages. The story of a little onion Cipollino who together with his friends—old Pump-kin, shoemaker Grapes, little Strawberry, and Lame Spider—opposed the wicked Prince Lemon, Cavalier Pomodoro, and Countesses Cher-ries was first published in the Soviet Union in the translation of Zlata Potapova in 1955 and enjoyed a long life, being later transformed into a cartoon, a movie, and a ballet.[26] Works of the South African writer, struggler with apartheid, and political exile Alex la Guma, however, did not share the success of Rodari's fairy tale. *A Walk in the Night* by La Guma was the first among his works to be published in the Soviet Union as a separate book.[27] In 1985, the publishing house Pravda published a collection of La Guma's works in three hundred thousand copies.[28] This gigantic number of copies, however, hardly attested to the popularity of the writer, who barely enjoyed popularity in the perestroika-minded Soviet Union, or later in the independent Russian Federation. Printed in large numbers, original and translated books of officially approved con-tent secured the unhampered work of publishing houses in the Soviet Union. Sales of politically charged books were ensured, for instance, by making the purchase of one of them a condition for obtaining a copy of widely popular and desired book (Alexandre Dumas, Jack London, John Galsworthy)—a process that was nicknamed "extra-load purchase." The year of publication of La Guma's book coincided with the beginning of perestroika in the country, whose turbulent events make the fate of the edition difficult to trace.

The chances of foreign authors being translated and published in the Soviet Union did not depend purely on their political views and social activity, but also on their ethnic background. The following story told by Larisa Bespalova serves as a good illustration to this statement.

LARISA BESPALOVA: In the end of the 1960s, translator Elena Surits came up with the idea to translate *Seize the Day* and *Dangling Man* by Saul Bellow. I was working in the Molodaia Gvardiia publishing house at that time, and I included Bellow into the publishing plan. Unfortunately, the director of Molodaia Gvardiia Valerii Ganichev went on a trip to the United States at that point. There he learnt that Bellow was a Jew, and thus Bellow was removed from the publishing plan. Only much later, in the

1980s, I was able to publish my translations of *The Bellarosa Connection* and *Cousins* by Bellow in *Inostrannaia literatura*. And Elena Surits translated both *Dangling Man* and *Seize the Day*. Her translation of *Seize the Day* was published in 1990 by *Novyi mir*, where I was working at that time.

The seeming freedom of publishing houses in compiling publishing plans and choice of translators was, as we can already see, nonexistent. Any decision of a publishing house could be disputed and banned at any time by different departments of Glavlit at any stage of approval. The dismissal of the publication could be done indirectly—that is, the ban could be initiated not by a censor or a Glavlit office, but by an influential literary institution, which could give a negative review of the book under consideration. Evgenii Witkowsky describes this period of time as a challenge for translators and anthologists who had to work with a careful eye to Glavlit activities.

EVGENII WITKOWSKY: Publishing houses were virtually unable to make independent decisions. Their decisions could be disputed by anyone, even by the Institute of World Literature. The only way to get around the policy of the publishing house was to write an application for something people in the publishing house had no idea about. I always tried to be an expert on something no one else knew. This is why I worked with the literatures of smaller European countries like Luxembourg and Malta. Later, I learned Gaelic and Mirandese. In 1974, I came up with my translations from Afrikaans. Therefore, when I applied for a book on something no one knew, there was a hundred percent guarantee the application would pass. The application response could take a long time, but eventually my applications would always be granted approval.

The constant reforms of censoring organizations were supposed to optimize and coordinate their activity; however, these reforms were so numerous that they eventually started to impede the work of the huge bureaucratic machine. Translators and publishers could not keep up with the reforms that regularly shook Glavlit and sometimes did not comply with the regulations due to their frequent changes. For example, in January 1969, the Central Committee of the Communist Party circulated the classified regulation entitled "On the Rising Responsibility of Administrations of Print, Radio, Television, Cinematography, Culture, and

Arts Organizations for the Ideological and Political Level of Published Materials and Repertories," which established the personal responsibility of authors and publishers for the contents of publications and thus made self-censorship a guiding principle of the Soviet culture.[29] Issued by the central government authority, the regulation required immediate compliance; however, self-censorship had by then already become an integral part of the publishing process. All interviewed translators were unanimous in their response that the regulation of 1969 did not affect their literary activity. Eventually, publishers had to invent measures to demonstrate fulfillment of requirements.

> EVGENII WITKOWSKY: Self-censorship as a strategy proclaimed in 1969 came to naught by 1973, because publishing houses had to imitate activity in this regard. It was anyway assumed that translators would censor themselves.
>
> As an editor, I faced all kinds of bans. For example, one day we were told at the daily briefing that the word *cryptogram (shifrovka)* was not allowed to be used anymore. One could expect changes of requirements at any time. There once came a day when they stopped publishing Sartre. Then they stopped publishing Theun de Vries, but at the same time they maintained the relationship with Theun de Vries because he was a translator of Pushkin into Dutch. His translations of Pushkin into Dutch continued to be published in the USSR by Raduga and Progress publishing houses, because there was no other Dutch translator of Pushkin available.

Personal biographies of authors were not the only factor that decided the fate of translated literature in the Soviet Union; the longevity of the translation was equally determined by the biography of its translator. The requirements for selection of the authors of the original material also applied to translators to the full extent. Loyalty to the Communist Party or, at least, absence of an anticommunist record, was an absolute must. Renegades, former political prisoners, and emigrants were often banned from publication. This was a serious impediment for editors and publishing houses, because many high-quality literary translations were produced by politically undesirable persons.

After the 1930s, when names of repressed translators were forever erased from publications, with their translations further published without their names, the period after World War II, especially the time of the Thaw, looked much more favorable in terms of publishing and acknowledgment of translators' achievements. Nonetheless, a considerable number of names of well-qualified translators were committed to oblivion. Thus, for example, the repressed translator Isai Mandel'shtam remained unpublished, even despite his posthumous rehabilitation in 1962. His biggest work—the translation of Shakespeare's *Henry IV*— remained unknown even to specialists until its manuscript was accidentally discovered in 2006.

Disfavored translators resorted to different ways of getting their translations published. Active search for publication opportunities was not a search for literary fame in these cases: sneaking translations into print was a means of survival for those who went through labor camps and public dispraise. Such was the fate of Iulii Daniel', who in the 1960s served a sentence for publishing in tamizdat. In 1966, writers Andrei Siniavskii and Iulii Daniel' were sentenced to seven and five years, respectively, of strict-regime labor camp for publishing their works abroad under the names of Abram Tertz and Nikolai Arzhak. After their release, Siniavskii emigrated to Paris, whereas Daniel' remained in the Soviet Union. A talented writer and translator, he was officially excluded from the Soviet literary world as a politically unreliable person. His translations made before the scandalous trial were banned from any publication, and his new translations could not be published under his own name. To ensure income, Daniel' took the pen name of Iu. Petrov—Petrov being the most common last name in Russia—and published quite regularly till the 1980s. The authorship of translations was an open secret; as Maiia Kviatkovskaia mentioned, all editors and translators knew who stood behind the pen name but according to their silent agreement this fact was never discussed. Sometimes Daniel' literally had to "rent" his friends' names to publish his translations. This meant that friends of his published his translations under their names, got paid for these translations, and then passed the money over to Daniel'.

At the same time, as we have already seen, many former political prisoners gained universal respect as gifted translators: they not only published their translations, but also chaired translation seminars, as in the cases of El'ga Linetskaia, Ivan Likhachev, Tat'iana Gnedich, and

Sergei Petrov. It is notable that with the denouncement of the personality cult of Stalin many political prisoners of the 1930s through the 1940s
were restored in their rights, yet political prisoners of the 1960s through
the 1970s (Siniavskii, Daniel', Kheifets, Maramzin, Brodsky, etc.) were
unable to get back to their regular activities even after they had served
their terms.

From the 1960s on, one could clearly observe the intersection of two
main tendencies in Soviet literary translation and publishing. On the
one hand, there existed a complex and powerful system of control that
dictated its terms to publishers. On the other hand, publishers were
ready to take risks selecting politically unreliable but gifted authors and
translators. With this perseverance of publishers, some of the names initially defined as politically insecure gradually became officially accepted.
Glavlit and its controlling organs researched biographies of translators
much less than biographies of original authors, as long as publishing
houses kept quiet about the past of their translators.

EVGENII WITKOWSKY: When I compiled anthologies, I regularly
included translations made by immigrants. I started doing that in
1974 when I published the book of translations of Rilke in the Molodaia Gvardiia publishing house where I worked at that time. I included
the translations made by Aleksandr Bisk who emigrated from Russia
in 1919. Then I started doing this regularly, and I got away with it. I
kept publishing Russian emigrants, and all I had to do was abstain from
talking about it.

Bans on original works and translations by particular individuals
were inseparable from bans on particular styles, genres, and subjects.
Sometimes it was not the personal biography and political preferences
of the author but the contents of his/her literary works that gave the
impression of political insecurity. The definition of suspicious contents was not reduced to anticommunist statements, for there existed a
wide range of subjects that gave rise to political suspicions. Such works
could, for instance, infringe on morality, national achievements, or
social values. Below, politically inconvenient literary subjects will be
conventionally grouped into political, sexual, religious, national, and
anti-Soviet.

UNWANTED SUBJECTS
Politics

This choice of a foreign literary work was not determined purely by the reputation of its author in the Soviet Union and his/her relations with the Communist Party, but also by the contents of the work considered for publication. Politically undesirable subjects included, but were by all means not restricted to, sex, religion, anticommunist statements, and comparisons of the Soviet Union with other countries. It is striking that these subjects could be classified into the same categories as initially mentioned in the 1917 Decree on Press: refusal to subordinate to the government, sedition, calls for criminal activity.[30] Sex and religion clearly qualified as marginal criminal activity; promotion of these subjects for translation, as we shall see, regularly proved unsuccessful. Bold political statements incompatible with the general guideline of the Communist Party of the Soviet Union and comparisons of the Soviet Union with other countries were looked upon as sedition and refusal to subordinate. Literary works of controversial political content were carefully screened; even if the permission for translation and publication was eventually granted, suspicious and questionable pieces had to be removed from the text of the translation.

The fate of the Soviet publication of Ernest Hemingway's novel *For Whom the Bell Tolls* serves as a vivid example. The novel was first published in the United States in 1940, and its first translation into Russian was prepared in 1941 by Natalia Volzhina and Evgeniia Kalashnikova to be published by the Goslitizdat publishing house and *Znamia* journal. The novel in translation was considerably abridged and even renamed (the published version was entitled *Robert Jordan: Chapters from the novel "For Whom the Bell Tolls"*). Despite the careful selection of episodes for the abridged version, the translation was rejected for publication due to its "particularly 'criminal' places."[31] Reasons for the publication ban included the sympathetic depiction of Karkov, whose prototype, journalist Mikhail Kol'tsov, had fallen victim to political repression in the Soviet Union and was sentenced to death and shot in 1940.[32] Another reason for the ban was the unflattering description of André Marty, a French communist, Political Commissar of the International Brigades during the Spanish Civil War.[33] It is notable, however, that some chapters of the unpublished translation somehow reached the general public: in 1941 the soldiers of the frontlines were known to read "a partisan story."[34]

The death of Stalin in 1953, the posthumous rehabilitation of Kol'tsov, and the expulsion of André Marty from the French Communist Party gave the translators hope for publication of the novel. The publication, however, was dismissed several more times in 1958, 1962, and 1963, despite the fact that the text was carefully censored: political ideas were carefully brought in line with the views of the Communist Party of the Soviet Union, sexual scenes were considerably abridged.[35] The novel eventually got published in 1968, twenty-seven years after it had first been prepared for publication. The years of continuous efforts to get the translation into print could not but affect not only the contents, but also the style, which eventually became more smooth and polished. The version of 1968[36] was still published with over twenty omissions: many of the removed passages related to political figures, like Dolores Ibárruri, leader of the Spanish Civil War, General Secretary of the Communist Party of Spain in 1942–60 (see appendix A).

Ekaterina Kuznetsova, who compared four versions of the Volzhina-Kalashnikova translation of *For Whom the Bell Tolls* (that is, two rejected versions dated 1941, the version dated 1963, and the finally published version of 1968), points out that the final version looks fundamentally different compared with the unpublished versions of 1941 and 1963. On the one hand, the 1968 version has the smallest number of omissions, and the text therefore looks more complete. On the other hand, the ideological influence brings forth the strategy of estrangement: that is, the focus is on the subjectivity of Hemingway's views and the "foreignness" of his attitude to the events described. This effect was enhanced by the preface that was written by the famous writer and poet Konstantin Simonov and that had been thoroughly censored before it was published, as Kuznetsova mentions.[37] Thus, for instance, the preface states that Robert Jordan "makes judgments from his own points of view, the points of view unshared by us . . . The novel of the civil war in Spain was written by an American who made his main character an American upon having seen the Spanish people and the Spanish revolution through his own eyes. One must not forget this when reading the novel and forming judgments of its different aspects, for this feature lies in the very basis of the novel and determines a great number of things in it."[38]

Politically controversial content, as we can see, could create serious obstacles to the implementation of translation projects. Political subjects presented difficulties to publishers even in cases when the subject of the book did not have any direct links to Russian or Soviet history. As Viktor Golyshev noted in his interview, publishers were apprehensive of new themes and subjects that could potentially cause complications. It took Viktor Golyshev a great deal of effort and perseverance to convince the publishers to accept his translation of the novel by Robert Penn Warren *All the King's Men.*

VIKTOR GOLYSHEV: The story of the publication of my translation of *All the King's Men* in *Novyi mir* journal was a peculiar one. It was 1967, the editors did not know the author and they did not know me, which is why they asked me to provide them with a sample twenty-page-long translation. So I did, and they requested another hundred pages. After a hundred they asked for more sample pages, and still would not sign a contract with me. At that point I got angry. Then an editor told me that an influential literary critic and specialist in American literature had advised them to stay away from this fascist novel. What is fascist about this novel, I wonder? I was surprised. Some people had the strangest aberrances in those days.

Robert Penn Warren was just one of those writers who were yet unknown in the country, and every new name was treated with caution. My mother attempted to translate Warren's stage adaptation of *All the King's Men,* and she was talked out of it. I was also advised against translating this novel: I was told that the novel would put both the publishers and me in an awkward spot. I could not understand this. In what way could it affect the publishers? If the publishers did not want the book, they would not publish it, this is all. And the novel was published without any omissions.

The situation described by Golyshev was far from being a solitary case. Translators who wrote individual applications often had to translate long sections of the book at their own risk, while the publishing house took time making a decision about whether the publication of the proposed literary work was reasonable. This practice continued till late in the 1980s, even after the fall of communism. Viktor Golyshev remembers clearly the procrastination of the publishing house Progress in 1989 in regards to his translation of George Orwell's *1984*.

> VIKTOR GOLYSHEV: Upon learning that I was translating *1984* by Orwell, an editor of the Progress publishing house asked me to give them my translation once it was finished. This was already the perestroika times. I first read the novel in the 1960s, but translated it only in 1987—probably, the time was due. The publishing house accepted the novel unofficially, and even at the point when the novel had been paginated the publishing house would not sign an official contract with me. They must have been worried that the political situation might change again, they were afraid of what might possibly happen.[39] Since there was no contract, I gave my translation to a different publisher, and this is why it happened that *1984* was published by two different publishers almost at the same time.[40]

The lack of guidelines for approval of publications made it especially difficult to define the degree of harmlessness of literary works. Sometimes translators had trouble promoting translations of quite innocent works of literature, which were in no way contradictory to the Soviet ideology. For example, Ignatii Ivanovskii, the renowned translator of the Robin Hood ballads, described the ballads' review process as an unnerving experience. The caution and reluctance of publishers came as a surprise to Ivanovskii, who considered Robin Hood a very safe literary character for his being the protector of the poor.

> IGNATII IVANOVSKII: I brought my *Robin Hood* to Detgiz and went to see the director. His name was Dmitrii Chevychelov, and he was famous for being suspicious of everything new and for his reluctance in promoting applications. For this he was nicknamed "Chevychelov-see-what-problems-we-might-have."[41] Chevychelov looked at the manuscript and said, "The translation needs improvement. You need to take a couple of years to work on it." I objected, saying that I had been working on the translation for several years. "Good," he replied, "let it sit in your desk drawer for another five years."
>
> I finally got my translation published in Detgiz. Vladimir Admoni and the members of his translation seminar of the Union of Writers put in a good word for me. I also made it a rule to recite my translation of *Robin Hood* whenever and wherever it was possible, and gradually it became known to people.

Chevychelov's fear of anything new was notorious, and people started to use his fear to get their works passed. For example, illustrator Iurii Vasnetsov would add something ridiculous to his illustrations, like a third ear on a human head. Chevychelov would take a look at the picture and scream: "How come there are three ears here?!" Vasnetsov would appear to be at a loss and would humbly explain that the third ear had got into the picture by mistake. The third ear would eventually be removed, and Chevychelov would be so content his comments had produced an effect that he would not look at the picture any closer.

The director of Detgiz Dmitrii Chevychelov had an outstanding career: he started as a literary censor in the 1930s and was known to write denunciations of his colleagues. He occupied the post of the director of Detgiz for almost twenty years—from 1941 until 1960—and created the most oppressive professional atmosphere for children's writers, poets, and translators.[42] His actions rarely resulted, as Ivanovskii assumed, from fear or suspicion: the actions of Chevychelov were motivated by long-standing habit of fighting any novelty. As Blium observed, the mere fact of forbidding the text is by definition more important for a totalitarian censorship system than the contents of the text as such: repressive activities are given higher priority and possess a self-contained value.[43]

Sexuality

Whereas the subject of Robin Hood was neutral enough to be defended and finally granted permission for publication, there were multiple subjects that were unable to gain approval under any circumstances. Thus, many Soviet translators faced the dilemma of either omitting or rephrasing candid scenes in their translations or being banned from publication altogether. Undisguised sexuality in the arts was almost a complete taboo, no matter in what context sexuality was depicted. For example, when the novel *One Hundred Years of Solitude* by Gabriel García Márquez was first published in the translation of Valerii Stolbov and Nina Butyrina in 1970 in *Inostrannaia literatura*, most candid scenes and descriptions were either abridged or taken out, thus presenting the reader with more "virtuous" characters. The version of 1970 modestly omits the description of José Arcadio's tattooed body, as well as most detail of the relationship between Aureliano José and Amaranta.[44] The first Russian publication of the novel abounds in mitigations: thus, for instance, the description of Santa Sofia de la Piedad is followed by the sentence "She was a girl" *(Она была девушкой),* which looks quite out of place.[45] The later publications of the translation of the novel correct the initial substitution and formulate the sentence as "She was a virgin" *(Она была девственницей).* The omissions and substitutions of 1970 were still present in the subsequent edition by the Khudozhest-vennaia Literatura publishing house[46]; however, in 1979, the Progress publishing house published the complete text of the translation without omissions.[47] Viktor Andreev explains this brave decision of Progress by the close correspondence of García Márquez with Soviet publishers, his visits to the USSR, and his extraordinary popularity among the younger readers. Abridging the novel meant impairing the relatively stable relationship with the author, which the publishers did not want to risk. The publication of the complete version of *One Hundred Years of Solitude* was yet an exception to the general rule: sexual scenes and images continued to be severely censored years later, as it happened, for instance, with the novel of William Styron *Set This House on Fire.*

LARISA BESPALOVA: In 1985, *Novyi mir* published the translation by Viktor Golyshev of the novel by William Styron *Set This House on Fire.* At one point in the novel, Styron gives a brilliant satirical description of the collection of pornographic pictures owned by one of the characters. The Soviet censorship would have never passed that piece, even though the description of the collection contributed to the image of its owner—a downright scoundrel. This is why Viktor Golyshev himself suggested we abridge the piece. It is amazing that the book version of the novel was later shortened even more. That means that the book publisher turned out to be much more cautious than our journal, though it was usually journals that exercised the right for using abridged versions and therefore abridged texts more freely.

The piece Viktor Golyshev and Larisa Bespalova had to abridge occupies three quarters of a page of the third chapter of Styron's novel.[48] The *Novyi mir* version of Golyshev's translation omits all the detail of Mason's collection of erotica, making the description general and almost scientific.[49] The decision made by Golyshev and Bespalova presents us with a case of what Maria Tymoczko calls *strategic self-censorship*, that is, a form of self-censorship "in which some cultural elements of a source text are given zero translation because of goal-driven decision-making procedures consciously chosen by translator."[50] Such strategic decision-making combines resistance with complicity with oppressive cultural norms.[51] It should be noted here that the mere publication of a novel of such candidness was an act of courage. Despite the necessity of mitigation, the translator and the editor preserved other highly controversial moments of the novel, including, for instance, the detailed and explicit description of a sexual act and Mason's reflections on sex as the last frontier.[52] The omissions made in the translation were in some places indicated by elision marks, which sent a clear message to the reader.[53]

> IRINA KOMAROVA: In my time, literary works with any kind of "indecencies" were not approved for translation in the first place. Although, when Meri Bekker and I were working on the translation of *The French Lieutenant's Woman*, it was I who got the chapter about the indecent performance, and my editor Antonina Slavinskaia found the scene so indecent that she insisted these three pages had to be taken out. I did not agree to do it without having consulted the author first and sent a letter to John Fowles with whom I was corresponding at that time, as he was advising me on the translation of his novel. I told Fowles the editor had found the Soviet reader unprepared for such sexually explicit scenes. Fowles responded promptly, saying that not much harm would be done to the book if these three pages were taken out. And this is how the translation of the novel looked till recently when the editor of Azbuka noticed the gap and commissioned the translation of the missing scene.

The chapter Komarova is talking about here is chapter 39, which describes a sexually explicit scene at old Ma Terpsichore's. The scene was completely omitted in the Bekker-Komarova's translation starting with the words "What particularly pleases me about the unchangingness of this ancient and time-honored form of entertainment is that it allows one to borrow from someone else's imagination" down to "their abandoned Obscenity had quite stifled all thoughts of lying with them, yet now his Desires were as strong as if they had been modest Virgins, and he had seen nothing of their Wantonness; so that he became as earnest to oblige them to comply as any Man in the Company," the expurgation thus making over two pages in length.[54] The published translation included an indication of the omission: the use of brackets—< . . . >—informed the reader that a part of the translated text had been withdrawn.[55] This withdrawal, however, was not the only interference with the translated text on the behalf of its editors and censors: for instance, the mention of a phallus was modestly omitted at several instances.[56] The mere reference to sexual arousal, regularly used in the novel, is treated with caution. Thus, for instance, the directness of the original in the phrase ". . . so was he sexually irritated" was mitigated in the translation: ". . . he was feeling a certain arousal" (. . . *он испытывал известное возбуждение*).[57] In the latter case, the omission of the adverb affected the general tone of the sentence: originally neutral and descriptive, the narration acquired additional emotive connotations and became more playful.

The efforts of Irina Komarova and Meri Bekker and their brave resistance to the pressure eventually resulted in the publication of their translation, albeit with omissions, in 1985.[58] The life of this translation in Russia is quite notable: enjoying tremendous popularity among Russian readers, it changed its name three times in the course of twenty years. In 1985, the translation was published by Khudozhestvennaia Literatura under the title *Podruga franzuzskogo leitenanta,* the Russian word *podruga* being very obscure in the given context. *Podruga* in Russian means "friend" or "girlfriend" and can either imply sexuality or be used for description of a purely platonic relationship. An association clearly triggered by the combination of the Russian words *podruga* and *leitenanta* is that of a female comrade-in-arms, the image of a female soldier being extremely popular in Soviet literature and cinematography. This means that the title of the first edition of the translation of Fowles's novel was misleading to Russian readers. Komarova and Bekker tried to protest and protect the original title but could not persuade the publishing house.

IRINA KOMAROVA: Meri Bekker and I wanted to entitle the translation *Liubovnitsa franzuzskogo leitenanta* (The French lieutenant's mistress). We persevered till the very end; however, the editor stood her ground. She said such a sexually explicit title was improper and unbecoming.

The wish of Komarova and Bekker to substitute the word *woman* for *mistress* might seem overexplicit; however, from the point of view of the Russian language it is well motivated: in the Russian language, the word *woman*, apart from gender and sexual semantics, may also contextually imply the semantics of age (i.e., "not particularly young") and can function as a form of direct address (cf. *Madam*), however informal and detested by many women. The word *mistress (liubovnitsa)* therefore is less charged with connotations; it is quite straightforward and focuses the attention on the central semantics of sexuality. It is the explicitness of the word *liubovnitsa* that was deemed absolutely inappropriate in the 1980s and made the publisher experiment with other words that were charged with additional and misleading connotations.

It is interesting that the title of the eponymous 1981 film directed by Karel Reisz was later translated into Russian as *The French Lieutenant's Woman (Zhenshchina frantsuzskogo leitenanta)*. It was only in 1993 that the novel was published without omissions by Khudozhestvennaia Literatura under the title *Liubovnitsa frantsuzskogo leitenanta* (The French lieutenant's mistress), thus reconciling the wishes of its translators and publishers.[59]

Religion

Religious subjects could also become a serious impediment for the promotion and publication of literary translations. The state propaganda of atheism abated during World War II, when Soviet citizens were given a chance to worship in the times of calamity. Religious persecutions were stirred up in the country when the government under Nikita Khrushchev encouraged the increase of atheist propaganda. Many Russians still remember Khrushchev's bold forecast made in 1961, in which he promised that the last priest would be shown on Soviet TV in 1980. Even though the belligerent campaign against religion subsided with the removal of Khrushchev in 1964, apprehension toward religious subjects remained strong till the end of the 1980s. The cautious approach of publishers impeded publications of books of religious subjects; even a mere mention of religion was at times sufficient for the book or translation to be rejected.

MAIIA KVIATKOVSKAIA: I had a hard time with my translation of the Portuguese poet Luís Vaz de Camões. I translated his elegy, which was 360 lines long and quite difficult to translate. This elegy was based on Psalm 136, which also serves as an epigraph to the poem, starting with the words, "By the rivers of Babylon, there we sat down, yea, we wept, when we remembered Zion. We hanged our harps upon the willows in the midst thereof. For there they that carried us away captive required of us a song; and they that wasted us required of us mirth, saying, Sing us one of the songs of Zion. How shall we sing the Lord's song in a strange land? If I forget thee, O Jerusalem, let my right hand forget her cunning . . ."[60] In his elegy, Camões creates an extended metaphor where he compares his own fate with the sufferings of a Zion singer in the Babylonian captivity. The word *Zion* is mentioned several times in the poem; it is a metaphor with a deep philosophic and religious meaning. My translation of this elegy was rejected because of the word *Zion:* it made the poem looks like Zionist propaganda to censors.[61]

It is notable that rejection of religious subjects and allusions did not have a universal nature. Publishers and censors eagerly approved of the works of François Rabelais and Jonathan Swift, despite their religious activities at different times of their lives. For many years, Maiia Kviatkovskaia was engaged in translating the Spanish poet Luis de Góngora y Argote, a canon of Córdoba Cathedral, and, as she notes, Góngora's occupation did not create obstacles for publications of her translations of his poetry.

Works on religious subjects were granted permissions for publication in cases where the originals were very well known and particularly important for world literature. This particularly concerned those literary works that had already been translated into Russian in the tsarist times and therefore were known to Russian readers. Such texts were allowed to be retranslated and published: circulations of old translations that were made under a hostile regime were deemed worse than bans on new translations. This is how the brilliant translation of Milton's *Paradise Lost* got published in 1982 by Arkadii Steinberg. Steinberg cherished the idea of publication since the moment he had started working on the translation in the 1960s. Evgenii Witkowsky, who calls Steinberg his teacher, remembers the process of the translation approval quite well.

EVGENII WITKOWSKY: When Arkadii Steinberg submitted his application for Milton's *Paradise Lost* it turned out that this book was on the syllabus of many universities. Yet there was no Soviet translation of it—that is, all existing translations of *Paradise Lost* had been published before 1917. This is why the application was approved and the translation was successfully published.

Racial Issues

Despite the active Soviet propaganda on the friendship of nations, the ethnic issue in the country was far from being completely resolved. Ethnic discrimination existed both in the professional sphere and in everyday life; there existed ethnic division of labor and mutual grievances of the peoples of the Soviet Union.[62] References to racial and ethnic conflicts, as well as discussions of individual ethnicities, however, were often perceived as manifestations of bad taste. This controversial attitude toward ethnic issues regularly affected literature and publishing and made controlling organs exercise special caution in selecting works of literature containing references to race or ethnicity.

VIKTOR GOLYSHEV: Of all my translations only one got seriously censored—it was Truman Capote's *Breakfast at Tiffany's*. When the novella was first published in 1965 in *Moskva* journal, the magazine cut out several pages in the beginning of the novel because it went on about the white woman living with a black man in Africa. For some reason, it embarrassed the journal—despite the fact that the country openly campaigned against racism. Before that, I had been offering this translation to different journals, but no one wanted to accept it, and eventually *Moskva* did. Soon afterwards, the novella was published in the Biblioteka Ogon'ka series, and this time the text was published without omissions. But I learned my lesson well—one must not agree to such things.

The first publication of Golyshev's translation of the novella in *Moskva* starts with the same paragraph as the original; however, the second paragraph of the translation begins with the phrase "I'd been living in the house about a week," which means that the scene in the bar and the conversation with Joe Bell was omitted completely.[63] This example of Golyshev's translation alone is very demonstrative of the fact that the issues of skin color and race was a very delicate matter in the Soviet Union. The official attitude toward the question swung from one extreme to the other. If in 1965 *Breakfast at Tiffany's* was censored due to the mere mention of a mixed-race relationship, in 1987 Golyshev's translation of Ken Kesey's *One Flew over the Cuckoo's Nest* faced a rejection for racial reasons again, but in this case the reasons for rejection clearly opposed the reasons that were offered Golyshev in 1965.

VIKTOR GOLYSHEV: I offered my translation of Ken Kesey's *One Flew over the Cuckoo's Nest* to Raduga and got rejected for completely opposite reasons: the publishers thought black people were depicted too negatively in the novel. They meant the two hospital aides in the first chapter, however small their role was in the book.[64] But, eventually, the novel was accepted and published by *Novyi mir*.

Soviet Realities

Publication of literary works that could evoke negative associations with the Soviet realities or lifestyle was not possible in the Soviet Union. The proofs of this are numerous: from the ban on the works of Orwell, Kipling, and Huxley to the headline-making trial of Siniavskii and Daniel'. For a literary work to be rejected its author did not need to engage in direct criticism of the system; the use of politically inappropriate cultural realities or references to politically inconvenient facts could also be taken as slanderous of the reputation of the USSR. Translators and publishers were required to pay close attention to any elements of the text that were able to cast a shadow on the image of the Soviet way of living and to make alterations in texts in order to make them appropriate for publication.

LARISA BESPALOVA: I remember how my publishing house Molodaia Gvardiia was working on the publication of Kurt Vonnegut's novel *Cat's Cradle*. The translation of the novel was made by the distinguished translator Rita Rait-Kovaleva. In the novel, there is a character—a Soviet female spy named Zinka. Rait-Kovaleva was requested to change the name of the spy into Zika to obscure the nationality of the character. To make sure the novel got published, Rait-Kovaleva agreed to the renaming of the character, and the spy was called Zika when the novel was first published in the Soviet Union. And yet the novel was a tremendous success. It was so popular that young people spoke in quotations from Vonnegut.[65]

The Russian theme of Vonnegut's novel *Cat's Cradle*, as Larisa Bespalova notes, underwent serious transformations. These transformations affected, however, much more than the name of the female character: the whole image of the Soviet spy became more obscure and indefinite. At the instant Zinka is introduced to the reader in chapter 8, Vonnegut states her country of origin, occupation, and theater she worked for quite clearly: "Zinka was a Ukrainian midget, a dancer with the Borzoi Dance Company."[66] The name of the character—Zinka—together with Zina is a diminutive form of the name Zinaida, which was quite popular in the Soviet Union in the middle of the twentieth century. Not only the name and the nationality, but also the dance company's name is very symbolic of the Soviet Union: Borzoi Dance Company is a clear allusion to the Bolshoi Opera and Ballet Theatre. It is quite notable that the word *borzoi* exists in the Russian language as an adjective used to describe both a type of a hunting dog and, with a stress on a different syllable, an audacious, shameless, and aggressive person.[67] Both meanings are characteristic of Zinka: a spy hunting for information and a shameless liar. The Russian translation of 1970 reduced the sentence to "Zika was a Lilliput, a ballet dancer of a foreign dance company."[68] Apart from the omissions and the change in the name, the word *midget* in the translation is substituted by the word *Lilliput*, which in the Russian language is used to define a person of an extremely small height, and which, in describing the small height of Zinka, makes it look rather like a medical condition.[69]

Other references to Zinka and her country of origin were also mitigated in the translation of Rait-Kovaleva. In chapter 58, Vonnegut calls Zinka a "Russian midget dance friend," but, again, the translation omits the adjective and introduces the description of "a Lilliput-friend, a little ballerina."[70] The omissions made to avoid the mention of the Soviet Union eventually interfered with the key point of the novel, when the translator was forced to omit the explanation of the way the Republic of

San Lorenzo and the three Hoenikkers lost ice-nine. A substantial part of chapter 110 was omitted as shown below.

> From what Frank had said before he slammed the door, I gathered that the Republic of San Lorenzo and the three Hoenikkers weren't the only ones who had *ice-nine*. Apparently the United States of America and the Union of Soviet Socialist Republics had it, too. The United States had obtained it through Angela's husband, whose plant in Indianapolis was understandably surrounded by electrified fences and homicidal German shepherds. And Soviet Russia had come by it through Newt's little Zinka, that winsome troll of Ukrainian ballet.
>
> I was without comment.
>
> I bowed my head and closed my eyes; and I awaited Frank's return with the humble tools it would take to clean up one bedroom—one bedroom out of all the bedrooms in the world, a bedroom infested with *ice-nine*.
>
> Somewhere, in the violet, velvet oblivion, I heard Angela say something to me. It wasn't in her own defense. It was in defense of little Newt. "Newt didn't give it to her. She stole it."
>
> I found the explanation uninteresting
>
> "What hope can there be for mankind," I thought, "when there are such men as Felix Hoenikker to give such playthings as *ice-nine* to such short-sighted children as almost all men and women are?"[71]

Omissions and substitutions in the chapters devoted to Zinka are not the only interferences with the plot of *Cat's Cradle*. Thus, the title of chapter 54 "Communists, Nazis, Royalists, Parachutists, and Draft Dodgers," which stands for the five major events of the life of Nestor Aamons described in the chapter, was translated with the omission of the first word.[72] It is not purely the omission of the word that is important here: Nestor Aamons is a native Finn, a citizen of the country that had territorial disputes with the Soviet Union. By Vonnegut's words, Nestor was "captured by the Russians, then liberated by the Germans during the Second World War,"[73] which means that Aamons's family was living on the territory ceded by Finland to the Soviet Union in 1940 in accordance with the Moscow Peace Treaty that ended the Winter War (1939–40); the liberation by the Germans relates to the Continuation War (1941–44) when Finland tried to reclaim the territory lost to the

Soviet Union. In Rait-Kovaleva's translation of 1970, the accents are shifted: Nestor Aamons is first captured by the Russians and then by the Germans in course of the same war—World War II: "Nestor Aamons during the Second World War was first captured by the Russians and then by the Germans."[74] The mere change of the grammatical word order and the omission of the verb *liberated* targets the omission of a painful political issue of the Winter War: the translation ignores the issue of seizure of 11 percent of the Finnish territory by the Soviet Union and reduces the problem to the captivity of a single individual.

In some cases, translators and publishers had to remove pieces that could be found too disagreeable, unpleasant, or incompatible with the Soviet reality. For example, when publishing the translation of *A Hall of Mirrors* by Robert Stone, the journal *Inostrannaia literatura* had to abridge the text. The abridgement was mainly done because each issue of the journal could afford only a limited number of pages for each publication. However, it is notable that the decrease of the number of pages was not made by mere withdrawal of sections less important for the plot.

> VIKTOR GOLYSHEV: The text of *A Hall of Mirrors* was split between three translators, including me, because the journal needed the translation urgently. The journal abridged the novel in advance: they were short of space. They also needed to take out some dialogs of either some rambling drunks, or drug addicts. This is how one secondary character disappeared from the novel completely.

Contents of literary works were relatively easy to identify as incompatible with the Soviet reality. Publications, however, were proofread much closer for the employment of certain words or expressions that could raise suspicions of controlling organs. These buzz words could range from those having a derogatory meaning to the words associated with particular contexts. For example, Maiia Kviatkovskaia told an emotional story about her struggle for her translation, which she eventually lost because a single word was disapproved of by the censors.

> MAIIA KVIATKOVSKAIA: I translated the Cuban Romantic poet Juan Clemente Zenea. Zenea was a fighter against the Spanish government, for which he was eventually shot to death in 1871. Zenea was an active

journalist; he also supplied the Cuban rebels with arms. Therefore his poetry naturally has social content. In his poem "In the days of slavery" (*En días de esclavitud*) he addresses God with the words

> Tengo el alma, ¡Señor!, adolorida
> por unas penas que no tienen nombres;
> y no me culpes, no, porque te pida
>   otra patria, otro siglo y otros hombres.

> [Take the soul, Lord, which has suffered
> Its punishments which have no names,
> And it is not my fault, no, I would have asked you
> For other motherland, other century, and other people.]

I translated these lines as:

> Прими же душу, что всегда страдала,
> И не суди—усталую, больную,–
> Когда б могла, она себе избрала
> Иных сограждан, родину иную!

> [Take the soul that has always suffered,
> And do not judge it—tired, aching,—
> If it could, it would have chosen
> Other fellow-countrymen, other motherland.]

This version never got into print, for the word *fellow-countrymen* (*sograzhdane*) that I used evoked rejection. I had to change the last line into "Other century, other motherland" (*I vek inoi, i rodinu inuiu*). I never liked this version, because the next stanza in the translation starts with the words "Other times I call mine," so it turns out that time is mentioned twice, and people are omitted.

The thing is that language is a very mysterious thing. "Other fellow-countrymen" sounds extremely straight-from-the-shoulder, whereas "other century" is rather bland.

The words *fellow-countrymen* that Kviatkovskaia never got passed were strongly associated with civil and public contexts that were predominantly optimistic. The pessimistic mode of Zenea's poem and the direct proximity of the mention of the fellow countrymen to the mention of God and human soul created a sufficient reason for rejecting this wording.[75]

As we can see, unwanted subjects varied in the degree of their relat-
edness to the main principles of Soviet power. Issues directly related to
politics and sexuality were taboo, whereas the attitude to other issues
strongly depended on changes in the political climate. Thus, a blind eye
was turned to religious subjects after World War II, during which Stalin
made a decision to improve the relations between the Soviet state and the
Russian Orthodox Church.[76] Lenience toward religious subjects was done
away with during the time in office of Nikita Khrushchev, who launched
an aggressive antireligious campaign. The removal of Khrushchev from
his office in 1964 and the appointment of Leonid Brezhnev put an end to
massive persecutions against religion and eased restrictions on religious
practices. The same dependence applies to nationalities —thus, for example, the Sino-Soviet Treaty of Friendship, Alliance and Mutual Assistance
signed in 1950 marked the beginning of the era of friendship between
China and the USSR. This friendship ended abruptly at the end of 1950s in
the course of the so-called Sino-Soviet split. Chinese themes, welcome in
the 1950s, lost their appeal in the 1960s and were strongly discouraged. This
resulted in a decrease in the number of Chinese books published in the
Soviet Union and literary translations made from Chinese into Russian.[77]

The situation also applied to the styles of translated literature. Attitudes toward literary forms changed under the influence of the political and social context. As we shall see, any literary form or genre could
be proclaimed decadent, and translators and editors at times had to
resort to cunning or seek the protection and recommendations of more
reputed people of letters.

UNWANTED STYLES

The promotion of books on controversial subjects was a risky enterprise
for editors and translators. Yet it was not purely the contents of books
and the biographies of their authors that could evoke suspicion of censoring structures in the Soviet Union. The style of the selected literary
work and the expressive means employed by the author were of the same
importance as the subject. Style was paid close attention to as it was a
means of individual expression.

A foreign author had better chances of being promoted for publication in the Soviet Union if his/her works and style could be related to the socialist realism doctrine. This concerned not only contemporary writers and poets, but also foreign classics. Thus, for instance, in 1956, in describing the style of Byron, the Soviet critic Anna Elistratova noted that Byron "from the very beginning was foreign to the hypocritical humility of the Lake Poets, as well as their religious mysticism and cult of the feudal past."[78] Such characteristics were double-edged: they validated the importance of the reviewed work in front of literature and publishing specialists and, at the same time, influenced public opinion. It was yet quite impossible to describe all existing literary works in terms of socialist realism. Distinct dissimilarities or even clashes with the governing approach to literary styles gave censors another reason to slow down the process of approval of literary work.

In this regard, it is interesting to see which literary works had difficulty getting into print purely for reasons of their stylistic individuality. These works varied in their genres and contents. Thus, for example, it took Irina Komarova much time to get her brilliant and extremely witty translations of the poetry of Ogden Nash to the Soviet reader. The translator well remembers her struggle for the right of publication of her translations of Nash.

IRINA KOMAROVA: I was engaged in translating Ogden Nash for many years. The first chance to publish my translation of Nash came about in 1963, when my translations appeared in *Novyi mir*. This publication turned out to be very important as it got noticed by no one other than Kornei Chukovskii, who wrote a letter of praise to the editorial board of *Novyi mir*.

The publication of my own volume of translations was very important to me. I needed a published book to be admitted into the Union of Writers. I decided to apply for a publication of the book of my translations of Nash to Lenizdat, and Nina D'iakonova and El'ga Linetskaia were eager to give me their recommendations. The female editor who dealt with my application was clearly afraid of Nash. She was deeply concerned about the unusual rhymes and neologisms I was planning to reconstruct in my translations. Luckily, in the course of lengthy disputes, D'iakonova, Linetskaia, and I managed to convince her.

The year Komarova is referring to here is 1988, which is a quarter of a century after her first publication of Nash in *Novyi mir*. The end of the 1980s was marked by the growing feeling of social freedom, and a publication of the politically moderate poetry of Nash was quite possible. Nevertheless, the fear of the possible return of the Soviet system urged publishers to exercise care. Strong recommendations remained a safe way to secure publications, and the name of the recommender was able to change the fate of many unconventional works.[79] A similar story was told, for instance, by Maiia Kviatkovskaia. Despite the fact that the publication of Komarova's translations of Nash took place fifteen years later than the publication of Edgar Allan Poe, the system of approval, as we can see, barely changed with the years.

MAIIA KVIATKOVSKAIA: Edgar Allan Poe was planned for publication in the Sokrovishcha liricheskoi poezii (Treasures of lyrical poetry) series in the 1960s. The series was edited by Boris Tomashevskii. Edgar Poe was planned to be presented in the translations of Georgii Ben, Vasilii Betaki, Mikhail Donskoi, and several others; I was invited to take part in this volume, too. But the publication of the book was suspended for eleven years because Poe's poetry was criticized for being decadent and moribund. Opponents of Tomashevskii wrote that Soviet literary translation did not need poetry like that. After eleven years, the book was eventually edited and published by Natalia Tolstaia. Once Tolstaia called and invited me for a meeting. When I came, she showed me the manuscript: my translations were underlined, and below it stood: "Symbolist interpretation." But Tolstaia found a way to convince the right people to let my translations get the approval.

One of the most controversial publications in terms of style modifications was the novel by J. D. Salinger, *The Catcher in the Rye*, translated by Rita Rait-Kovaleva. Rait-Kovaleva's application for the translation and publication of *The Catcher in the Rye* in the journal *Inostrannaia literatura* in 1960 was approved despite the controversy and emotional instability of the protagonist and the highly colloquial language employed by Salinger in his novel (for examples, see appendix A). The approval of the publication of Salinger looks quite unexpected, as the novel includes many more controversial points than the relatively "harmless" poems of Nash in the translation of Komarova, who had difficulties publishing them a quarter of a century later. The publication of Salinger's novel became a literary event in the Soviet Union; its immense popularity among the literati made the translation almost canonical. The next translation of the novel made by Maksim Nemtsov followed half a century later, in 2008. The translation evoked an outcry of criticism for its rough "uncivilized" language, as well as for the mere attempt to rival Rait-Kovaleva: some outraged readers even compared the new translation with the impudent "doodling over Leonardo's masterpiece."[80] The Soviet translation of Rait-Kovaleva gradually began to be perceived as the original work, the invariant that could not be contested.

The mere entry of *The Catcher in the Rye* into the Russian translation market and its ability to pass all the stages of censorial approval can be considered a remarkable achievement on the behalf of the translator and her editors, especially given the fact that *The Catcher in the Rye* was for many years considered one of the most controversial books in the United States and the focal point of heated disputes for several decades after its first publication in 1951.[81]

EVGENII WITKOWSKY: The Soviet translation of *The Catcher in the Rye* done by Rait-Kovaleva is extremely different from the original. The translation was well adapted for Soviet reality. Rait-Kovaleva mitigated *The Catcher in the Rye* till it became unrecognizable—otherwise the translation would not have been published. Once I even attended Rait-Kovaleva's lecture on transfer of euphemisms in translation. I never understood where she had found euphemisms in Salinger's original text.

Direct rendering of style and content of translated foreign literature could result in a long-term publication ban and affect the reputation of the translator and his/her publishers. Therefore, the domesticating approach of Rait-Kovaleva can be justified by her desire to introduce the Soviet reader to modern American prose, in which she by all means succeeded. Aleksei Semenenko rightfully places Rait-Kovaleva among the ones "who shaped the literary horizon for several generations of Soviet people."[82] The language employed by Rait-Kovaleva, as well as other translators of American literature, was quite distinct and strikingly different from the Soviet mainstream language, which ensured the keen interest of Soviet readers. Alexander Burak, for example, speaks about a special American literary substyle that existed in Soviet literature and Russian everyday speech. Burak to a great degree ascribes this substyle to the wide popularity of Hemingway translations into Russian in the Soviet Union.[83]

The practice of text alterations was a general one; it was not limited purely to foreign literature, but to original works of Soviet writers as well. The process of deconstruction of original prose was described by Aleksandr Solzhenitsyn in his note to the novel *In the First Circle*: "Such is the fate of Russian books today: They bob up to the surface, if ever they do, plucked down to the skin . . . So also with this novel of mine: In order to give it even a feeble life, to dare show it, and to bring it to a publisher, I myself shortened and distorted it—or, rather, took it apart and put it together anew, and it was in that form that it became known."[84]

Solzhenitsyn here referred to the mitigated version of his novel, which he prepared in 1964 hoping to publish *In the First Circle* legally. He was, however, denied publication, and the novel was later circulated in samizdat. Deconstruction of translated literature followed in the footsteps of domestic literature. The mere fact of bringing an unconventional literary work to light to be read by the general public was much more important than the complete rendering of its content or its stylistic features. Simply translating Western literature in the Soviet Union was an act of courage—but there also were cases of extreme courage, when translators refused to change originals and protected the right of foreign writers to be translated into other languages with full respect for the original plots and philosophy.

CHAPTER 8

A FAREWELL TO FEAR

Translation Activism

As we have already seen in the cases of Evgenii Witkowsky, who published translations by emigrants and political prisoners, or Arkadii Steinberg, who was able to promote his translation of *Paradise Lost*, official publications of controversial literature took place in the Soviet Union despite obvious difficulties in its promotion. To obtain permissions for such literary works, translators and their editors had to ensure the positive pro-Soviet reputation of the prospective publications. Apart from official literary reviews and the complete set of necessary signatures, each publication had to be ensured by the appropriate accompanying material—prefaces and commentaries written by well-respected literary specialists, whose reputation was above suspicion. This entourage of published works played an important role already in the 1930s, when forewords began to determine the decision-making process regarding the future of a publication. For instance, after the fall of Lev Trotsky and his deportation from the Soviet Union in 1929, all books with prefaces written by Trotsky were withdrawn from libraries and classified as restricted-access items. The book by Andrei Belyi *Gogol's Artistry* published in 1934 later joined the restricted-access list due to the introductory notes to the volume written by Lev Kamenev, a Bolshevik revolutionary and politician, who had been tried for his allegiance to Trotsky and shot in 1936.[1] Forewords and commentators could therefore determine the future of a book, which is why they were sarcastically nicknamed "convoy." This gave cause for even more sarcastic slogans such as "The art is at the head of the procession, the convoy follows."[2]

It was, however, not purely the biography of the commentator that could decide the fate of the book. It was mainly the content of the preface or commentaries, or rather, intentional or unintentional remarks that they contained. Thus, in 1968, the publishing house Sovetskii Pisatel' commissioned the distinguished professor, specialist in translation, and chair of one of the translation seminars of the Union of Writers Efim Etkind to write commentaries and a foreword to a big two-volume anthology entitled *Mastera russkogo stikhotvornogo perevoda* (Masters of Russian poetic translation). Etkind prepared a detailed foreword "Stikhotvornyi perevod v istorii russkoi literatury" ("Poetic translation in the history of Russian literature") in which he elaborately spoke about the importance of translation for the development of Russian literary views and styles. Commenting upon the contemporary state of Soviet translation, Etkind noted, "In the Soviet epoch, there is taking place a remarkable process in which a number of great poets are becoming professional translators. This can be said about B. Pasternak, A. Akhmatova, N. Zabolotskii, L. Martynov, P. Antokol'skii . . . The social reasons for this process are clear: deprived of the possibility to express themselves completely in their original works, the Russian poets—especially between the Seventeenth and the Twentieth Congress [of the Communist Party]—spoke to their readers through the lips of Goethe, Orbeliani, Shakespeare, Hugo. One way or another, the 1930s, 1940s, and 1950s turned out to be miraculously fruitful for poetic translation in the USSR. This art raised itself to such a high level as was seen nowhere else in the world."[3] However innocent this statement might seem nowadays, it became the reason for the already printed anthology to be rejected and destroyed—twenty-five thousand volumes in total. The next version of the anthology was strictly censored; the scandalous phrase about poets who dedicated themselves to literary translation due to the inability to publish their original works was removed. The censors also removed other parts of the preface that they found inappropriate, including

Etkind's praise of Pasternak's translations.[4] As was required in such cases, Etkind was publicly condemned at the general meeting of the university where he was teaching, but he continued his academic and literary activity in the Soviet Union for another five years. This period was nothing but a reprieve, for on April 25, 1974, the mutinous phrase was recalled many times when Etkind was stripped of his academic titles and expelled from the Union of Writers. Half a year later, Etkind left the Soviet Union; his Soviet academic titles were returned to him by the new Russian government only after the collapse of the USSR.

The preface therefore was able to decide the fate of the book and affect the life of the author and the commentator himself. A great number of published translations in the Soviet Union were made possible due to the effort of commentators who created prefaces that catered both to the political demands and to the public interest. A well-written preface was often used to divert the attention of censors during the final approval of the paginated book, which in the case of some books was extremely important. Along with general information about the author, the literary merits, and the contents, prefaces highlighted particular features of the literary work and ignored anything that the publishers wanted censors to overlook.

Sometimes the system of ideas and values of the reviewed work became completely reprioritized in the preface. Such reprioritization, as well as harsh criticism of the novel or characters in the preface, had a strategic nature: it was resorted to in order to anticipate the wish of the controlling organs to look closer into the published work. Equipping literary translations with politically convenient prefaces was practiced both in Moscow and Leningrad, publishers and translators in both cities placing a high value on the importance of prefaces in those years.

INNA STREBLOVA: Controversial or semicontroversial contents of the novel could be covered up by a smart introduction with an appropriate ideological tinge. A proper preface was able to become a good smoke screen, which would distract the censors and increase the chances of the book being published without major changes.

LARISA BESPALOVA: The administration of the Molodaia Gvardiia publishing house barely read books; they mainly acquainted themselves with books by means of prefaces: this was less time-consuming. This is why when preparing a preface we mainly targeted the editor-in-chief's office. Of course, there was information for readers in prefaces, too, but their main addressee was the editor-in-chief. We made special efforts to find such a specialist to write the preface, whose opinion would look solid to the editor-in-chief. We would also request the author of the preface to pay special attention to antibourgeois motives of the reviewed work. And one can always find antibourgeois motives in every serious literary work.

Forewords, concluding remarks, and commentaries written in line with the communist ideology were able to distract the attention of censors and help translators and their publishers avoid disputes with controlling organs over controversial content of published translations. Thus, for instance, the concluding remarks of the editor to the 1970 Russian publication of *Salamina* by Rockwell Kent spoke about the "dangerous vicinage of the United States of America which deprives Greenlanders of their confidence in the future."[5] The preface to a collection of stories by Jack London published in 1984 mentioned that Vladimir Lenin, Maksim Gor'kii, and Anatole France were keenly interested in London's works.[6] The volume of Ray Bradbury's works, which included *Fahrenheit 451*, *The Martian Chronicles*, and short stories and which was published in Moscow as late as 1987, was prefaced by astronaut-pilot Vladimir Dzhanibekov, a universally adored figure, like all astronauts in the 1980s. The preface included comments on "military ambitions and deadly plans of cosmic neo-Crusaders" of America and described Bradbury as an adversary of "anti-humanism of the modern capitalist society of the United States."[7] As one can see, even in the times of perestroika at the end of the 1980s, publishers remained apprehensive of the possible effect the publication of Bradbury might have in the case of a sudden return to the Soviet past and secured the publication by a politically charged preface.

When publishing literature of controversial content or written by "politically unreliable" individuals, publishers did their best to find reliable commentators to create politically appropriate prefaces. But the risks that could be taken by publishers were quite limited: being part of the system, publishing houses were not always able or willing to protect literary works selected for publication. This lack of power of publishing houses regularly resulted in professional disputes between publishers and individual translators who were adamant in protecting their work. As institutions, publishing houses naturally exercised more power, and the resistance of translators was often ineffective. Nonetheless, there were notable cases of brilliant victories of translators over publishing houses. One of the most notable cases is the lawsuit of translator Viktor Golyshev against the publishing house Molodaia Gvardiia at the end of the 1960s to the beginning of the 1970s.

> VIKTOR GOLYSHEV: Molodaia Gvardiia tried to cut some phrases out of my translation of the novel *The Day of the Locust* by Nathanael West. At that point the translation had already passed the second proof, and it was a proofreader who rushed to complain about the "bad phrases" in the novel all of a sudden. One of those "bad phrases" concerned prostitution, which was ironically called a profitable business.

Here Golyshev talks about the paragraph in chapter 17 of the novel, which ends with the following passage: "The economic didn't make sense either. Whoring certainly paid. Half of the customer's thirty dollars. Say ten men a week."[8] Neither the paragraph nor the quoted passage serves as a determinative factor of the narrative; however, the attempt of the publishing house to withdraw it made the translator rebel and oppose the situation.

> VIKTOR GOLYSHEV: I objected and said I was not going to change a word, because the author was dead by then. I wrote an official refusal, and the publishing house decided to use it against me. They decided to withhold 150 rubles they still owed me, and though my contract stated the sum clearly, they would not pay. And this was when I sued. I did not file the lawsuit because of money: it was not the matter of money, but the matter of principle. We lost the case in the district court, and my lawyer appealed, even though I told her, "To hell with it!" But she took her job seriously. The Moscow city court returned the case to the district court, and this is when we won the case against the publishing house.
>
> During the first court hearing the lawyer of the publishing house lost his temper and said that I was a shady character and a censor was closely watching my activity. This, of course, was a sheer lie used to make an impression on the judges who had no idea of the publishing business. It was actually the first time when I heard the word "censor" spoken aloud.

Resisting the publishing house for several years in the beginning of the 1970s was an extremely daring act: strengthening of Glavlit requirements and public persecution of Solzhenitsyn and Brodsky gave substantial grounds for a person engaged in literary activity to be careful. Golyshev, however, protected the principles of his trade by openly opposing the publishing house.

It must be noted here that not only translators resisted the interference of publishers with the content and style of translated works, but also many publishers demonstrated resolution when rejecting ideologically corrected and retouched translations. This concerned translations both by unknown translators and by reputed masters in the field.

LARISA BESPALOVA: When the well-known translator Osiia Soroka brought his translation of *Brave New World* by Huxley to *Novyi mir*, the journal had to reject his translation. The thing is that the criticism by Huxley in the novel targets both capitalism and socialism. Soroka's translation matched the original where Huxley criticized capitalism; but to blur the antisocialist moods of the novel, the translator altered some proper names (for example, Bernard Marks became Maerks, etc.). With this approach, the Huxley's double-edged criticism was lost, the message of the novel was distorted, and *Novyi mir* decided against the publication.

The rejection of Soroka, who by that time had already translated *The Last Tycoon* by Fitzgerald, short stories by Faulkner, and *The Watchers and the Watched* by Sid Chaplin, might have seemed surprising: by the beginning of 1980s, Soroka had already gained the reputation of an extremely gifted translator with an acute sense of style. Despite his reputation, the editors required from him an appropriate representation of Huxley's imagery. It should be noted that after the rejection, Soroka revised his translation of *Brave New World*. When his translation of the novel was eventually published in 1989, most of the names, including the aforementioned Bernard Marks, were rendered by means of transliteration or transcription in the forms traditionally accepted and recognized in Russian culture.[9] One of the exceptions, however, was the name of Lenina Crowne, whose name was rendered as *Linaina Kraun (Линайна Краун)*. The vowel substitution in the root of the name made it difficult for the Russian speaker to see the similarity of the names *Lenina* and *Lenin* and to recognize the allusion.[10]

As an editor, Larisa Bespalova was consistent in her strategy of selections and rejections of literature. She describes an earlier case of a translation rejection, explaining the reason in the following way:

LARISA BESPALOVA: In 1973, when I had just come to *Novyi mir* as an editor, I was editing the translation of a Polish novel—I do not remember the title, unfortunately. When I started reading the translation and checking it against the original I realized that the translator had left out important facts. Thus, the novel described the military atrocities of both the Home Army [*Armia krajowa*] and the pro-Soviet military forces; however, the translator left out everything concerning the pro-Soviet units, so it looked as if it was only the Home Army that committed atrocities. I convinced the editorial board of the journal to abstain from publishing that translation: I do not think one has the right to distort the author's original ideas.

So far we have seen cases of translators and publishers standing guard for the appropriate rendering of originals. Translators and publishers, as was stated earlier, occupied lower steps of the censoring ladder. Translators traditionally dealt with editors and administrations of publishing houses, the latter occupying the neighboring steps in the hierarchy. Approaching other steps was difficult and unwise: even gaining access to higher structures of the hierarchy did not guarantee the success of the publication but could have a negative impact on the translator's career. However, in their desire to introduce the reader to new authors and ideas, some translators resorted to the help of influential institutions that could advise Glavlit on its decisions

EVGENII WITKOWSKY: Glavlit had to put up with the decisions of the Ministry of Foreign Affairs. If, for instance, one submitted an application for a book from or about the country that had not been much mentioned in the publications of recent years, the Ministry of Foreign Affairs could command Glavlit to allow the publication. Therefore, when submitting an application to a publishing house, I would ask the publishing house to contact institutions other than Glavlit to make sure the book was topical and of current interest. This is how I received the approval of my application for the book of my translations of Luxembourg poets.

Sometimes translators had to take personal risks in their wish to get their translations published. One of such stories was described by Evgenii Witkowsky, who had to develop a complex strategy to get his translations accepted by controlling institutions and published.

EVGENII WITKOWSKY: One had to be inventive in those days. I resorted to cunning when I decided to publish my translations of the South African writer Breyten Breytenbach. Breytenbach, an active opponent of apartheid, was thrown into prison for seven years. While he was in prison, he was belied and slandered: some people wrote that Breytenbach had betrayed his employ, and so forth. The officer of the Central Committee of the Communist Party of the USSR for questions of southern Africa, Vladimir Shubin, forbade all publications of Breytenbach in the USSR, because he found Breytenbach politically inconvenient, or, as they would also put it in Glavlit, politically incompatible. So I waited patiently, and chose the moment when Shubin went to Angola to attend the funeral of some official. And with the help of my friends, I published half a page of my translations of Breytenbach in the newspaper *Literaturnaia gazeta*. Shubin returned back from Angola and got very annoyed, but eventually had to put up with the situation. The thing is that there was an institution called the Committee for Control that was higher than Glavlit itself and that could take the side of the translator. The effective publication in the newspaper predetermined the decision of the Committee for Control, and Glavlit complied with the committee's decision.

What Witkowsky means here is that *Literaturnaia gazeta* had to obtain the approval of the typeset pages before sending each issue into print. First approved in Shubin's absence by Glavlit officials, who were obviously unaware of Shubin's views on Breytenbach, and then—possibly—by the Committee for Control, the poetry of Breytenbach was officially accepted and encouraged for further publication. With the precedent created, the change of the situation was only possible with the new interference of the Committee for Control, which was clearly not in the interests of Glavlit.

Translation activism did not always take the form of an open protest, disagreement, or daring actions. Activism took an extremely peaceful but nonetheless dangerous turn in the case of Irina Komarova, who was engaged in the long correspondence with the authors of originals she was translating. As was mentioned above, Komarova corresponded with John Fowles, their correspondence eventually growing into a friendship. In the beginning of the 1990s, when the Soviet system became a relic of the past, Fowles invited his Russian translator Irina Komarova to his place in Dorset, England, for the New Year celebration and personally showed her the landscapes, the descriptions of which she had translated before.

Whereas the correspondence with Fowles took place in the relatively lenient 1980s, Komarova's correspondence with Ogden Nash unfolded in the 1960s. A young language specialist, Komarova first saw Nash's poetry in an anthology of American poetry and made up her mind to translate his poems into Russian. As she could not get access to originals, she decided to write to the author personally. Nash replied; along with the letter he sent the unknown Soviet translator a box full of books that included an almost complete collection of his poetry published by then. Komarova kept informing Nash of her progress in translating his poetry, and he replied with letters "full of wit, charm, and genuine friendliness."[11] This acute desire for honesty and transparency, the wish to understand and embrace the author's intention, and the sincere interest in the personality of the author were by all means a revolutionary approach to the task of a translator, a form of resisting conventions, and a contribution into the development of literary translation methodology.

The pressure of controlling institutions and the strict subordination of the Soviet publishing system invoked the natural resentment of all parties involved in the publishing process, which conforms to the well-known formula of Michel Foucault, "where there is power, there is resistance."[12] The formula allows us to assume that a closed society exercising a high degree of control over its citizens and their activities would also tend to resist this control. The resistance demonstrated by Soviet writers, translators, and publishers was predominantly tacit and can be described in terms of everyday resistance, the translation and publishing industry in the Soviet Union thus building up the space of resistance.[13] In describing the phenomenon of the space of resistance, Gennadii Zhirkov pointed out such characteristic features as circumlocution, ample use of parables, and platform oratory in creative writing;

he also indicated the proneness of the general situation to conflict.[14] In translation, circumlocution and parables as well as oratory type narratives could not be introduced at random, for the style and genre of target texts were naturally determined by their originals. The proneness of the translation situation to conflict, however, is a clear distinctive feature of the translation process in the USSR. Literary translation in the Soviet Union, as we have seen, was steeped in confrontation: the struggle of young translators for their first commissions, the struggle of translators for their membership in the Union of Writers, high competition in the field of translation, competition between Moscow and Leningrad translators and publishers, the struggle of translators and publishers in their promotion of texts for publication, the struggle of publishing houses for the right to include modern and controversial works of literature into their publishing plans. In this web of confrontation there was a central big battle that did not leave aside anyone who was in any way related to the world of Soviet literature and publishing. This was a battle for gaining the freedom of literary activity, the freedom of following one's true vocation, and the freedom of selection of literatures and authors.

The blossoming of Soviet literary translation in the 1960s through the 1980s was not only due to social circumstances, which turned the best poets and writers to translating other people's works. The literary renaissance was also due to the massive advent of young, brave, talented people into Soviet literature. As Maiia Kviatkovskaia stated in her interview, "For poetry to work in translation there must be some inner force in the translator." This statement applies, in fact, to translations of all literary genres. At the end of 1950s, the Soviet translation community welcomed back into the fold people who had gone through long imprisonments, camps, and misery and who continued to serve their calling even in captivity. These people educated several generations of Soviet translators, teaching them both translation skills and the translator's social role. And despite the fact that the interviewed translators almost invariably said in their interviews at some point, "We did not do or plan anything extraordinary, we just translated," the second half of the twentieth century saw the extraordinary results of literary endeavors and social resistance in Soviet literary translation.

CONCLUSION

How Far That Little Candle Throws His Beams

L iterary translation in the Soviet Union was an activity performed in a highly politicized context. The closedness of Soviet society created conditions for the construction of the pyramid-type structure of the Soviet publishing system, as well as censorship and control of styles and content of translated works. Close surveillance of literature by censoring organs did not purely consist in censorship—it provided for self-censorship as a means of promotion of translated literary works. Self-censorship manifested itself both in the choice of literary works for translation, because there were always some subjects that were difficult to promote, and in interference with the style and content of translated texts.

The decisions of Soviet literary translators to resort to self-censorship were not determined solely by fear of punishment or loss of career opportunities. As we have seen, the mere fact of engagement in literary translation in a closed society can be perceived of as a statement, even in cases when translators share the views of the ruling circles. This is mainly because translation implies the knowledge of another language and culture. The translator as a mediator of otherness is always a half-alien, who raises the suspicions of fellow citizens in a closed society, thus risking becoming a target of criticism and even persecution. This is why entering the profession of a literary translator in a closed society is a form of activism as such. Literary translation is very seldom able to build up a person's career in the traditional sense, nor is it able to ensure considerable and steady income. People become literary translators driven by the desire to feel and to share their feelings. In a closed society, literary translation can also be seen as a refuge—access to an alternative reality reconstructed in foreign-language literary texts. This means that literary translators of closed societies are aware of the possible difficulties the clash of two realities might offer. And it is the awareness of the difference that most often turns translators to self-censorship. Translators censor themselves when choosing the text for translation, as they try to make sure the form and content of the original are compatible with the norms and regulations imposed on them. In the process of translation and subsequent editing, translators agree to text modifications in order to get the translation through the process of approval. As the interviews have shown, even abridged and edited versions of translations were highly valued both by general readers and literature specialists; publications of censored translations were almost invariably soon followed by improved, noncensored translations. Therefore, in the case of a closed society, self-censorship cannot be looked upon as an absolute evil—but rather as a means of promotion, a way of first presentation, a promise of more to come, and, eventually, an activist strategy.

Another important issue in this regard is the way the translators see their role. Not a single interviewed translator described his/her work as dangerous. Quite the contrary, all translators demonstrated calm awareness of the rules imposed on them—and, at the same time, a passion for the literature they translated. Sharing the work of a favorite writer or poet with others was a common passion for translators; it was not political opposition, dissident activity, or any other form of open resistance the translators had in mind, but the mere engagement in the literary process. Active protests took place more seldom and at a later stage—mainly as a reaction to injustice on the behalf of publishers, censoring organs, or other controlling bodies.

In describing their literary activity, translators readily spoke about themselves not as individuals but as members of groups of fellow thinkers. However individual their translation tasks might have been, translators in the Soviet Union were group oriented. A high value was set on the opinion of colleagues; respect for opinions of other translators was a quality fostered by older, well-respected translators, chairs of translation seminars. Regular tandem work, open discussions of translations, and translation readings made Soviet translators well familiar with the work of others; awareness of being part of a wide literary world made translators both more critical of their own work and respectful of their colleagues. Communication was by all means the leitmotif of the whole historic period described in this book, be it gatherings of seminars in the Union of Writers or in Linetskaia's apartment or traveling to Chişinău to consult the author of the original, as was done by Mikhail Yasnov, or writing to John Fowles to ask for permission to make changes, as Irina Komarova did when translating *The French Lieutenant's Woman*. Literary translation in the Soviet Union was not an individual quest, but an activity performed in front of the colleagues by professionals open to criticism and ready for self-perfection. This unity of translators can also be seen as a special feature of Soviet translation activism: despite official prescriptions and control, translators jointly developed their own aesthetic and moral values and principles, which they continue to conform to nowadays and which they try to pass on to younger generations of translators.

Openness to criticism was particularly important for Soviet literary translators, because the demand for translated foreign literature in the Soviet Union was exceptionally high, and the Soviet reader found solace in foreign literature. And the higher the demand, the more heated were the discussions of translations and debates on the quality of translations in translation seminars. Collective discussions of translations ensured the steady growth and improvement of translation skills and techniques, notwithstanding the growth of demand and, therefore, work load.

The last decades of Soviet history took literary translation to a new level. Translation continued to attract talented people with a profound passion for literature, who joined literary groups and, despite political obstacles, developed new literary approaches and translation philosophies. Made under pressure, Soviet literary translation was yet built on passion for literature and yearning for communication with colleagues, literatures, cultures, and authors separated from the Soviet Union by the Iron Curtain.

LITERARY TRANSLATION UNDER RESTRICTIONS

Two Case Studies

The study of Soviet bans on original works and translations, in my view, would be incomplete without some illustrations. This appendix includes two case studies that demonstrate the transfer of literary works into the Russian language under political and social restrictions. The first example focuses on the presentation of Communist Party members in the first Russian translation of Ernest Hemingway's *For Whom the Bell Tolls* by Natalia Volzhina and Evgenia Kalashnikova. The second example addresses the issues of style and lexical choice in Rita Rait-Kovaleva's first Russian translation of *The Catcher in the Rye* by J. D. Salinger.

The translation of *For Whom the Bell Tolls* by Natalia Volzhina and Evgenia Kalashnikova was first published in Moscow in 1968 in the third volume of the collection of works of Ernest Hemingway.[1] It took the translators and their publishers a quarter of the century to make the publication of the translation possible. Despite numerous omissions made by censors, the mere fact of the publication was an achievement as such, and the novel immediately had tremendous success among Russian readers.

Most censorial omissions were made for political reasons. The examples studied here relate to two controversial political figures, whose representation in the novel evoked particular concern for Soviet censors. One of them is Dolores Ibárruri, leader of the Spanish Civil War, General Secretary of the Communist Party of Spain in 1942–60. The other is Political Commissar of International Brigades, Secretary of Comintern, French communist André Marty.

Dolores Ibárruri does not appear in the novel as an active participant; however, she is described quite vividly in the conversation of Karkov and a nameless journalist in chapter 32. According to Ekaterina Kuznetsova, the conversation about Ibárruri in chapter 32 was omitted completely in the unpublished version of 1941.[2] The first edition of the translation in 1968 preserved the dialog of Karkov with the puffy-eyed journalist with small omissions, the effect of which was yet so considerable that it changed the general tone of the conversation.

"That is true," the puffy-eyed man said. "Dolores brought the news herself. She was here with the news and was in such a state of radiant exultation as I have never seen. The truth of the news shone from her face. That great face," he said happily.

"That great face," Karkov said with no tone in his voice at all.

"If you could have heard her," the puffy-eyed man said. "The news itself shone from her with a light that was not of this world. In her voice you could tell the truth of what she said. I am putting it in an article for *Izvestia*. It was one of the greatest moments of the war to me when I heard the report in that great voice where pity, compassion and truth are blended. Goodness and truth shine from her as from a true saint of the people. Not for nothing is she called La Pasionaria."

"Not for nothing," Karkov said in a dull voice. "You better write it for *Izvestia* now, before you forget that last beautiful lead."

"That is a woman that is not to joke about. Not even by a cynic like you," the puffy-eyed man said. "If you could have been here to hear her and to see her face."

"That great voice," Karkov said. "That great face. Write it," he said. "Don't tell it to me. Don't waste whole paragraphs on me. Go and write it now."[3]

The omissions made in the passage mitigate the contrast between the words of the exalted journalist and the ironic remarks of Karkov.

The anadiploses are removed in both cases: Karkov's dull and inexpressive reiteration of the words of the interlocutor devaluates them, making them sound empty, and focuses the reader's attention on Karkov's annoyance with the situation and with Dolores Ibárruri herself. The fact that the puffy-eyed journalist finally realizes Dolores Ibárruri was being mocked is also removed from the translation. The same is true of the mention of the Soviet newspaper *Izvestia* that was at the time the main source of political information for Soviet readers. Therefore, the use of its title in an ironic context or an assumption that it could receive information from unreliable and hyperemotional journalists was deemed improper and was crossed out.

It is striking that the passage starting with *"Not for nothing," Karkov said in a dull voice* and down to *If you could have been here to hear her and to see her face* is also missing in the Soviet publication of *For Whom the Bell Tolls* in English, published by Progress publishing house in 1981.[4] The fact is clearly demonstrative of the interference of censors; the thoroughly censored text of the translation by Volzhina and Kalashnikova functioned here as a reliable reference, against which the later publication of the English original in the Soviet Union was censored.

Another notably amended place of the 1968 version is the conversation between Karkov and André Marty—that is, the two most inconvenient characters, the mere existence of whom in the novel impeded the publication of the translation for a long time (see also chap. 7). By 1968, André Marty had already been expelled from the French Communist Party (this happened in 1952), and his unjustified cruelty and suspicion were no longer kept a secret. Yet the negative image of Marty was still found to be too inappropriate for a political commissar leading the heroic struggle, which is why the most unpleasant characteristics of Marty were mitigated in the version of 1968. In the first description of Marty in chapter 41, we see three omissions in two consecutive sentences:

The tall, heavy old man looked at Gomez with his outthrust head and considered him carefully with his watery eyes. Even here at the front in the light of a bare electric bulb, he having just come in from driving in an open car on a brisk night, his gray face had a look of decay [inserted: "had something dead in it"]. His face looked as though it were modeled from the waste material [inserted: "the dead skin"] you find under the claws of a very old lion.[5]

The omissions and substitutions made in this passage target partial improvement of the image of André Marty. It is notable that three of the removed and substituted elements relate to the semantic field *death*: Marty is described as old and decaying; his face looks as if it were made of the waste material. Already in this introductory description, Marty is shown as an obstacle in the furious struggle against fascism. However cruel and suspicious, a communist of this rank could definitely not produce such a depressing impression, therefore the description was mitigated. But the most considerable changes to Hemingway's original were made several pages later, where Karkov challenges Marty, forcing him to admit the fact of hiding the dispatch delivered to him by Gomez and Andrés.

> "What dispatch?" Marty asked. It was a very stupid thing to say and he knew it. But he was not able to admit he was wrong that quickly and he said it anyway to delay the moment of humiliation. "And the safe-conduct pass," [inserted: "'The one which is in your pocket. Jordan's dispatch to Golz,'"] Karkov said through his bad [inserted: "clenched"] teeth.
>
> André Marty put his hand in his pocket and laid the dispatch on the table. He looked Karkov squarely in the eye. All right. He was wrong and there was nothing he could do about it now but he was not accepting any humiliation.
> "And the safe-conduct pass," Karkov said softly.[6]

The seemingly unmotivated substitution of the words of Karkov targets mitigation of the described situation. In the original, Karkov does not condescend to explanations: his knowledge of Marty and his ways is absolute, and he merely repeats his demand of the self-conduct pass, because the fact of Marty hiding the dispatch is obvious to him. Karkov's clarity of expression adds to Marty's humiliation. In the 1968 translation, Karkov goes into explanations, thus condescending to Marty and showing much more respect and subordination than he does in the original, which allows Marty to "save face" in the translation.

The confrontation of Karkov and Marty ends with a highly sarcastic remark of Karkov, which also got shortened in the translation by one sentence.

> "This is something else," Karkov went on, "but it is the same principle. I am going to find out just how untouchable you are, Comrade Marty. I would like to know if it could not be possible to change the name of that tractor factory."[7]

The fact that "tractor factories, villages and cooperatives" were named after Marty is mentioned several pages before chapter in the internal speech of Golz; this section was rendered in Russian without omissions.[8] Despite that, Karkov's speech is abridged, and the last sarcastic remark is removed from the translation. Indeed, the cut-out piece was able to evoke unnecessary associations, because two shipyards in the Soviet Union bore the name of André Marty: one in Leningrad (1922–57), another in Nikolaev (1922–56). By the time the translation was published, both shipyards had already been renamed, thus the remark of Karkov in this context could look prophetic and much more sarcastic than intended in the original. The sentence was also omitted in the Soviet 1981 edition of the English original by the Progress publishing house in Moscow, the translation of Volzhina and Kalashnikova again functioning here as a reference point more reliable than the original itself.[9] This dominance of the translated text over the original for the reason of being better censored demonstrates the capacity of the translation to create information that would be accepted as the ultimate truth even in comparison with the original source.

It is notable that the translation also avoids mentioning Karkov's bad teeth. Omissions of this small detail were, however, far from being accidental: it is a strategy religiously followed throughout the whole text of translation. In the translation, Karkov's teeth are once described as yellow;[10] the other two times the mention of bad teeth is omitted.[11] One can make assumptions why this was done; in all probability, the censors considered this mention of bad teeth trivial and incompatible with an image of a hero.

Such intentional lexical substitutions took place quite frequently in rendering works of unconventional content and style. The degree of the novelty and modernity of such works commanded the closer attention of the controlling organs and individuals, whose decision could suspend or even stop the publication of the book. In this regard, the translation of *The Catcher in the Rye* by Rita Rait-Kovaleva was a very difficult and daring project, as the degree of speech informality, the density of slang use, and the directness of the protagonist required caution on the behalf of the translator. Given that the protagonist expresses his negative views quite regularly, it would be interesting to start with more neutral situations, like the following one where Holden Caulfield expresses his admiration for a grown-up.

> SALINGER: All of a sudden, this lady got on at Trenton and sat down next to me. Practically the whole car was empty, because it was pretty late and all, but she sat down next to me, instead of an empty seat, because she had this big bag with her and I was sitting in the front seat. She stuck the bag right out in the middle of the aisle, where the conductor and everybody could trip over it. She had these orchids on, like she'd just been to a big party or something. She was around forty or forty-five, I guess, but she was very good looking. Women kill me. They really do. I don't mean I'm oversexed or anything like that—although I am quite sexy. I just like them, I mean.[12]

> RAIT-KOVALEVA: And suddenly a lady got on at Trenton and sat down next to me. Practically the whole car was empty, it was pretty late and all, but she sat down next to me, instead of an empty seat, because I was sitting in the front seat and she had a big bag. She stuck the bag right out in the aisle, so that the conductor or someone else could trip over it. She must have been returning from a reception or a ball—there were orchids on her dress. She must have been around forty or forty-five, but she was very beautiful. I just go crazy about women. Honestly. I don't mean I'm such a womanizer, but I am quite sensitive. I just like them.[13]

The key connotations employed in the original text became subject to mitigation in the translation; the barely noticeable realities of the Western culture were brought in accordance with the Soviet realities. First, this concerns the mention of "a big party or something": the Russian word for a party—*vecherinka*—has the connotation of light-heartedness, which is intensified grammatically by the diminutive suffix. Such light-heartedness was obviously deemed inappropriate for a mother of a teenager, and Rait-Kovaleva substituted the word "party" with the phrase "a reception or a ball," which sounds much more official and therefore suitable for a woman in her forties. This substitution automatically changes the gender identity of the text: in the original, the text is clearly produced by a teenage male: "a big party or something" is vague; it does not indicate much interest. Holden is more interested in the woman herself: the dress with orchids is the focus of his attention, and the reason for wearing it is secondary. The translation of Rait-Kovaleva employs teenage girls' language. Topic and comment are shifted, and the party is clearly more important, as the translator provides two synonyms, neither of which is an indicator of the colloquial style. Whereas the word "reception" is merely official, the word "ball" belongs to a different social context; it is also important that it is more associated with the lexicon of a teenage girl. The same can be said of the word "beautiful" used in the translation for rendering the word combination "good-looking": a teenage boy would be too shy to speak about the looks of an older woman with such openness. It is also notable that the substitution of the word "party" for a "reception or a ball" contradicts the situation described: the woman is carrying a big bag unacceptable for official receptions and is traveling by train, which is not a usual means of transportation from a ball.

Second, the speech of the protagonist in general looks much more official in the translation. The grammatical structures employed in the translation (as "she must have" instead of "she was, I guess") transfer Holden Caulfield to a different age category. But the most serious deformation of the original concerns the transfer of sexual connotations. The very mention of the protagonist's sexuality is removed from the translation; Holden Caulfield describes his feelings in a way untypical for a teenager. The use of such words as "womanizer" and "sensitive" are also indicators of an older age—in fact, at this point in the translation the protagonist sounds much older and reasonable than the woman he is describing. It is interesting that two pages after this paragraph the word "sensitive" is actually used by Salinger, but the use is ironic:

Holden Caulfield reiterates the words of the woman traveling with him: "Sensitive. That killed me. That guy Morrow was about as sensitive as a goddam toilet seat."[14]

Another feature of Rait-Kovaleva's translation is the active mitigation or omission of slang, swear words, as well as grammatical pleonasms, which intensify derogatory meanings. This was necessary to ensure the novel passed censorship. Euphemisms and periphrases are a very common translation technique in Rait-Kovaleva's approach to Salinger's original. For example, soon after the paragraph analyzed above, Holden Caulfield gives the extremely derogatory characteristics of the woman's son who turns out to be his schoolmate.

> SALINGER: Her son was doubtless the biggest bastard that ever went to Pencey, in the whole crumby history of the school. He was always going down the corridor, after he'd had a shower, snapping his soggy old wet towel at people's asses. That's exactly the kind of a guy he was.[15]

> RAIT-KOVALEVA: Her son was the biggest bastard in the whole of this lousy school. He would always go down the corridor after the shower and hit everyone with his wet towel. That's the kind of bastard he was.[16]

Rait-Kovaleva removes all intensifiers apart from the word "bastard" which she uses twice in order to compensate for the omissions. She takes out the parenthesis in the first sentence, shortens the second sentence by a clause, making the sentence more compact, and turns the complex third sentence into a simple one. The mention of the body part targeted by the towel blows is also omitted. The active compression results in a hastiness of narration and loss of colloquial redundancy, which is a distinctive feature of the protagonist's speech.

The changes made to texts, which we have seen in the examples above, cannot be ascribed to the translators' attempts to bring the translated works in line with the requirements of socialist realism; neither were they made out of fear of censors and publishers. The wish to get the readership acquainted with the work of foreign culture, which the translators thought important, valuable, and timely, made them look for new approaches to text transfer. In this regard, the twenty-five-year-long story of the first publication of *For Whom the Bell Tolls* is proof in itself. For more than two decades, Volzhina and Kalashnikova attempted to bring the novel to the Russian audience. This required considerable alterations to the text; however, the response of the readership to the first publication of the Russian version in 1968 was tremendous, as well as to the translation of *The Catcher in the Rye* by Rait-Kovaleva. Quotes from both novels became part of everyday speech; for several decades, Hemingway's works enjoyed iconic status among Soviet intellectuals, and the story of Holden Caulfield continued to excite new generations of readers. For those born in the 1970s, *The Catcher in the Rye* is invariably associated with its 1983 edition and its cover featuring *Albert's Son* by Andrew Wyeth.[17] Salinger's story and Wyeth's image taken together contributed to educating the generation of dreamers and passionate travelers, who were the youngest voters when the Soviet Union collapsed and its republics went their separate ways.

APPENDIX B

PERSONALIA

AKHMADULINA, BELLA AKHATOVNA (1937–2010), Soviet poet, writer, translator, and social activist.

AKHMATOVA, ANNA ANDREEVNA (1889–1966), Russian poet, one of the major Russian literary figures of the twentieth century. Her poetry ranged from the lyrical works of the Silver Age to the solemn *Requiem* and unparalleled *Poem without a Hero*. Akhmatova was actively engaged in poetic translation in the 1950s and 1960s, mainly working with inter-linear trots from Serbian, Czech, Bulgarian, Romanian, Korean, and other languages.

ANIKST, ALEKSANDR ABRAMOVICH (1910–88), distinguished theorist of literature and theater, author of the seminal *Istoriia angliiskoi literatury* (History of English literature). One of the most prominent Shakespeare specialists in the Soviet Union, founder of the Shakespeare Commission of the History of the World Literature Scientific Council of the Academy of Sciences. Founder of the symposium Shakespeare Readings, editor-in-chief of the journal *Shekspirovskie chteniia* (Shakespeare readings).

ASTAF'EVA NATALIA GEORGIEVNA (1922–2016), poet, translator from Polish.

AZADOVSKII, KONSTANTIN MARKOVICH (b. 1941), literary critic, specialist in Germanic and Slavic languages.

211

BEKKER, MERI IOSIFOVNA (1920–2010), Leningrad/St. Petersburg literary translator of William Thackeray, Edgar Allan Poe, Jonathan Swift, Edith Wharton, William Faulkner, John Updike, and John Fowles.

BEN, GEORGII EVSEEVICH (1934–2008), Leningrad translator and critic, student of Tat'iana Gnedich. Translated British and American poetry and prose: Lord Byron, Henry Longfellow, Walter Scott, Edgar Allan Poe, Rudyard Kipling, Langston Hughes. In 1973, Ben emigrated to Israel; he later moved to London where he worked at the BBC and continued translating literature (Howard Fast, Arthur Koestler, Aldous Huxley).

BETAKI, VASILII PAVLOVICH (1930–2013), Leningrad translator of poetry, writer, student of Tat'iana Gnedich. In 1973, Betaki emigrated to France, where he worked at radio Freedom. He continued translating poetry— Sylvia Plath, Rudyard Kipling, T. S. Eliot, Dylan Thomas.

BOGOSLOVSKAIA, MARIIA PAVLOVNA (1902–74), Moscow translator, member of the Kashkin circle. Known for her translations of English, American, and French prose: Charles Dickens, Stendhal, Thomas Hardy, Jack London, Bernard Shaw, Edgar Allan Poe, Honoré de Balzac, James Joyce, Theodore Dreiser, William Faulkner.

CHEZHEGOVA, INNA MIKHAILOVNA (1929–90), literary translator of Sor Juana Inés de la Cruz, Juan de Arguijo, Manoel de Oliveira, and other Spanish and Portuguese poets. Student of El'ga Linetskaia. Wife of translator Mikhail Donskoi.

CHUKOVSKAIA, LIDIIA KORNEEVNA (1907–96), Soviet poet, writer, critic, and political activist. Daughter of Kornei Chukovskii. Close friend and biographer of Anna Akhmatova. Took active part in the defense of Aleksandr Solzhenitsyn and Andrei Sakharov, as a consequence losing her own right to publish in the USSR and getting expelled from the Union of Writers.

CHUKOVSKII, KORNEI IVANOVICH (1882–1969), poet, translator, children's writer, journalist, essayist, and literary critic. Author of several books on translation, translation practice, and children's language. Known for his translations of Walt Whitman, Daniel Defoe, Mark Twain, Robert Louis Stevenson, Oscar Wilde, H. G. Wells, and O'Henry.

DANIEL', IULII MARKOVICH (1925–88), pseudonyms—Nikolai Arzhak and Iu. Petrov. Soviet writer, poet, translator, dissident, and political prisoner. Together with Andrei Siniavskii, Daniel' wrote stories and novels and published them illegally in France under a pseudonym. In 1965, Daniel' and Siniavskii were arrested and tried, their trial later becoming universally known as the Siniavskii-Daniel' trial. In 1966, Daniel' was sentenced to five years of hard labor for anti-Soviet activity. After release, Daniel' refused to emigrate; he earned his living by translating poetry, which he published under a pen name, his official name being under a publishing ban.

DARUZES, NINA LEONIDOVNA (1899–1982), Moscow translator of English, American, and French prose, member of the Kashkin circle. Translated Charles Dickens, Mark Twain, William Thackeray, Guy de Maupassant, Henry James, Bret Harte, Jack London, Rudyard Kipling, Ernest Hemingway, and Bernard Shaw.

D'IAKONOVA, NINA IAKOVLEVNA (1915–2013), professor of philology and English literature of Leningrad/St. Petersburg State University, influential English literature specialist. Author of academic research works on Shakespeare, Lord Byron, Percy Bysshe Shelley, John Keats, Charles Dickens, Robert Louis Stevenson, John Galsworthy, Bernard Shaw, and Aldous Huxley. Collected several volumes of classic English literature.

DONSKOI, MIKHAIL ALEKSANDROVICH (1913–96), Leningrad translator from English, French, and Spanish. Widely known for his translations of Molière, Pierre Corneille, Jean Racine, Shakespeare, Lope de Vega, Tirso de Molina, Pedro Calderón, Juan Ruiz, Victor Hugo. Student of El'ga Linetskaia. Husband of translator Inna Chezhegova, at whose death he abandoned translation.

ETKIND, EFIM GRIGOR'EVICH (1918–99), Leningrad philologist, translation theorist, literature specialist, and literary translator. Professor of Herzen State Pedagogical Institute. Chair of the German translation seminar of the Union of Writers. Witness for the defense in the trial of Joseph Brodsky in 1964 and was a friend of Aleksandr Solzhenitsyn even after Solzhenitsyn's exile from the USSR. In April 1974, Etkind was stripped of his professorship, deprived of all academic titles, and expelled from the Union of Writers on the charges of dissident and anti-Soviet activity. Half a year later, Etkind was forced to emigrate and moved to France, where he became a professor at Paris X Nanterre University.

FEDOROV, ANDREI VENEDIKTOVICH (1906–97), Leningrad philologist, major translation theorist of twentieth-century Russia, professor of Leningrad/St. Petersburg State University. Fedorov was the first in the Soviet Union to declare the linguistic approach to translation studies.

GALICH, ALEKSANDR ARKAD'EVICH (1918–77), Soviet poet, playwright, screenwriter, writer of songs. One of the founders of the genre of "bard song" in the Soviet Union. Expelled from the Union of Writers and the Union of Cinematographers on the charges of dissident activity, Galich was forced to leave the Soviet Union in 1974 and lived in France until his accidental death in 1977.

GASPAROV, MIKHAIL LEONOVICH (1935–2005), philologist, specialist in antique literature and Russian prose, member of the Russian Academy of Sciences. Famous translator of goliardic poetry.

GELESKUL, ANATOLII MIKHAILOVICH (1934–2011), Moscow translator from Romance, Germanic, and Slavic languages, widely known for his translations of poetry: Juan de la Cruz, Antonio Machado, Juan Ramón Jiménez, Frederico García Lorca, César Vallejo, Octavio Paz, Pablo Neruda, Théophile Gautier, Gérard de Nerval, Charles Baudelaire, Paul Verlaine, Guillaume Apollinaire, Fernando Pessoa, Rainer Maria Rilke, Adam Mickiewicz, Konstanty Gałczyński, Czesław Miłosz.

GNEDICH, TAT'IANA GRIGOR'EVNA (1907–76), Leningrad literary translator. Spent over a year in solitary confinement, and then over six years in labor camps on treason charges; in prison she translated Byron's *Don Juan* from memory. From 1957, Gnedich chaired the English translation seminar of the Union of Writers. Also known as a translator of William Shakespeare and Walter Scott.

GOLYSHEVA, ELENA MIKHAILOVNA (1906–84), an accomplished Soviet translator of Ernest Hemingway, Thornton Wilder, William Saroyan, William Faulkner, J. D. Salinger, James Aldridge, Somerset Maugham, and many others. Mother of translator Viktor Golyshev.

GRUDININA, NATALIA IOSIFOVNA (1918–99), Leningrad poet, translator, activist. Chaired the poetic club for literary youth and the seminar on translation from the languages of the Extreme North. Grudinina is also known for her active participation in the defense of Joseph Brodsky.

JURJEW, OLEG ALEKSANDROVICH (1959–2018), St. Petersburg translator, poet, and literary critic. Student of El'ga Linetskaia. Since 1991, he lived and worked in Germany.

KALASHNIKOVA, EVGENIIA DAVYDOVNA (1906–76), Moscow translator of English and American prose and drama, member of the Kashkin circle. Universally known for her translations of *A Farewell to Arms, For Whom the Bell Tolls, To Have and Have Not,* and *The Fifth Column* by Ernest Hemingway, *Pygmalion* by Bernard Shaw, *The Great Gatsby* by F. Scott Fitzgerald, and *Martin Eden* by Jack London. She also translated Thornton Wilder, James Aldridge, John Updike, Charles Dickens, William Thackeray, Theodore Dreiser, Nathaniel Hawthorne, Ambrose Bierce, James Joyce, and O. Henry.

KASHKIN, IVAN ALEKSANDROVICH (1899–1963), Moscow translator, poet, and literary critic; educated a group of female literary translators who became leading Soviet translators of the third quarter of the twentieth century known under the name of the Kashkin circle, or *kashkinki.* Translated Ernest Hemingway, James Joyce, and Ambrose Bierce. His major translation work is considered to be the translation of Chaucer's *Canterbury Tales.*

KHEIFETS, MIKHAIL RUVIMOVICH (b. 1934), writer, journalist. In 1974, Kheifets was sentenced for four years of imprisonment and two years of exile for dissident activity, namely, for writing a preface to the works of Joseph Brodsky, illegally collected for publication by Vladimir Maramzin. Continued to write in prison and emigrated to Israel after his release in 1980.

KHVOSTENKO, LEV VASIL'EVICH (1915–59), literary translator, founder and chair of the English prose translation seminar in the Leningrad department of the Union of Writers. Translated works of Mark Twain and Theodore Dreiser and poetry of Henry Longfellow.

KOPELEV, LEV ZINOV'EVICH (1912–97), philologist, literary critic, dissident, and human rights activist. Prototype for Rubin in the novel by Solzhenitsyn *In the First Circle*. Stripped of his Soviet citizenship in 1980; since then lived in Germany where he was a professor at the University of Wuppertal.

KORNEEV, IURII BORISOVICH (1921–95), Leningrad translator from English, German, French, Spanish, and Portuguese. His best-known translations are *Cantar de mío Cid, Das Nibelungenlied, La Chanson de Roland,* and *La Chançun de Willame*, as well as plays of Pierre Corneille, Lope de Vega, and Shakespeare, and numerous poetic works.

KORNILOV, VLADIMIR NIKOLAEVICH (1928–2002), Moscow poet, writer, and literary critic. Expelled from the Union of Writers in 1977 for dissident activity: samizdat publications and support of Andrei Siniavskii and Iulii Daniel'. Was first published again only in 1986. Husband of translator and editor Larisa Bespalova.

KOSS, ALEKSANDRA MARKOVNA (1934–2010), philologist, translator from Spanish and Portuguese. Mainly translated poetry: Cervantes, Luís vas de Camões, Fernando Pessoa, Francisco de Quevedo, Luis Carrillo, Miguel de Unamuno.

LOZINSKII, MIKHAIL LEONIDOVICH (1886–1955), the leading Soviet translator, one of the most accomplished Russian translators of the twentieth century. Among his translations are *The Divine Comedy* by Dante, *Don Quixote* by Cervantes, dramas by Shakespeare, *Le Cid* by Corneille, fragments of *Shahnameh* by Ferdowsi, *The Autobiography of Benvenuto Cellini* and *Les Caves du Vatican* by André Gide, plays by Molière, Lope de Vega, and Tirso de Molina, novellas by Prosper Mérimée, and numerous lyrical works.

LIKHACHEV, IVAN ALEKSEEVICH (1902–72), Leningrad translator. Political prisoner; spent over seventeen years in labor camps, where he also translated Charles Baudelaire's *Fleurs du mal* from memory. Chaired the English prose translation seminar after the death of Lev Khvostenko. Likhachev translated from English and French; his most known translations are *Waverley* by Walter Scott, *Lavengro* by George Borrow, and the poetry of Jean-Antoine de Baïf, Philippe Desportes, Emily Dickinson, and Gerard Manley Hopkins.

LINETSKAIA, EL'GA L'VOVNA (1909–97), Leningrad translator, teacher, inspirer of several generations of Leningrad translators. In 1937–46,

Linetskaia was exiled to Kazakhstan, charged with counterrevolutionary activity. After her return to Leningrad, Linetskaia became chair of the Romance poetry seminar, which she headed for over thirty-five years until her death in 1997. Linetskaia is widely known for her translations of Blaise Pascal, François de La Rochefoucauld, Jean Racine, François-René de Chateaubriand, Alexandre Dumas, Guy de Maupassant, Jerome K. Jerome, Lion Feuchtwanger, and William Faulkner.

LORIE, MARIIA FEDOROVNA (1904–92), Moscow translator, member of the Kashkin circle. Actively translated from the English language: Charles Dickens, William Thackeray, F. Scott Fitzgerald, John Galsworthy, Somerset Maugham, Evelyn Waugh, Bernard Shaw, Iris Murdoch, Herman Melville, O. Henry, Jack London, Virginia Woolf, Thomas Hardy, Ernest Hemingway, Katherine Mansfield.

MAKSIMOV, VLADIMIR EMEL'IANOVICH (1930–95), writer, editor, and critic. Politically persecuted, he emigrated to Paris in 1974. Founder of the émigré dissident journal *Kontinent*.

MANDEL'SHTAM, ISAI BENEDIKTOVICH (1885–1954), translator of Shakespeare, Heinrich Heine, Stefan Zweig, Honoré de Balzac, Joris-Karl Huysmans, Anatole France, Detlev von Liliencron, and Leo Perutz.

MARAMZIN, VLADIMIR RAFAILOVICH (b. 1934), writer. Was conditionally sentenced for compiling a five-volume samizdat edition of the exiled Joseph Brodsky. Was allowed to emigrate to France in 1975.

MARSHAK, SAMUIL IAKOVLEVICH (1887–1964), an influential Soviet poet, playwright, translator, and literary critic. One of the most active and admired translators of his time. As a translator, he is best known for his translations of all the sonnets of Shakespeare and the poetry of Robert Burns, William Wordsworth, John Keats and Rudyard Kipling.

OKUDZHAVA, BULAT SHALOVICH (1924–97), poet, writer, musician, author of songs. One of the founders of the genre of "bard song" in the Soviet Union.

PASTERNAK, BORIS LEONIDOVICH (1890–1960), one of the most influential Russian-language poets, writers, and translators of the twentieth century, Nobel Prize winner for literature, for which he became target of a ruthless bullying campaign in the Soviet Union. As a translator, Pasternak is honored for his translations of Shakespearean histories and tragedies, *Faust* by Goethe, *Maria Stuart* by Friedrich Schiller, *The Alchemist* by Ben Johnson, and the plays of Pedro Calderon and Heinrich von Kleist.

PETROV, SERGEI VLADIMIROVICH (1911–88), Leningrad translator, famous for his phenomenal knowledge of more than twelve languages. Petrov started to translate literature in prison, where he was confined for political reasons from 1933–43. Since 1960, Petrov has chaired the Scandinavian translation seminar of the Leningrad department of the Union of Writers. Among his best-known translations are the works of Walter Scott, Lord Byron, Robert Burns, Stéphane Mallarmé, Charles Leconte de Lisle, Théophile Gautier, Francisco de Quevedo, and Carl Bellman.

REVICH, ALEKSANDR MIKHAILOVICH (1921–2012), Moscow poet and translator. Predominantly translated poetry: Paul Verlaine, Agrippa d'Aubigné, Stéphane Mallarmé.

RAIT-KOVALEVA, RITA IAKOVLEVNA (1898–1988), famous Moscow translator of Heinrich Böll, Franz Kafka, J. D. Salinger, John Steinbeck, William Faulkner, Kurt Vonnegut, Graham Greene, Sinclair Lewis, and Seán O'Casey.

SERGEEV, ANDREI IAKOVLEVICH (1933–98), Russian poet, writer, and translator. Author of brilliant translations from W. B. Yeats, James Joyce, T. S. Eliot, Robert Frost, Bertolt Brecht, Rainer Maria Rilke, E. E. Cummings, Dylan Thomas, and Robert Graves. Perished in a car accident at the height of his literary activity.

SHENGELI, GEORGII ARKAD'EVICH (1894–1956), poet, writer, literature specialist, and translator. As a researcher, specialized in the theory of poetry. As a translator is widely known for his translations from Lord Byron, Charles Baudelaire, Paul Verlaine, and Victor Hugo.

SHMAKOV, GENNADII GRIGOR'EVICH (1940–88), poet, writer, critic, translator of Paul Verlaine, Jean Cocteau, Rubén Darío, Marcel Proust, Nathaniel Hawthorne, and Henry James.

SHOR, VLADIMIR EFIMOVICH (1917–71), Leningrad translator and literature specialist, chair of French prose translation seminar of the Union of Writers. Translated from English, German, and French: novels by Walter

Scott, Horace Walpole, George Sand, tragedies by Jean Racine, poems by Victor Hugo, Charles Baudelaire, Paul Verlaine, Jules Laforgue.

STEINBERG, ARKADII AKIMOVICH (1907–84), poet, translator, and painter. Widely recognized in Russia for his translation of Milton's *Paradise Lost*, as well as numerous works of English and German poetry.

SIL'MAN, TAMARA ISAAKOVNA (1909–74), Leningrad philologist, writer, and translator of Rainer Maria Rilke.

SINIAVSKII, ANDREI DONATOVICH (1925–97), pseudonym—Abram Tertz. Soviet writer, dissident, and political prisoner. Together with Iulii Daniel', Siniavskii wrote stories and novels and published them in illegally in France under his pseudonym. In 1965, Siniavskii and Daniel' were arrested and tried, their trial later becoming universally known as the Siniavskii-Daniel' trial. In 1966, Siniavskii was sentenced to seven years of hard labor for anti-Soviet activity. After release, Siniavskii emigrated to France, where he continued his literary and social activity.

SNETKOVA, NINA PAVLOVNA (1923–2010), editor of the French and Spanish section of Khudozhestvennaia Literatura publishing house. Literary critic, translator from Spanish, known for her translations of Julio Cortázar and Julio Ramón Ribeyro.

SOROKA, OSIIA PETROVICH (1927–2001), translator from the English language, best known for his translation of *The Sound and the Fury* by William Faulkner. Soroka translated ten plays by Shakespeare, *East of Eden* by John Steinbeck, *The Last Tycoon* by F. Scott Fitzgerald, and *Brave New World* by Aldous Huxley.

STOLBOV, VALERII SERGEEVICH (1913–91), translator, editor, specialist in Spanish-language literature. Translated the poetry of Antonio Machado, León Felipe, Pablo Neruda, Ángel González; compiled the volumes of poetry of Rubén Darío and César Vallejo. The main translation work of Stolbov was his joint project with his wife Nina Butyrina—the translation of *One Hundred Years of Solitude* by Gabriel García Márquez. In tandem with Butyrina, Stolbov also translated *La Dame de Monsoreau* by Alexandre Dumas.

STUKALIN, BORIS IVANOVICH (1923–2004), head of the State Committee of the Council of Ministers of the USSR (since July 1978—State

Committee of the USSR) for Publishing, Print, and Book Trade from 1972–82. Later in 1982, Stukalin was promoted to the post of the head of the Propaganda Department of the Central Committee of the Communist Party of the USSR, which he occupied until 1985.

TOLSTAIA, NATALIA IVANOVNA (1926–2003), Leningrad/St. Petersburg editor, literature specialist, and translator. Specialist in Sanskrit and Punjabi.

TERTERIAN, INNA ARTUROVNA (1933–86), Moscow editor, specialist in Spanish and Latin American literature. Member of the Real Academia Española.

TOPER, VERA MAKSIMOVNA (1890–1964), Moscow translator of English, American, Austrian, and French prose, member of the Kashkin circle. Known for her translations of Ernest Hemingway, Charles Dickens, Jack London, Guy de Maupassant, James Joyce, O. Henry, and Franz Kafka.

TOPOROV, VIKTOR LEONIDOVICH (1946–2013), St. Petersburg translator, writer, and literary critic. Translator from English, German, and Dutch; known for his translations from the poetry of John Donne, Lord Byron, Rudyard Kipling, T. S. Eliot, Robert Frost, Goethe, Rainer Maria Rilke, Paul Celan, Lucebert, Gerbrand Bredero, and Hugo Claus.

VASIL'EV, VLADIMIR EFIMOVICH (1929–2014), literary translator of Spanish and French poetry, specialist in literary epigrams.

VAKHTIN, BORIS BORISOVICH (1930–81), Leningrad researcher, playwright, philosopher, renowned translator of Chinese poetry. Chaired the Asian languages translation seminar of the Union of Writers.

VOLZHINA, NATALIA ALBERTOVNA (1903–81), Moscow translator of English, American, Austrian, and French prose, member of the Kashkin circle. Well known for her translation of *The Grapes of Wrath* by John Steinbeck, *The Old Curiosity Shop* by Charles Dickens, and *The Hound of the Baskervilles* by Arthur Conan Doyle. Also translated John Galsworthy, Graham Greene, Ernest Hemingway, Bret Harte, Mark Twain, Robert Louis Stevenson, James Joyce, O. Henry, H. G. Wells, Harriet Beecher Stowe, Ambrose Bierce, and Sherwood Anderson.

VOINOVICH, VLADIMIR NIKOLAEVICH (1932–2018), writer and political activist exiled from the Soviet Union in 1980. From 1980–92 lived in Germany and the United States. After being restored as a Russian citizen, Voinovich returned to Russia, where he continued his engagement in social and political activity.

VYSOTSKII, VLADIMIR SEMENOVICH (1938–80), actor, poet, widely known and adored for his songs and unique performance style.

WACHSMACHER, MAURICE NIKOVAEVICH (1926–94), distinguished poet-translator, known for his brilliant translations from French—Paul Verlaine, Georges Rodenbach, Guillaume Apollinaire, Paul Éluard, Louis Aragon. Chair of one of the translation seminars of the Moscow Union of Writers. The annual literary prize for the best translation of the French literature into Russian awarded by the French embassy in Russia since 1996 bears his name—Prix Maurice Wachsmacher.

ZABOLOTSKII, NIKOLAI ALEKSEEVICH (1903–58), Moscow poet, translator of Georgian poetry. Translated the Georgian medieval epic poem *The Knight in the Panther's Skin*.

ZHIRMUNSKII, VIKTOR MAKSIMOVICH (1891–1971), Leningrad philologist, member of the Russian Academy of Sciences, honorary member of the British Academy, Bavarian Academy of Sciences and Humanities, and Saxon Academy of Sciences and Doctor Honoris Causa of Oxford University. Specialist in Germanic and Turkic languages, comparative literature, and theory of verse.

WORKS CITED

Admoni, Vladimir, and Tamara Sil'man. *My vspominaem* [We are remembering]. St. Petersburg: Kompozitor, 1993.

Akhmadulina, Bella. "Stikhotvorenie, podlezhashchee perevodu . . ." [A poem undergoing translation . . .] In *Perevod—sredstvo vzaimnogo sblizheniia narodov: Khudozhestvennaia publitsistika*, edited by Anatolii Klyshko, 456–59. Moscow: Progress, 1987.

Akhmatova, Anna. *The Complete Poems of Anna Akhmatova.* Vol. 1. Translated by Judith Hemschemeyer. Edited by Roberta Reeder. Sommerville: Zephyr Press, 1990.

———. "V to vremia ia gostila na zemle . . ." *Stikhotvoreniia. Poemy* ["In those days I was a guest on earth . . ." Poetry]. St. Petersburg: Lenizdat, 1995.

Antochi, Roxana-Mihaela. "Communist Ideology and Drama Translation in Romania." In *Aspects of Literary Translation: Building Linguistic and Cultural Bridges in Past and Present*, edited by Eva Parra-Membrives, Miguel Ángel García Peinado, and Albrecht Classen, 251–64. Tübingen: Narr, 2012.

Asimakoulas, Dimitris. "Translation as Social Action: Brecht's 'Political Texts' in Greek." *TTR: Traduction, Terminologie, Rédaction* 1 (2007): 113–40.

Azov, Andrei. *Poverzhennye bukvalisty: Iz istorii khudozhestvennogo perevoda v SSSR v 1920–1960-e gody* [Prostrate bukvalists: From the history of literary translation in the USSR in the 1920–1960s]. Moscow: Dom Vysshei Shkoly Ekonomiki, 2013.

Baer, Brian James. "Literary Translation and the Construction of a Soviet Intelligentsia." *Massachusetts Review* 3 (2006): 537–60.

———. *Translation and the Making of Modern Russian Literature*. New York and London: Bloomsbury, 2016.

Baer, Brian James, and Natalia Olshanskaya, eds. *Russian Writers on Translation: An Anthology*. Manchester: St. Jerome, 2013.

Bagriana, Elisaveta. *Stikhi* [Poems]. Translated from Bulgarian. Moscow: Khudozhestvennaia Literatura, 1979.

Bagryana, Elisaveta. *Izbrani proizvedeniia v dva toma. Pervi tom* [Selected works in two volumes. First volume]. Sofia: Bŭlgarski Pisatel, 1983.

Bairon, Dzhordzh G. [Byron, George G.] *Don Zhuan* [Don Juan]. Translated by Georgii Shengeli. Moscow: Goslitizdat, 1947.

———. *Don Zhuan* [Don Juan]. Translated by Tat'iana Gnedich. Moscow-Leningrad: Khudozhestvennaia Literatura, 1964.

Baker, Mona. *Translation and Conflict: A Narrative Account*. London and New York: Routledge, 2006.

Barenbaum, Iosif. *Istoriia knigi* [The history of the book]. Moscow: Kniga, 1984.

Belinskii, Vissarion. "Letter to Gogol." In *Readings in Russian Civilization. Vol. II: Imperial Russia 1700–1917*, edited by Thomas Riha, 315–20. Chicago and London: University of Chicago Press, 2009.

Bell, Daniel. *The End of Ideology: On the Exhaustion of Political Ideas in the Fifties*. Cambridge, MA, and London: Harvard University Press, 1962.

Bergson, Henri. *Les deux sources de la morale et de la religion* [Two sources of morality and religion]. Paris: Félix Aclan, 1932.

Betaki, Vasilii. "Red'iard Kipling i russkaia poeziia XX veka" [Rudyard Kipling and the Russian poetry of the 20th century]. Concluding remarks to *Izbrannye stikhi iz vsekh knig* by Red'iard Kipling. Edited by Vasilii Betaki, 256–305. B.m.: Salamandra P.V.V., 2011.

Blium, Arlen. *Kak eto delalos' v Leningrade: Tsenzura v gody ottepeli, zastoia i perestroiki. 1953–1991* [The way it was done in Leningrad:

Censorship in the years of Thaw, stagnation, and perestroika. 1953–1991]. St. Petersburg: Akademicheskii Proekt, 2005.

———. *Sovetskaia tsenzura v epokhu total'nogo terrora. 1929–1953* [Soviet censorship in the epoch of total terror 1929–1953]. St. Petersburg: Akademicheskii Proekt, 2000.

———. "Zarubezhnaia literatura v spetskhrane" [Foreign literature in *spetskhran*]. *Inostrannaia literatura* 12 (2009): 131–46.

Bolotnikov, Nikita. Editor's concluding remarks to *Salamina* by Rockwell Kent, 374–77. Moscow: Mysl', 1970.

Borisenko Aleksandra. "Selindzher nachinaet i vyigryvaet" [Salinger begins and wins]. *Inostrannaia literatura* 7 (2009): 223–31.

Briusov, Valerii, ed. *Poeziia Armenii s drevneishikh vremen do nashix dnei v perevode russkikh poetov* [Poetry of Armenia from ancient times until our days in the translations of Russian poets]. Moscow: Moskovskii Armianskii Komitet, 1916.

Burak, Alexander. "The 'Americanization' of Russian Life and Literature through Translations of Hemingway's Works." *Translation and Interpreting Studies* 1 (2013): 50–72.

Byron, George G. N. *The Works of Lord Byron. Poetry.* Vol. VI. Edited by Ernest Hartley Coleridge. London: John Murray, 1903.

Calvani, Alessandra. *Traduzioni e traduttori. Gli specchi dell'originale* [Translations and translators. Mirrors of the originals]. Padova: Libreriauniversitaria.it Edizioni, 2012.

Calzada-Pérez, María. Introduction to *Apropos of Ideology.* Edited by María Calzada-Pérez, 1–22. Manchester: St. Jerome, 2003.

Capote, Truman. *Breakfast at Tiffany's.* Harmondsworth: Penguin Books, 1977.

Chekhov, Anton. *Perepiska A.P. Chekhova v trekh tomakh. T. 2* [Letters of A. P. Chekhov in three volumes. Vol. 2]. Moscow: Nasledie, 1996.

———. *The Sea Gull.* New York: Dover Publications, 1999.

Chernetsky, Vitaly. "Nation and Translation: Literary Translation and the Shaping of Modern Ukrainian Culture." In *Contexts, Subtexts, Pretexts: Literary Translation in Eastern Europe and Russia,* edited by Brian James Baer, 33–53. Amsterdam/Philadelphia: John Benjamins, 2011.

Choldin, Marianna Tax. "Closing and Opening and Closing: Reflections on the Russian Media." In *The Space of the Book: Print Culture in the Russian Social Imagination*, edited by Miranda Remnek, 281–99. Toronto: University of Toronto Press, 2011.

Chukovskaia, Lidiia. *Zapiski ob Anne Akhmatovoi. V 3 tomakh* [Notes on Anna Akhmatova. In 3 volumes]. Moscow: Vremia, 2013.

Chukovskii, Kornei. *Sobranie sochinenii. T. 3* [Collection of works. Vol. 3]. Moscow: TERRA-Knizhnyi klub, 2001.

——. *Vysokoe iskusstvo: O printsipakh khudozhestvennogo perevoda* [A high art: Toward the principles of literary translation]. Moscow: Iskusstvo, 1964.

Clark, Katerina. *Moscow, the Fourth Rome: Stalinism, Cosmopolitanism, and the Evolution of Soviet Culture, 1931–1941*. Cambridge, MA: Harvard University Press, 2011.

——. *Petersburg: Crucible of Cultural Revolution*. Cambridge, MA: Harvard University Press, 1996.

Cooper, David L. "Vasilii Zhukovskii as Translator and the Protean Russian Nation." In *Contexts, Subtexts, Pretexts: Literary Translation in Eastern Europe and Russia*, edited by Brian James Baer, 55–77. Amsterdam, Philadelphia: John Benjamins, 2011.

Danylenko, Andrii. "The Ukrainian Bible and the Valuev Circular of July 18, 1863." *Acta Slavica Iaponica* 28 (2010): 1–21.

Dashtents, Khachik. "Shekspir v Armenii" [Shakespeare in Armenia]. In *Masterstvo perevoda*, edited by Kornei Chukovskii, 60–68. Moscow: Sovetskii Pisatel', 1968.

Dekrety Sovetskoi vlasti. T. I [Decrees of the Soviet Power. Vol I]. Moscow: Gosudarstvennoe Izdatel'stvo Politicheskoi Literatury, 1957.

Dekrety Sovetskoi vlasti. T. IV [Decrees of the Soviet Power. Vol IV]. Moscow: Gosudarstvennoe Izdatel'stvo Politicheskoi Literatury, 1968.

"Doklad tov. A. A. Zhdanova o zhurnalakh *Zvezda* i *Leningrad*" [Report of comrade A. A. Zhdanov on the journals *Zvezda* and *Leningrad*], *Pravda*, 225 (10307), September 21, 1946.

Dostoevskii, Fedor. *Polnoe sobranie sochinenii. Kanonicheskie teksty. T. III* [Complete works. Canonical texts. Vol. 3]. Petrozavodsk: Petrozavodsk University, 1997.

Dostoevsky, Fyodor. *Writer's Diary. Vol. I: 1873-1878*. Translated by Kenneth Lantz. Edited by Gary Saul Morson. Evanston, IL: Northwestern University Press, 1994.

Dzhanibekov, Vladimir. "Verit' budushchemu" [Believing in the future]. Introduction to *O skitan'iakh vechnykh i o Zemle* by Rei Bredberi, 3–4. Moscow: Pravda, 1987.

Efimov, Boris. *Sud'ba zhurnalista* [The fate of a journalist]. Moscow: Pravda, 1988.

Eichenbaum, Boris. "Teoriia formal'nogo metoda" [Theory of the formal method]. In *O literature* by Boris Eichenbaum, 375–408. Moscow: Sovetskii Pisatel', 1987.

Elistratova, Anna. *Bairon* [Byron]. Moscow: AN SSSR, 1956.

Etkind, Efim. *Poeziia i perevod* [Poetry and translation]. Moscow-Leningrad: Sovetskii Pisatel', 1963.

———. *Razgovor o stikhakh* [A talk about poems]. Moscow: Detskaia Literatura, 1970.

———. *Russkie poety-perevodchiki ot Trediakovskogo do Pushkina* [Russian poet-translators from Trediakovskii to Pushkin]. Leningrad: Nauka, 1973.

———. *Zapiski nezagovorshchika [Notes of a Non-Conspirator]*. Kharkiv: Prava Liudini, 2013.

Evtushenko, Evgenii. *Vse poemy*. Moscow: Zebra E, 2015.

Faulz, Dzhon [Fowles, John]. *Liubovnitsa frantsuzskogo leitenanta* [The French lieutenant's mistress]. Translated from English by Meri Bekker and Irina Komarova. St. Petersburg: Khudozhestvennaia Literatura, 1993.

———. *Podruga frantsuzskogo leitenanta* [The French lieutenant's girlfriend]. Translated from English by Meri Bekker and Irina Komarova. Leningrad: Khudozhestvennaia Literatura, 1985.

Fedorov, Andrei. *Vvedenie v teoriiu perevoda* [Introduction to the theory of translation]. Moscow: Izdatel'stvo Literatury na Inostrannykh Iazykakh, 1953.

———. *Iskusstvo perevoda i zhizn' literatury* [Art of translation and life of literature]. Leningrad: Sovetskii Pisatel', 1983.

———. *Osnovy obshchei teorii perevoda (lingvisticheskie problemy)*

[Fundamentals of the general translation theory (linguistic problems)]. Moscow: Vysshaia Shkola, 1983.

Folkner, Uil'iam [Faulkner, William]. *Avessalom, Avessalom!* [*Absalom, Absalom!*]. Translated by Meri Bekker. *Novyi mir* 9–10 (1980).

Forrester, Sibelan. "The Water of Life. Resuscitating Russian Avant-Garde Authors in Croatian and Serbian Translations." In *Contexts, Subtexts, Pretexts: Literary Translation in Eastern Europe and Russia*, edited by Brian James Baer, 117–36. Amsterdam/Philadelphia: John Benjamins, 2011.

Foucault, Michel. *The History of Sexuality. Volume 1: An Introduction.* New York: Random House, 1978.

Fowles, John. *The French Lieutenant's Woman.* London: Vintage, 1996.

Friedberg, Maurice. *Literary Translation in Russia: A Cultural History.* University Park: Pennsylvania State University Press, 1997.

Gal', Nora. *Slovo zhivoe i mertvoe* [The word living and dead]. Moscow: Vremia, 2007.

Gao, Khu. *Perevodnaia kitaiskaia kniga v SSSR, 1949–1990 gg.: Problemy izdaniia i tematiko-tipologicheskii analiz* [The translated Chinese book in the USSR, 1949–1990: Publishing problems and a thematical and typographical analysis]. Moskovskii gosudarstvennyi universitet kul'tury i iskusstv, 2001.

Gavruk, Iurii. "Nuzhen li novyi perevod *Gamleta* na russkii iazyk?" [Is a new translation of *Hamlet* into the Russian language needed?]. In *Masterstvo perevoda*, edited by Kornei Chukovskii, 119–33. Moscow: Sovetskii Pisatel', 1968.

Genzler, Edwin, and Maria Tymoczko, eds. *Translation and Power.* Amherst: University of Massachusetts Press, 2002.

Gogol, Nikolai. *Perepiska N.V. Gogolia v dvukh tomakh. T. 1* [Correspondence of N. V. Gogol in two volumes. Vol. 1] Moscow: Khudozhestvennaia Literatura, 1988.

Goriaeva, Tat'iana. *Politicheskaia tsenzura v SSSR. 1917–1991 gg.* [Political censorship in the USSR. 1917–1991.] Moscow: ROSSPEN, 2009.

Gor'kii, Maksim. "Iz pis'ma k K. I. Chukovskomu" [From a letter to K. I. Chukovskii]. In *Perevod—sredstvo vzaimnogo sblizheniia narodov: Khudozhestvennaia publitsistika*, edited by Anatolii Klyshko, 302. Moscow: Progress, 1987.

———. "Iz zametok" [From the sketchbook]. In *Perevod—sredstvo vzaimnogo sblizheniia narodov: Khudozhestvennaia publitsistika*, edited by Anatolii Klyshko, 289–300. Moscow: Progress, 1987.

———. "O rabote neumeloi, nebrezhnoi, nedobrosovestnoi" [Upon the work unskillful, negligent, slack]. In *Perevod—sredstvo vzaimnogo sblizheniia narodov: Khudozhestvennaia publitsistika*, edited by Anatolii Klyshko, 302–3. Moscow: Progress, 1987.

Gorkii, Maxim. "World literature." In *Russian Writers on Translation: An Anthology*. Edited by Brian James Baer and Natalia Olshanskaya, 65–66. Manchester: St. Jerome, 2013.

Green, Jonathon, and Nicholas J. Karolides. *Encyclopedia of Censorship, New Edition*. New York: Facts on File, 2005.

Hatim, Basil, and Ian Mason. *The Translator as Communicator*. London and New York: Taylor & Francis, 2005.

Hemingway, Ernest. *For Whom the Bell Tolls*. Harmondsworth: Penguin Books, 1966.

Hornsby, Robert. *Protest, Reform and Repression in Khrushchev's Soviet Union*. Cambridge: Cambridge University Press, 2013.

Iasin, Evgenii. "Shestidesiatniki: nostal'giia ili aktual'nost'?" [Shestide-syatniks: nostalgia or reality?] In *Shestidesiatniki*, edited by Mark Barbakadze, 5–13. Moscow: Fond Liberal'naia Missiia, 2007.

Iasnov, Mikhail [Yasnov, Mikhail], ed. *El'ga L'vovna Linetskaia (1909–1997). Materialy k biografii. Iz literaturnogo naslediia. Vospominaniia. Bibliografiia. Fotodokumenty* [El'ga L'vovna Linetskaia (1909–1997). Biographic materials. From Literary Heritage. Memoirs. Bibliography. Photographs]. St. Petersburg: Simpozium, 1999.

———. "*Khranitel' chuzhogo nasledstva* . . . Zametki o leningradskoi (peterburgskoi) shkole khudozhestvennogo perevoda" ["The keeper of foreign possessions . . ." Notes of the Leningrad (St. Petersburg) school of literary translation]. *Inostrannaia literatura* 12 (2010): 222–41.

———. "Uroki frantsuzskogo" [Lessons of French]. *Sobaka.ru* 11 (2008). http://kn.sobaka.ru/n71/05.html.

Iur'ev, Oleg [Jurjew, Oleg]. "Gorlitsa sovetskoi nochi" [The turtledove of the Soviet night]. *Booknik*, January 23, 2009. http://booknik.ru /today/reports/gorlitsa-sovetskoy-nochi.

Ivanovskii, Ignatii. "Vospominaniia o Mikhaile Lozinskom" [Memoirs of Mikhail Lozinskii]. *Neva* 7 (2005): 197–207.

———. "Fragmenty (iz knigi *Pochtovaia loshad'*)" [Fragments (from the book *Stage Horse*]. *Zarubezhnye zapiski* 7 (2006): 137–45.

———. "Fragmenty (iz knigi *Pochtovaia loshad'*)" [Fragments (from the book *Stage Horse*]. *Zarubezhnye zapiski* 8 (2006): 138–48.

Kapote, Truman [Capote, Truman]. *Zavtrak u Tiffani* [*Breakfast at Tiffany's*]. Translated from English by Viktor Golyshev. *Moskva* 4 (1965): 97–137.

Karatzogianni, Athina, and Andrew Robinson. *Power, Resistance and Conflict in the Contemporary World: Social Movements and Hierarchies.* London and New York: Routledge, 2009.

Kashkin, Ivan. "Lozhnyi printsip i nepriemlemye rezul'taty (O bukvalizme v russkikh perevodakh Ch. Dikkensa)" [The false principle and unacceptable results (Upon bukvalism in the Russian translations of C. Dickens)]. In *Dlia chitatelia-sovremennika (Stat'i i issledovaniia)* by Ivan Kashkin, 377–410. Moscow: Sovetskii Pisatel', 1968.

———. "Traditsiia i epigonstvo (Ob odnom perevode baironovskogo "Don-Zhuana")" [Tradition and epigony (on one translation of Byron's *Don Juan*)]. In *Dlia chitatelia-sovremennika (Stat'i i issledovaniia)* by Ivan Kashkin, 411–34. Moscow: Sovetskii Pisatel', 1968.

———. "V bor'be za realisticheskii perevod" [In the struggle for the realistic translation]. In *Dlia chitatelia-sovremennika (Stat'i i issledovaniia)* by Ivan Kashkin, 473–513. Moscow: Sovetskii Pisatel', 1968.

———. "Voprosy perevoda" [Questions of translation]. In *Dlia chitatelia-sovremennika (Stat'i i issledovaniia)* by Ivan Kashkin, 435–72. Moscow: Sovetskii Pisatel', 1968.

Khaksli, Oldos [Huxley, Aldous]. *O divnyi, novyi mir* [*Brave New World*]. Translated from English by Osiia Soroka. In *Antiutopii XX veka: Evgenii Zamiatin, Oldos Khaksli, Dzhordzh Oruell*, 131–271. Moscow: Knizhnaia Palata, 1989.

Kheminguei, Ernest [Hemingway, Ernest]. *Po kom zvonit kolokol* [*For Whom the Bell Tolls*]. Translated by Natalia Volzhina and Evgeniia

Kalashnikova. In *Sobranie sochinenii. T. 3* by Ernest Kheminguei, 107–610. Moscow: Khudozhestvennaia Literatura, 1968.

———. *Po kom zvonit kolokol. Na angliiskom iazyke [For Whom the Bell Tolls.* In English]. Moscow: Progress, 1981.

Kesey, Ken. *One Flew Over the Cuckoo's Nest.* New York: Viking Press, 1970.

Kipling, Red'iard [Kipling, Rudyard]. *Izbrannye stikhi* [Selected poems]. Edited by Valentin Stenich. Leningrad: Khudozhestvennaia Literatura, 1936.

———. *Red'iard Kipling v perevodakh Bena i Betaki* [Rudyard Kipling in translations of Ben and Betaki]. Paris: Ritm, 1986.

———. *Stikhotvoreniia* [Poems]. Translated by Ada Onoshkovich-Iatsyna. Petrograd: Mysl', 1922.

———. *Stikhotvoreniia. Roman. Rasskazy* [Poems. A novel. Short stories]. Edited by Evgenii Vitkovskii. Moscow: Ripol Klassik, 1998.

Kipling, Rudyard. *The Complete Verse.* London: Kyle Cathie Limited, 1990.

———. *Mine Own People: The Works of Rudyard Kipling.* New York, Philadelphia, Chicago: Nottingham Society, 1909.

Komarova, Irina. Translator's Note to *Vse, krome nas s toboi: Sto izbrannykh stikhotvorenii* by Ogden Nash, translated by Irina Komarova, 3–8. Leningrad: Lenizdat, 1988.

"Konstitutsiia (Osnovnoi Zakon) Rossiiskoi Sotsialisticheskoi Federativnoi Sovetskoi Respubliki, priniataia 5 Vserossiiskim S"ezdom Sovetov v zasedanii ot 10 iiulia 1918 goda" [Constitution (Fundamental Law) of the Russian Socialist Federative Soviet Republic passed by the Fifth All-Russian Congress of Soviets in the Session of 10 July 1918]. In *Pervaia Sovetskaia Konstitutsiia (Konstitutsiia RSFSR 1918 goda). Sbornik dokumentov,* edited by Andrei Vyshinskii, 423–39. Moscow: NKIU SSSR, 1938.

"Konstitutsiia (Osnovnoi Zakon) Soiuza Sovetskikh Sotsialisticheskikh Respublik 1977/Redaktsiia ot 24 iiunia 1981 goda" [Constitution (Fundamental Law) of the Union of Soviet Socialist Republics 1977/revised July 24, 1981]. In *Konstitutsiia (Osnovnoi Zakon) Soiuza Sovetskikh Sotsialisticheskikh Respublik, Konstitutsii (Osnovnye*

Zakony) Soiuznykh Sovetskikh Sotsialisticheskikh Respublik, 3–49. Moscow: Izvestiia Sovetov Narodnykh Deputatov SSSR, 1985.

Korolenko, Vladimir. *Stat'i, retsenzii, ocherki* [Articles, reviews, essays]. Moscow: Direkt-Media, 2014.

Kostadinova, Vitana. "Meaningful Absences: Byron in Bulgarian." In *Contexts, Subtexts, Pretexts: Literary Translation in Eastern Europe and Russia,* edited by Brian James Baer, 219–32. Amsterdam/Philadelphia: John Benjamins, 2011.

Kundzich Oleksei. "Perevodcheskii bloknot" [The translator's sketchbook]. In *Masterstvo perevoda,* edited by Kornei Chukovskii, 199–238. Moscow: Sovetskii Pisatel', 1968.

Kuznetsova Ekaterina. "Sposoby ideologicheskoi adaptatsii perevodnogo teksta: O perevode romana E. Khemingueia *Po kom zvonit kolokol*" [Means of ideological adaptation of the translated text: towards the translation of the novel of E. Hemingway *For Whom the Bell Tolls*]. *Logos* 3 (2012): 153–71.

Kviatkovskaia, Maiia, trans. *Poesiás ibericas: Perevody Maii Kviatkovskoi s ispanskogo, portugal'skogo, katalanskogo i galisiiskogo iazykov* [Poesiás Ibericas: translations of Maiia Kviatkovskaia from the Spanish, Catalan, and Gallegan languages]. St. Petersburg: Znak, 2013.

——, trans. *Poetas latinoamericanos: Poety Latinskoi Ameriki v perevodakh Maii Kviatkovskoi* [Poetas Latinoamericanos: poets of Latin America in Translations of Maiia Kviatkovskaia]. St. Petersburg: Znak, 2014.

La Guma, Aleks [La Guma, Alex]. *Skitaniia v nochi [A Walk in the Night].* Translated by Solomon Guterman. Moscow: Progress, 1964.

——. *Izbrannoe* [Selected works]. Moscow: Pravda, 1985.

Lange, Anne. "Performative Translation Options under the Soviet Regime." *Journal of Baltic Studies* 3 (2012): 401–20.

Lapidus, Gail W. "The Nationality Question and the Soviet System." *Proceedings of the Academy of Political Science* 3 (1984): 98–112.

Lefevere, André, ed. *Translation/History/Culture: A Sourcebook.* London and New York: Routledge, 1992.

——. *Translation, Rewriting and the Manipulation of Literary Fame.* London: Routledge, 1992.

Lefevere, André, and Susan Bassnett. "Where Are We in Translation Studies?" Introduction to *Constructing Cultures: Essays on Literary Translation*, edited by Susan Bassnett and André Lefevere, 1–11. Clevedon: Multilingual Matters, 1998.

Lenin, Vladimir. "Ocherednye zadachi Sovetskoi vlasti" [Immediate tasks of the Soviet power]. In *Polnoe sobranie sochinenii. T. 36*, by Vladimir Lenin, 165–208. Moscow: Izdatel'stvo Politicheskoi Literatury, 1974.

———. "O proletarskoi kul'ture" [On proletariat culture]. In *O literature i iskusstve*, by Vladimir Lenin, 444–45. Moscow: Khudozhestvennaia Literatura, 1976.

———. "O znachenii voinstvuiushchego materializma" [Toward the importance of warring materialism]. In *Polnoe sobranie sochinenii. T. 45*, by Vladimir Lenin, 23–33. Moscow: Izdatel'stvo Politicheskoi Literatury, 1970.

———. "Partiinaia organizatsiia i partiinaia literatura" [Party organization and party literature]. In *O literature i iskusstve*, by Vladimir Lenin, 92–96. Moscow: Khudozhestvennaia Literatura, 1976.

Levik, Vil'gel'm. "Nuzhny li novye perevody Shekspira?" [Are new translations of Shakespeare needed?]. In *Masterstvo perevoda*, edited by Kornei Chukovskii, 93–104. Moscow: Sovetskii Pisatel', 1968.

Linthout, Ine Van. *Das Buch in der nationalsozialistischen Propagandapolitik* [The book in the National Socialist propaganda politics]. Berlin/Boston: Walter de Gruyter, 2012.

Logosh, Ol'ga. "My do sikh por sovetuemsia s El'goi L'vovnoi Linetskoi" ["We still consult with El'ga L'vovna Linetskaia"]. *Viperson*, January 23, 2009. http://viperson.ru/wind.php?ID=608570.

Lozinskii, Mikhail. "Iskusstvo stikhotvornogo perevoda" [The art of poetic translation]. In *Perevod—sredstvo vzaimnogo sblizheniia narodov: Khudozhestvennaia publitsistika*, edited by Anatolii Klyshko, 91–106. Moscow: Progress, 1987.

Lygo, Emily. *Leningrad Poetry, 1953–1975: The Thaw Generation (Russian Transformations: Literature, Culture and Ideas)*. Bern: Peter Lang, 2010.

Markes, Gabriel' Garsiia [Márquez, Gabriel García]. *Sto let odinochestva* [*One Hundred Years of Solitude*]. Translated by Nina Butyrina and Valerii Stolbov. *Inostrannaia literatura* 6 (1970): 5–69.

———. Sto let odinochestva [*One Hundred Years of Solitude*]. Translated by Nina Butyrina and Valerii Stolbov. *Inostrannaia literatura* 7 (1970): 140–99.

———. *Sto let odinochestva* [*One Hundred Years of Solitude*]. Translated by Nina Butyrina and Valerii Stolbov. Moscow: Khudozhestvennaia Literatura, 1971.

———. *Sto let odinochestva. Povesti i rakksazy* [*One Hundred Years of Solitude*. Short Stories and Novellas]. Moscow: Progress, 1979.

Medvedev, Roi. *Liudi i knigi. Chto chital Stalin? Pisatel' i kniga v totalitarnom obshchestve* [People and books. What did Stalin read? The writer and the book in a totalitarian state]. Moscow: Prava Cheloveka, 2004.

Mesthrie, Rajend, Joan Swann, Ana Deumert, and William L. Leap. *Introducing Sociolinguistics*. Edinburgh: Edinburgh University Press, 2009.

Miller, Aleksei. *"Ukrainskii vopros" v politike vlastei i russkom obshchest-vennom mnenii (vtoraia polovina XIX veka)* [The "Ukrainian question" in state policy and in Russian public opinion (second half of the XIX century)]. St. Petersburg: Aleteiia, 2000.

Miller-Budnitskaia, Rashel'. "Poeziia Red'iarda Kiplinga" [Poetry of Rudyard Kipling]. Introduction to *Izbrannye stikhi* by Red'iard Kipling. Edited by Valentin Stenich, 3–28. Leningrad: Khudozhestvennaia Literatura, 1936.

Mingjian, Zha. "Modern China's Translated Literature." In *A Companion to Modern Chinese Literature*, edited by Yingjin Zhang, 214–27. Southern Gate: John Wiley and Sons, 2015.

Møller, Peter Ulf. *Postlude to "The Kreutzer Sonata": Tolstoj and the Debate on Sexual Morality in Russian Literature in the 1890s*. Translated from Danish by John Krendal. Leiden, New York, Copenhagen, Cologne: E. J. Brill, 1988.

Monticelli, Daniele. "Translation under Totalitarianism. Soviet Estonia, Johannes Semper and Translation History." *Novyi Protei* 1 (2015): 204–9.

Monticelli, Daniele, and Anne Lange. "Translation and Totalitarianism: The Case of Soviet Estonia." *Translator* 20 (2014): 95–111.

Morozov, Mikhail. "*Gamlet* v perevode B. Pasternaka" [*Hamlet* in the translation of B. Pasternak]. *Teatr* 2 (1941): 144–47.

Naiman, Anatolii. *Rasskazy o Anne Ahmatovoi* [Stories about Anna Akhmatova]. Moscow: AST: Zebra E, 2008.

"Nase s'ogodni" (Our today), *Vaplite* 3 (1927): 131–40.

Neliubin, Lev, and Georgii Khukhuni. *Nauka o perevode (istoriia i teoriia s drevneishikh vremen do nashikh dnei)* [The science of translation (history and theory from the ancient times until our days)]. Moscow: Flinta MPSI, 2006.

Nemirovskii, Evgenii, and Viktor Kharlamov. *Istoriia knigi v SSSR. 1917–1921. T. 1* [History of the book in the USSR. 1917–1921. Vol. 1]. Moscow: Kniga, 1983.

O partiinoi i sovetskoi pechati, radioveshchanii i televidenii. Sbornik dokumentov i materialov [Of party and Soviet press, radiobroadcasting, and television. Collection of documents and materials], edited by L. Klimanova. Moscow: Mysl', 1972.

Pasternak, Boris. "Zametki o perevode" [Notes about translation]. In *Masterstvo perevoda*, edited by Kornei Chukovskii, 105–10. Moscow: Sovetskii Pisatel', 1968.

Phillipson, Robert. *Linguistic Imperialism*. Oxford: Oxford University Press, 2003.

Pokorn, Nike K. *Post-Socialist Translation Practices: Ideological Struggle in Children's Literature*. Amsterdam/Philadelphia: John Benjamins Publishing, 2012.

Popper, Karl. *The Open Society and Its Enemies*. Abingdon: Routledge Classics, 2011.

Pribytkov, Viktor. *Glavlit i tsenzura: Zapiski zamestitelia nachal'nika Glavnogo upravleniia po okhrane gosudarstvennykh tain v pechati pri Sovete ministrov SSSR* [Glavlit and censorship: notes of the Deputy Chief on the Main Administration for the Protection of State Secrets in the Press under the USSR Council of Ministers]. Moscow: Molodaia Gvardiia, 2014.

Pushkin, Aleksandr. *Polnoe sobranie sochinenii v desiati tomakh. T. 7. Kritika i publitsistika* [The complete works in ten volumes. Vol. 7. Literary criticism and journalism]. Leningrad: Nauka, 1978.

———. *Polnoe sobranie sochinenii v desiati tomakh. T. 10. Pis'ma [The complete works in ten volumes. Vol. 10. Letters].* Leningrad: Nauka, 1979.

Rayfield, Donald. *Anton Chekhov: A Life.* Evanston: Northwestern University Press, 1998.

Rossiiskii Gosudarstvennyi Arkhiv Noveishei Istorii. F. 89. Op. 6. Dok. 2.

Rodari, Dzhanni [Rodari, Gianni]. *Prikliucheniia Chipollino* [Adventures of Cipollino]. Translated by Zlata Potapova. Moscow: Detgiz, 1955.

Rossel's, Vladimir. "Estafeta slova" [The relay race of the word]. In *Skol'ko vesit slovo: Stat'i* by Vladimir Rossel's, 6–43. Moscow: Sovetskii Pisatel', 1984.

———. "Znanie, talant, trud" [Knowledge, talent, labor]. In *Skol'ko vesit slovo: Stat'i* by Vladimir Rossel's, 44–126. Moscow: Sovetskii Pisatel', 1984.

Rudnyckyj, Jaroslav. "Ukrainian Linguistics in Exile (1918–1984)." In *Papers in the History of Linguistics: Proceedings of the Third International Conference on the History of Language Sciences,* edited by Hans Aarsleff, Louis G. Kelly, and Hans-Josef Niederehe, 637–46. Amsterdam: John Benjamins, 1987.

Salinger, J. D. *The Catcher in the Rye.* New York: Modern Library, 1958.

Schäffner, Christina. "Politics and Translation." In *A Companion to Translation Studies,* edited by Piotr Kuhiwczak and Karin Littau, 134–47. Clevedon: Multilingual Matters, 2007.

Selindzher, Dzherom [Salinger, Jerome]. *Nad propast'iu vo rzhi [The Catcher in the Rye].* Translated by Rita Rait-Kovaleva. In *Nad propast'iu vo rzhi; Povesti; Deviat' rasskazov* by Dzherom Selindzher, 19–180. Moscow: Khudozhestvennaia Literatura, 1983.

Semenenko, Aleksei. *Hamlet the Sign: Russian Translations of Hamlet and Literary Canon Formation.* Stockholm: Stockholm Universitet, 2007.

———. "Smuggling the Other: Rita Rait-Kovaleva's Translation of J. D. Salinger's *The Catcher in the Rye.*" *Translation and Interpreting Studies* 1 (2016): 64–80.

Sherry, Samantha. *Discourses of Regulation and Resistance: Censoring Translation in the Stalin and Khrushchev Era Soviet Union.* Edinburgh: Edinburgh University Press, 2015.

Shekspir, Vil'iam [Shakespeare, William]. *Gamlet, prints datskii [Hamlet, Prince of Denmark]*. Translated by Boris Pasternak. Moscow: Goslitizdat, 1941.

———. *Tragicheskaia istoriia o Gamlete, printse datskom [The Tragedy of Hamlet, Prince of Denmark]*. Translated by Mikhail Lozinskii. Moscow: Goslitizdat, 1933.

Shkarovskii, Mikhail. "Russkaia Pravoslavnaia Tserkov' i religioznaia politika sovetskogo gosudarstva v gody voiny" [Russian Orthodox Church and religious policy of the Soviet state in the years of war]. *Khristianskoe chtenie* 12 (1996): 26–53.

Shklovskii, Viktor. *O teorii prozy* [Toward the theory of prose]. Moscow: Sovetskii Pisatel', 1983.

Shomrakova, Inga, and Iosif Barenbaum. *Vseobshchaia istoriia knigi* [The world history of the book]. St. Petersburg: Professiia, 2005.

Simonov, Konstantin. "Ispanskaia tema v tvorchestve Khemingueia [The Spanish theme in the works of Hemingway]. Introduction to *Sobranie sochinenii T. 3*, by Ernest Kheminguei, 5–16. Moscow: Khudozhestvennaia Literatura, 1968.

Solzhenitsyn, Aleksandr. *In the First Circle*. Translated by Harry T. Willetts. New York: Harper Perennial, 2009.

Spolsky, Bernard. *Language Policy. Key Topics in Sociolinguistics*. Cambridge: Cambridge University Press, 2004.

Sridhar, Kamal K. "Societal Multilingualism." In *Sociolinguistics and Language Teaching*, edited by Sandra Lee McKay and Nancy H. Hornberger, 47–70. Cambridge: Cambridge University Press, 1996.

Stairon, Uil'iam [Styron, William]. *I podzheg etot dom [Set This House on Fire]*. Translated by Viktor Golyshev. *Novyi mir* 1–6 (1985).

Steinle, Pamela Hunt. *In Cold Fear: The Catcher in the Rye Censorship Controversies and Postwar American Character*. Columbus: Ohio State University Press, 2000.

Strikha, Maksim. *Ukrains'kii khudozhnii pereklad: mizh literaturoiu i natsietvorenniam* [Ukrainian literary translation: between literature and nation-building]. Kiiv: Fakt-Nash Chas, 2006.

Strizhenko, Adel'. *Iazyk i ideologicheskaia bor'ba* [Language and ideological struggle]. Irkutsk: Izdatel'stvo Irkutskogo Universiteta, 1988.

Sturge, Kate. "Censorship of Translated Fiction in Nazi Germany." *TTR: Traduction, Terminologie, Rédaction* 2 (2002): 153–69.

Styron, William. *Set This House on Fire*. New York: Random House, 1960.

Sukhikh, Igor'. "Tynianov i Kiukhlia: izbiratel'noe srodstvo [Tynianov and Kiukhlia: The selective affinity]. *Zarubezhnye zapiski* 4 (2008): 174–81.

Terterian, Inna, and Lev Ospovat, eds. *Ispanskie poety XX veka* [Spanish poets of the twentieth century]. Moscow: Khudozhestvennaia Literatura, 1977.

Thornberry, Robert. "On the 'Built-In Obsolescence' of Literary Translation." In *On Translating French Literature and Film. Vol. 1*, edited by Geoffrey T. Harris, 145–60. Amsterdam/Atlanta: Rodopi, 1996.

Toporov, Viktor. *Dvoinoe dno. Priznaniia skandalista* [False bottom: Confessions of a trouble-maker]. Moscow: Zakharov, AST, 1999.

Toury, Gideon. *Descriptive Translation Studies and Beyond*. Amsterdam/Philadelphia: John Benjamins, 1995.

Tymoczko, Maria. *Enlarging Translation, Empowering Translators*. Manchester, UK, and Kinderhook, NY: St. Jerome Publishing, 2010.

———. "Postcolonial Writing and Literary Translation." In *Postcolonial Translation: Theory and Practice*, edited by Susan Bassnett and Harish Trivedi, 19–40. London and New York: Routledge, 1999.

———. "Translation, Ethics and Ideology in a Violent Globalizing World." In *Globalization, Political Violence and Translation*, edited by Esperanza Bielsa and Christopher W. Hughes, 171–94. London: Palgrave Macmillan, 2009.

———. "Translation, Ideology and Creativity." *Linguistics Antverpiensia. Translation as Creation: The Postcolonial Influence* 2 (2003): 27–45.

Uorren, Robert Penn [Warren, Robert Penn]. *Potop* [*Flood*]. Translated by Elena Golysheva. *Novyi mir* 4–8 (1982).

Usova, Galina. *I Bairona v soavtory voz'mu. Kniga o Tat'iane Grigor'evne Gnedich* [And we coauthor: Byron and myself. A book about Tat'iana Grigor'evna Gnedich]. St. Petersburg: DEAN, 2012.

Ustav Soiuza pisatelei SSSR [Charter of the Union of Writers of the USSR]. Moscow: Tipografiia "Literaturnoi Gazety," 1971.

"Ustav Soiuza Sovetskih Pisatelei SSSR" [Charter of the Union of Soviet

Writers of the USSR]. *In Pervyi Vsesoiuznyi S''ezd Sovetskikh Pisatelei 1934: Stenograficheskii otchet*, 712–14. Moscow: Khudozhestvennaia Literatura, 1934.

Uvarov, Valentin. "Paradoksy rolevogo povedeniia uchastnikov situatsii perevoda" [Paradoxes of the role behavior of the translation situation participants]. In *Tetradi perevodchika. Vyp. 18*, edited by Leonid Barkhudarov, 13–15. Moscow: Mezhdunarodnye Otnosheniia, 1981.

Van Dijk, Teun A. *Ideology. A Multidisciplinary Approach*. London/ Thousand Oaks/New Delhi: SAGE Publications, 1998.

———. "Ideology and Discourse Analysis." *Journal of Political Ideologies* 2 (2006): 115–40.

Venuti, Lawrence. *The Translator's Invisibility*. Taylor & Francis e-library, 2004.

Vid, Natalia Kaloh. "Censorship and Ideology in Literary Translations: The Case of Robert Burns Poetry in the Soviet Union." In *Perspectives in Translation Studies*, edited by Floriana Popescu, 77–94. Cambridge: Cambridge Scholars Publishing, 2009.

Vil'iam-Vil'mont, Nikolai. "*Gamlet* v perevode Borisa Pasternaka" [*Hamlet* in the translation of Boris Pasternak]. *Internatsional'naia literatura* 7–8 (1940): 284–85.

Vinthagen, Stellan, and Anna Johansson. "Everyday Resistance: Exploration of a Concept and Its Theories." *Resistance Studies Magazine* 1 (2013). www.rsmag.org.

Vitkovskii, Evgenii [Witkowsky, Evgenii]. "Imperiia po imeni Red'iard Kipling" [The empire named Rudyard Kipling]. Introduction to *Stikhotvoreniia. Roman. Rasskazy*, by Red'iard Kipling. Edited by Evgenii Vitkovskii, 5–20. Moscow: Ripol Klassik, 1998.

Vitkovskii, Evgenii [Witkowsky, Evgenii], ed. *Sem' vekov angliiskoi poezii: 3 t.* [Seven centuries of English poetry: 3 vol.]. Moscow: Vodoley Publishers, 2007.

———, ed. *Sem' vekov frantsuzskoi poezii v russkikh perevodakh* [Seven centuries of French poetry in Russian translations]. St. Petersburg: Evraziia, 1999.

———, trans. *Vechnyi slushatel': Sem' stoletii poezii v perevode Evgeniia Vitkovskogo. V 2 t.* [The eternal listener: seven centuries of poetry in translation of Evgenii Vitkovskii. In 2 vol.]. Moscow: Vodoley Publishers, 2013.

———, ed. *Vek perevoda: Antologiia russkogo poeticheskogo perevoda XXI veka* [Age of translation: anthology of Russian poetic translation of the twenty-first century]. Moscow: Vodoley Publishers, 2006.

———, ed. *Vek perevoda: Antologiia russkogo poeticheskogo perevoda XXI veka. Vtoroe desiatiletie* [Age of translation: anthology of Russian poetic translation of the twenty-first century. Second decade]. Moscow: Vodoley Publishers, 2012.

Vodop'ianova, Zoia, and Tat'iana Goriaeva, eds. *Istoriia sovetskoi politicheskoi tsenzury: Dokumenty i kommentarii* [History of Soviet political censorship: documents and commentaries]. Moscow: ROSSPEN, 1997.

Volchkevich, Maiia. *"Chaika". Komediia zabluzhdenii* ["Seagull." A comedy of errors]. Moscow: Probel, 2010.

Vulpius, Ricarda. "Language Policy in the Russian Empire: A Case of Translation of the Bible into Ukrainian, 1860–1906." *Ab Imperio* 2 (2005): 191–224.

Vonnegut, Kurt. *Cat's Cradle.* New York: A Delta Book, 1964.

West, Nathanael. *The Complete Works of Nathanael West.* New York: Farrar, Straus and Cudahy, 1957.

Witt, Susanna. "Between the Lines: Totalitarianism and Translation in the USSR." In *Contexts, Subtexts, and Pretexts: Literary Translation in Eastern Europe and Russia,* edited by Brian James Baer, 149–70. Amsterdam: John Benjamins, 2011.

———. "Byron's *Don Juan* in Russian and the 'Soviet School of Translation.'" *Translation and Interpreting Studies* 1 (2016): 23–43.

Zabolotskii, Nikolai. "Translator's Notes." In *Russian Writers on Translation: An Anthology,* edited by Brian James Baer and Natalia Olshanskaya, 109–10. Manchester: St. Jerome, 2013.

———. "Zametki perevodchika" [Translator's notes]. In *Perevod— sredstvo vzaimnogo sblizheniia narodov: Khudozhestvennaia publitsistika.* Edited by Anatolii Klyshko, 426–28. Moscow: Progress, 1987.

Zasurskii, Iasen, and Alla Paroiatnikova, eds. *Iazyk i stil' burzhuaznoi propagandy* [Language and style of bourgeois propaganda]. Moscow: Moscow State University, 1988.

Zelenov, Mikhail. "Glavlit i istoricheskaia nauka v 20–30-e gody" [Glavlit and the historic science in the 1920s to '30s]. *Voprosy istorii* 3 (1997): 21–36.

Zezina, Mariia. *Sovetskaia khudozhestvennaia intelligentsiia i vlast' v 1950-e—60-e gody* [Soviet artistic intelligentsia and power in the 1950s to the 1960s]. Moscow: Dialog-MGU, 1999.

Zhang, Mei. "Translation Manipulated by Ideology and Poetics—A Case Study of 'The Jade Mountain.'" *Theory and Practice in Language Studies* 2 (2012): 754–58.

Zhirkov, Gennadii. *Istoriia tsenzury v Rossii XIX—XX vv.* [History of censorship in Russia in XIX–XX c.]. Moscow: Aspekt Press, 2001.

Zhirmunskii, Viktor. "K voprosu o formal'nom metode" [Toward the question of the formal method]. In *Teoriia literatury. Poetika. Stilistika* by Viktor Zhirmunskii, 94–105. Leningrad: Nauka, 1977.

Zverev, Aleksei. "Dzhek London: Velichie talanta i paradoksy sud'by" [Jack London: greatness of talent and paradoxes of fate]. Introduction to *Rasskazy*, by Dzhek London, 3–16. Moscow: Pravda, 1984.

DICTIONARIES

Bol'shaia Sovetskaia Entsiklopediia. T. 10 [Big Soviet encyclopedia. Vol. 10]. Edited by Aleksandr Prokhorov. Moscow: Sovetskaia Entsiklopediia, 1972.

Bol'shaia Sovetskaia Entsiklopediia. T. 45 [Big Soviet encyclopedia. Vol. 45]. Edited by Sergei Vavilov and Boris Vvedenskii. Moscow: Bol'shaia Sovetskaia Entsiklopediia, 1956.

Bol'shaia Sovetskaia Entsiklopediia. T. 58 [Big Soviet encyclopedia. Vol. 1580]. Edited by Otto Schmidt. Moscow: OGIZ RSFSR, 1936.

Bol'shoi akademicheskii slovar' russkogo iazyka. T. 9 [Big academic dictionary of the Russian language. Vol. 9]. Edited by Kirill Gorbachevich. Moscow-St. Petersburg: Nauka, 2007.

Bol'shoi rossiiskii entsiklopedicheskii slovar' [Big Russian encyclopedic dictionary]. Moscow: Bol'shaia Rossiiskaia Entsiklopediia, 2005.

Bol'shoj tolkovyj slovar' russkogo iazyka [Definition dictionary of the Russian language]. Edited by Sergei Kuznetsov. St. Petersburg: Norint, 1998.

Dal', Vladimir. *Tolkovyi slovar' zhivogo velikorusskogo iazyka. T. 4* [Definition dictionary of the living Great Russian language. Vol. 4]. Edited by Ivan Boduen-de-Kurtene. St. Petersburg-Moscow: Tovarishchestvo M.O. Vol'f, 1909.

Elistratov, Vladimir. *Slovar' russkogo argo* [Dictionary of Russian argot]. Moscow: Russkie Slovari, 2000.

Kratkaia literaturnaia entsiklopediia. T. 2 [Brief literary encyclopedia. Vol. 2]. Edited by Aleksei Surkov. Moscow: Sovetskaia Entsiklopediia, 1964.

Literaturnaia entsiklopediia [Literary encyclopedia]. Moscow: Izdatel'stvo Kommunisticheskoi Akademii, 1931. http://dic.aca demic.ru/dic.nsf/enc_literature/2285.

Slovar' sovremennogo russkogo literaturnogo iazyka. T. 5 [Dictionary of the modern literary Russian language. Vol. 5]. Edited by Stepan Barkhudarov and Viktor Vinogradov. Moscow-Leningrad: Izdatel'stvo Akademii Nauk SSSR, 1956.

Slovar' sovremennogo russkogo literaturnogo iazyka. T. 6. [Dictionary of the modern literary Russian language. Vol. 6]. Edited by Aleksandr Babkin. Moscow-Leningrad: Izdatel'stvo Akademii Nauk SSSR, 1957.

NOTES

Introduction: A Round Unvarnished Tale of the Whole Course of Love

1. Samantha Sherry, *Discourses of Regulation and Resistance: Censoring Translation in the Stalin and Khrushchev Era Soviet Union* (Edinburgh: Edinburgh University Press, 2015), 1.
2. André Lefevere, ed., *Translation/History/Culture: A Sourcebook* (London and New York: Routledge, 1992), 11.
3. Edwin Gentzler and Maria Tymoczko, eds., *Translation and Power* (Amherst: University of Massachusetts Press, 2002), xxi.
4. www.vekperevoda.com. This website contains an extensive collection of the Russian poetic translation heritage from the end of the nineteenth century to the present time. It includes works of over a thousand translators.

Chapter 1: The Closed Society and Its Literary Translation Practices

1. Maria Tymoczko, "Translation, Ideology and Creativity," *Linguistica Antverpiensia* 2 (2003): 29.
2. Teun A. Van Dijk, *Ideology: A Multidisciplinary Approach* (London/Thousand Oaks/New Delhi: SAGE Publications, 1998), 2, 69.
3. María Calzada-Pérez, introduction to *Apropos of Ideology*, ed. María Calzada-Pérez (Manchester: St. Jerome, 2003), 3–4.
4. Calzada-Pérez, "Introduction," 5
5. Van Dijk, *Ideology*, 8–9, 29, 313.
6. Basil Hatim and Ian Mason, *The Translator as Communicator* (London and New York: Taylor & Francis, 2005), 120; Mei Zhang, "Translation Manipulated by Ideology and Poetics: A Case Study of *The Jade Mountain*," *Theory and Practice in Language Studies* 2 (2012): 754.
7. Maria Tymoczko, "Translation, Ethics and Ideology in a Violent Globalizing World," in *Globalization, Political Violence and Translation*, ed. Esperanza Bielsa and Christopher W. Hughes (London: Palgrave Macmillan, 2009), 183.

8. André Lefevere and Susan Bassnett, "Where Are We in Translation Studies?" introduction to *Constructing Cultures: Essays on Literary Translation*, ed. Susan Bassnett and André Lefevere (Clevedon: Multilingual Matters, 1998), 7.

9. Gideon Toury, *Descriptive Translation Studies and Beyond* (Amsterdam/Philadelphia: John Benjamins, 1995), 27.

10. André Lefevere, ed. *Translation/History/Culture: A Sourcebook* (London and New York: Routledge, 1992), 14.

11. Daniel Bell, *The End of Ideology: On the Exhaustion of Political Ideas in the Fifties* (Cambridge, MA, and London: Harvard University Press, 1962), 435–36.

12. *Slovar' sovremennogo russkogo literaturnogo iazyka. T. 5*, ed. Stepan Barkhudarov and Viktor Vinogradov (Moscow-Leningrad: Izdatel'stvo Akademii Nauk SSSR, 1956).

13. *Bol'shaia sovetskaia entsiklopediia. T. 10*, ed. Aleksandr Prokhorov (Moscow: Sovetskaia Entsiklopediia, 1972).

14. *Bol'shoi rossiiskii entsiklopedicheskii slovar'* (Moscow: Bol'shaia Rossiiskaia Entsiklopediia, 2005).

15. Bell, *The End of Ideology*, xi.

16. The term *communist ideology* is used, for instance, in Roxana-Mihaela Antochi, "Communist Ideology and Drama Translation in Romania," in *Aspects of Literary Translation: Building Linguistic and Cultural Bridges in Past and Present*, ed. Eva Parra-Membrives, Miguel Ángel García Peinado, and Albrecht Classen (Tübingen: Narr, 2012); Zha Mingjian, "Modern China's Translated Literature," in *A Companion to Modern Chinese Literature*, ed. Yingjin Zhang (Southern Gate: John Wiley and Sons, 2015); Nike K. Pokorn, *Post-socialist Translation Practices: Ideological Struggle in Children's Literature* (Amsterdam/Philadelphia: John Benjamins Publishing, 2012); Natalia Kaloh Vid, "Censorship and Ideology in Literary Translations: The Case of Robert Burns Poetry in the Soviet Union," in *Perspectives in Translation Studies*, ed. Floriana Popescu (Cambridge: Cambridge Scholars Publishing, 2009). For other terms, see, for example, Hatim and Mason, *The Translator as Communicator*, Christina Schäffner, "Politics and Translation," in *A Companion to Translation Studies*, ed. Piotr Kuhiwczak and Karin Littau (Clevedon: Multilingual Matters, 2007); Robert Thornberry, "On the 'Built-In Obsolescence' of Literary Translation," in *On Translating French Literature and Film. Vol. 1*, ed. Geoffrey T. Harris (Amsterdam/Atlanta: Rodopi, 1996).

17. Lawrence Venuti, *The Translator's Invisibility* (Taylor & Francis e-library, 2004).

18. Van Dijk, *Ideology*, 2. It should be noted, however, that the definition "Ours is the Truth, Theirs is the Ideology" precisely formulated by Van Dijk, finds terminological exceptions in Soviet history. The use of the word *ideology* in the Soviet Union, as was shown above, was directly related to the principles of the universally propagated Marxist-Leninist theory and was therefore used in a positive sense. See, for example, "Giving scientifically grounded solutions for the burning problems of the modern development of society, Marxist-Leninist ideology functions as the theoretical basis of the communist movement, as a powerful weapon of the revolutionary transformation of the world" (*Bol'shaia sovetskaia entsiklopediia*, 1972).

19. Henri Bergson, *Les deux sources de la morale et de la religion* (Paris: Félix Aclan, 1932).

20. Karl Popper, *The Open Society and Its Enemies* (Abingdon: Routledge Classics, 2011), 164.

21. Popper, *Open Society*, 164.
22. Popper, *Open Society*, 165.
23. See Popper, *Open Society*, 274.
24. For the asymmetric principle of multilingualism, see, for instance, Kamal K. Sridhar, "Societal Multilingualism," in *Sociolinguistics and Language Teaching*, ed. Sandra Lee McKay and Nancy H. Hornberger (Cambridge: Cambridge University Press, 1996), 52–56.
25. Robert Phillipson, *Linguistic Imperialism* (Oxford: Oxford University Press, 1992), 53–54.
26. Daniele Monticelli, "Translation under Totalitarianism. Soviet Estonia, Johannes Semper and Translation History," *Novyi Protei* 1 (2015): 205–6.
27. Monticelli, "Translation under Totalitarianism," 205.
28. Cited in "Nase s'ogodni" (Our today), *Vaplite* 3 (1927): 137.
29. Maksim Strikha, *Ukrains'kii khudozhnii pereklad: mizh literaturoiu i natsietvorenniam* (Kiiv: Fakt-Nash Chas, 2006), 208–9.
30. Bernard Spolsky, *Language Policy: Key Topics in Sociolinguistics* (Cambridge: Cambridge University Press, 2004), 65.
31. For more detail, see Susanna Witt, "Between the Lines: Totalitarianism and Translation in the USSR," in *Contexts, Subtexts, and Pretexts: Literary Translation in Eastern Europe and Russia*, ed. Brian James Baer (Amsterdam: John Benjamins, 2011), 156–63.
32. Kate Sturge, "Censorship of Translated Fiction in Nazi Germany," *TTR: Traduction, Terminologie, Rédaction* 2 (2002): 153.
33. Sturge, "Censorship of Translated Fiction in Nazi Germany," 156.
34. Ine Van Linthout, *Das Buch in der nationalsozialistischen Propagandapolitik* (Berlin/Boston: Walter de Gruyter, 2012), 24, 152–56.
35. Monticelli, "Translation under Totalitarianism," 207.
36. Alessandra Calvani, *Traduzioni e traduttori. Gli specchidell'originale* (Padova: Libreriauniversitaria.it Edizioni, 2012), 147.
37. Jonathon Green and Nicholas J. Karolides, *Encyclopedia of Censorship, New Edition* (New York: Facts on File, 2005), 11.
38. Vitana Kostadinova, "Meaningful Absences: Byron in Bulgarian," in *Contexts, Subtexts, Pretexts: Literary Translation in Eastern Europe and Russia*, ed. Brian James Baer (Amsterdam/Philadelphia: John Benjamins, Kostadinova 2011), 242.
39. Kostadinova, "Meaningful Absences," 229–31.
40. Brian James Baer, "Literary Translation and the Construction of a Soviet Intelligentsia," *Massachusetts Review* 3 (2006): 549.
41. Strikha, *Ukrains'kii khudozhnii pereklad*, 16–17, 213–14.
42. Gennadii Zhirkov, *Istoriia tsenzury v Rossii XIX—XX vv.* (Moscow: Aspekt Press, 2001), 31.
43. Maria Tymoczko, "Post-Colonial Writing and Literary Translation," in *Post-Colonial Translation: Theory and Practice*, ed. Susan Bassnett and Harish Trivedi (London and New York: Routledge, 1999), 30–31.
44. Teun A. Van Dijk, "Ideology and Discourse Analysis," *Journal of Political Ideologies* 2 (2006): 129.
45. Maria Tymoczko, *Enlarging Translation, Empowering Translators* (Manchester, UK, and Kinderhook, NY: St. Jerome Publishing, 2010), 208.
46. Mona Baker, *Translation and Conflict: A Narrative Account* (London and New York: Routledge, 2006), 25.

47. Tymoczko, *Enlarging Translation, Empowering Translators*, 196, 210–13.
48. Venuti, *The Translator's Invisibility*, 20.
49. Dimitris Asimakoulas, "Translation as Social Action: Brecht's 'Political Texts' in Greek," *TTR: Traduction, Terminologie, Rédaction* 1 (2007): 124–34.
50. Rajend Mesthrie et al., *Introducing Sociolinguistics* (Edinburgh: Edinburgh University Press, 2009), 39.
51. Strikha, *Ukrains'kii khudozhnii pereklad*, 77–79.
52. Baer, "Literary Translation and the Construction of a Soviet Intelligentsia," 459.
53. Van Dijk, "Ideology and Discourse Analysis," 128.
54. Sibelan Forrester, "The Water of Life. Resuscitating Russian Avant-Garde Authors in Croatian and Serbian Translations," in *Contexts, Subtexts, Pretexts: Literary Translation in Eastern Europe and Russia*, 120–23, 211.
55. Aleksei Zverev, "Dzhek London: Velichie talanta i paradoksy sud'by," introduction to *Rasskazy* by Dzhek London (Moscow: Pravda, 1984), 3–16.
56. Zverev, "Dzhek London: Velichie talanta i paradoksy sud'by," 9.
57. Witt, "Between the Lines," 165–67.
58. Forrester, "The Water of Life," 121.
59. Van Dijk, *Ideology*, 162, 168.
60. Tymoczko, *Enlarging Translation, Empowering Translators*, 211, 217.

Chapter 2: Censorship and the Russian Publishing System through History

1. Literally meaning *one hundred decisions;* the name is used to define both the volume *(Stoglav)* and the council of 1551 itself *(Stoglav council)*.
2. Gennadii Zhirkov, *Istoriia tsenzury v Rossii XIX–XX vv.* (Moscow: Aspekt Press, 2001), 8–9.
3. Literally, *apostle*.
4. Iosif Barenbaum, *Istoriia knigi* (Moscow: Kniga, 1984), 26–31.
5. Zhirkov, *Istoriia tsenzury v Rossii*, 11–13, 15–23.
6. I.e., *Vsiakaia vsiachina* (lit. *Omnium gatherum*).
7. Barenbaum, *Istoriia knigi*, 57–62.
8. Zhirkov, *Istoriia tsenzury v Rossii*, 29–31.
9. Zhirkov, *Istoriia tsenzury v Rossii*, 42, 48–49.
10. Zhirkov, *Istoriia tsenzury v Rossii*, 57.
11. Roi Medvedev, *Liudi i knigi. Chto chital Stalin? Pisatel' i kniga v totalitarnom obshchestve* (Moscow: Prava Cheloveka, 2004), 60.
12. Aleksandr Pushkin, *Polnoe sobranie sochinenii v desiati tomakh. T. 10. Pis'ma* (Leningrad: Nauka, 1979), 168, 189, 316.
13. Faddei Venediktovich Bulgarin (née Jan Tadeusz Krzysztof Bułharyn) (1789–1859) is a St. Petersburg publisher, critic, and journalist; publisher of the influential journals of the nineteenth century—*Russian Talia* (1825), *The Northern Archive* (1822–29), and *The Northern Bee* (1825–59), the latter being the one Pushkin is referring to in the quoted letter. The quote is taken from Pushkin, *Pis'ma*, 190.
14. Pushkin, *Pis'ma*, 286, 314, 316, 364.
15. "Journey from Moscow to St. Petersburg" was written by Pushkin as a counter to Aleksandr Radishchev's *Journey from St. Petersburg to Moscow*, written forty years earlier, in which Radishchev severely criticized the Russian absolutism, arbitrary rule, and oppression of peasants.

16. Aleksandr Pushkin, *Polnoe sobranie sochinenii v desiati tomakh. T. 7. Kritika i publitsistika* (Leningrad: Nauka, 1978), 207.

17. Pushkin, *Kritika i publitsistika*, 492.

18. Nikolai Gogol, *Perepiska N.V. Gogolia v dvukh tomakh. T. 1* (Moscow: Khudozhestvennaia Literatura, 1988), 238–39.

19. Gogol, *Perepiska*, 243; Vladimir Korolenko, *Stat'i, retsenzii, ocherki* (Moscow: Direkt-Media, 2014), 149.

20. Inga Shomrakova and Iosif Barenbaum, *Vseobshchaia istoriia knigi* (St. Petersburg: Professiia, 2005), 128; Zhirkov, *Istoriia tsenzury v Rossii XIX–XX vv.*, 84–99.

21. Vissarion Belinskii, "Letter to Gogol," in *Readings in Russian Civilization. Vol. II: Imperial Russia 1700–1917*, ed. Thomas Riha (Chicago and London: University of Chicago Press, 2009), 316–17.

22. Fedor Dostoevsky, *Writer's Diary. Vol. I: 1873–1878*, trans. Kenneth Lantz, ed. Gary Saul Morson (Evanston, IL: Northwestern University Press, 1994), 284–85.

23. Dostoevsky, *Writer's Diary*, 288–89.

24. Literally, *time*.

25. Fedor Dostoevsky, *Polnoe sobranie sochinenii. Kanonicheskie teksty. T. III* (Petrozavodsk: Petrozavodsk University, 1997), 689–90, 907–8.

26. In the last quarter of the nineteenth century, terrorist attacks were, unfortunately, numerous. The life of Tsar Alexander II himself was attempted upon eight times; the tsar was eventually assassinated in St. Petersburg on March 13 (March 1 old style), 1881.

27. Aleksei Miller, *"Ukrainskii vopros" v politike vlastei i russkom obshchestvennom mnenii (vtoraia polovina XIX veka)* (St. Petersburg: Aleteiia, 2000), 102.

28. Jaroslav Rudnyckyj, "Ukrainian Linguistics in Exile (1918–1984)," in *Papers in the History of Linguistics: Proceedings of the Third International Conference on the History of Language Sciences*, ed. Hans Aarsleff, Louis G. Kelly, and Hans-Josef Niederehe (Amsterdam: John Benjamins, 1987), 644.

29. Vitaly Chernetsky, "Nation and Translation: Literary Translation and the Shaping of Modern Ukrainian Culture," in *Contexts, Subtexts, Pretexts: Literary Translation in Eastern Europe and Russia*, ed. Brian James Baer (Amsterdam/Philadelphia: John Benjamins, 2011), 40–41.

30. Ricarda Vulpius, "Language Policy in the Russian Empire: A Case of Translation of the Bible into Ukrainian, 1860–1906," *Ab Imperio* 2 (2005): 193–94.

31. For the argumentation against the direct connection of Morachevs'kii's translation with the Valuev circular, see Andrii Danylenko, "The Ukrainian Bible and the Valuev Circular of July 18, 1863," *Acta Slavica Iaponica* 28 (2010).

32. Miller, *"Ukrainskii vopros" v politike vlastei i russkom obshchestvennom mnenii*, 101–3.

33. Peter Ulf Møller, *Postlude to "The Kreutzer Sonata": Tolstoj and the Debate on Sexual Morality in Russian Literature in the 1890s*, trans. John Krendal (Leiden, New York, Copenhagen, Cologne: E. J. Brill, 1988), 56–82.

34. Zhirkov, *Istoriia tsenzury v Rossii*, 170.

35. Anton Chekhov, *Perepiska A.P. Chekhova v trekh tomakh. T. 2* (Moscow: Nasledie, 1996), 361. English translation cited from Donald Rayfield, *Anton Chekhov: A Life* (Evanston, IL: Northwestern University Press, 2000), 382.

36. Chekhov, *Perepiska*, 362.

37. Maiia Volchkevich, *"Chaika." Komediia zabluzhdenii* (Moscow: Probel, 2010), 19, 81; Rayfield, *Anton Chekhov: A Life*, 382.

38. Chekhov, *Perepiska*, 362.

39. Anton Chekhov, *The Sea Gull* (New York: Dover Publications, 1999), 16.

Chapter 3: The Pyramid of Subordination

1. Maurice Friedberg, *Literary Translation in Russia: A Cultural History* (University Park: Pennsylvania State University Press, 1997).

2. Brian James Baer, *Translation and the Making of Modern Russian Literature* (New York and London: Bloomsbury, 2016).

3. Brian James Baer and Natalia Olshanskaya, eds., *Russian Writers on Translation: An Anthology* (Manchester: St. Jerome: 2013).

4. Vitaly Chernetsky, "Nation and Translation: Literary Translation and the Shaping of Modern Ukrainian Culture," in *Contexts, Subtexts, Pretexts: Literary Translation in Eastern Europe and Russia*, ed. Brian James Baer (Amsterdam/Philadelphia: John Benjamins, 2011); Anne Lange, Performative Translation Options under the Soviet Regime," *Journal of Baltic Studies* 3 (2012): 401–20; Daniele Monticelli and Anne Lange, "Translation and Totalitarianism: The Case of Soviet Estonia," *Translator* 20 (2014): 95–111; Daniele Monticelli, "Translation under Totalitarianism. Soviet Estonia, Johannes Semper and Translation History," *Novyi Protei* 1 (2015): 205–6; Natalia Kaloh Vid, "Censorship and Ideology in Literary Translations: The Case of Robert Burns Poetry in the Soviet Union," in *Perspectives in Translation Studies*, ed. Floriana Popescu (Cambridge: Cambridge Scholars Publishing, 2009); 77–94; Susanna Witt, "Between the Lines: Totalitarianism and Translation in the USSR," in *Contexts, Subtexts, and Pretexts: Literary Translation in Eastern Europe and Russia*, ed. Brian James Baer (Amsterdam: John Benjamins, 2011), 149–70; Susanna Witt, "Byron's *Don Juan* in Russian and the Soviet School of Translation," *Translation and Interpreting Studies: The Journal of the American Translation and Interpreting Studies Association* 1 (2016): 23–43; Maksim Strikha, *Ukrains'kii khudozhnii pereklad: mizh literaturoiu i natsietvorenniam* (Kiiv: Fakt-Nash Chas, 2006).

5. *Dekrety Sovetskoi vlasti. T. I* (Moscow: Gosudarstvennoe Izdatel'stvo Politicheskoi Literatury, 1957), 24–25.

6. *Dekrety Sovetskoi vlasti. T. I, 25.*

7. "Konstitutsiia (Osnovnoi Zakon) Rossiiskoi Sotsialisticheskoi Federativnoi Sovetskoi Respubliki, priniataia 5 Vserossiiskim S"ezdom Sovetov v zasedanii ot 10 iiulia 1918 goda," in *Pervaia Sovetskaia Konstitutsiia (Konstitutsiia RSFSR 1918 goda). Sbornik dokumentov*, ed. Andrei Vyshinskii (Moscow: NKIU SSSR, 1938), 425, 427.

8. Vladimir Lenin, "Ocherednye zadachi Sovetskoi vlasti," in *Polnoe sobranie sochinenii. T. 36* (Moscow: Izdatel'stvo Politicheskoi Literatury, 1974), 191; Vladimir Lenin, "O znachenii voinstvuiushchego materializma," in *Polnoe sobranie sochinenii. T. 45* (Moscow: Izdatel'stvo Politicheskoi Literatury, 1970).

9. In Russian, Главное управление по делам литературы и издательств (Главлит) Народного комиссариата просвещения РСФСР.

10. Sovnarkom, or Sovet Narodnykh Komissarov, lit. Council of People's Commissars, is the official name of the government cabinet of the Russian Federative Soviet Socialist Republic.

11. Quoted in Inga Shomrakova and Iosif Barenbaum, *Vseobshchaia istoriia knigi* (St. Petersburg: Professiia, 2005), 207.

12. Viktor Pribytkov, *Glavlit i tsenzura: Zapiski zamestitelia nachal'nika Glavnogo uprav-

leniia po okhrane gosudarstvennykh tain v pechati pri Sovete ministrov SSSR (Moscow: Molodaia Gvardiia, 2014), 46.

13. Vladimir Lenin, "Partiinaia organizatsiia i partiinaia literatura," in *O literature i iskusstve* (Moscow: Khudozhestvennaia Literatura, 1976), 93.

14. Vladimir Lenin, "O proletarskoi kul'ture," in *O literature i iskusstve*, 444–45; Lenin, "Partiinaia organizatsiia i partiinaia literatura," 94–96.

15. Arlen Blium, *Kak eto delalos' v Leningrade: Tsenzura v gody ottepeli, zastoia i perestroiki. 1953–1991* (St. Petersburg: Akademicheskii Proekt, 2005), 24.

16. Shomrakova and Barenbaum, *Vseobshchaia istoriia knigi*, 208.

17. Blium, *Kak eto delalos' v Leningrade*, 63.

18. Mikhail Zelenov, "Glavlit i istoricheskaia nauka v 20–30-e gody," *Voprosy istorii* 3 (1997): 33–34.

19. Pribytkov, *Glavlit i tsenzura*, 34–35.

20. Tat'iana Goriaeva, *Politicheskaia tsenzura v SSSR. 1917–1991 gg.* (Moscow: ROSSPEN, 2009), 146–47, 152–53.

21. Marianna Tax Choldin, "Closing and Opening and Closing: Reflections on the Russian Media," in *The Space of the Book: Print Culture in the Russian Social Imagination*, ed. Miranda Remnek (Toronto: University of Toronto Press, 2011), 283, 294–95.

22. Blium, *Kak eto delalos' v Leningrade*, 7–9.

23. Taken from Efim Etkind, *Zapiski nezagovorshchika* (Kharkiv: Prava Liudini, 2013), 237.

24. Blium, *Kak eto delalos' v Leningrade*, 46–47.

25. Etkind lived and worked in Leningrad, whereas Witkowsky is a Muscovite.

26. Committee of Party and State Control of the Central Committee of the Communist Party of the Soviet Union and the Council of Ministers of the USSR; founded November 27, 1962.

27. Shomrakova and Barenbaum, *Vseobshchaia istoriia knigi*, 208.

28. Blium, *Kak eto delalos' v Leningrade*, 47.

29. *Dekrety Sovetskoi vlasti. T. IV* (Moscow: Gosudarstvennoe Izdatel'stvo Politicheskoi Literatury, 1968), 68, 70.

30. Senator Eugene McCarthy (1916–2005), US Senator from Minnesota, member of the Minnesota Democratic Farmer-Labor Party, active opponent of the Vietnam War.

31. Maksim Gor'kii, "O rabote neumeloi, nebrezhnoi, nedobrosovestnoi," in *Perevod— sredstvo vzaimnogo sblizheniia narodov: Khudozhestvennaia publitsistika*, ed. Anatolii Klyshko (Moscow: Progress, 1987), 302–3.

32. "Ustav Soiuza Sovetskih Pisatelei SSSR," in *Pervyi Vsesoiuznyi S"ezd Sovetskikh Pisatelei 1934: Stenograficheskii otchet* (Moscow: Khudozhestvennaia Literatura, 1934), 712–13.

33. Venuti, Lawrence. *The Translator's Invisibility* (Taylor & Francis e-library, 2004), 20.

34. Khachik Dashtents, "Shekspir v Armenii," in *Masterstvo perevoda*, ed. Kornei Chukovskii (Moscow: Sovetskii Pisatel', 1968), 65.

35. Kornei Chukovskii, *Vysokoe iskusstvo: O printsipakh khudozhestvennogo perevoda* (Moscow: Iskusstvo, 1964).

36. Kornei Chukovskii, *Sobranie sochinenii. T. 3* (Moscow: TERRA—Knizhnyi Klub, 2001), 7–8.

37. Vladimir Dal', *Tolkovyi slovar' zhivogo velikorusskogo iazyka. T. 4*, ed. Ivan Boduen-de-Kurtene (St. Petersburg-Moscow: Tovarishchestvo M.O. Vol'f, 1909), 1150.

38. For the description of the formal method see, for instance, Viktor Zhirmunskii, "K voprosu o formal'nom metode," in *Teoriia literatury. Poetika. Stilistika* (Leningrad: Nauka, 1977), 94–105.

39. Boris Eichenbaum, "Teoriia formal'nogo metoda," in *O literature* (Moscow: Sovetskii Pisatel', 1987), 376.

40. *Bol'shaia sovetskaia entsiklopediia. T. 58,* ed. Otto Schmidt (Moscow: OGIZ RSFSR, 1936).

41. *Bol'shaia sovetskaia entsiklopediia. T. 45,* ed. Sergei Vavilov and Boris Vvedenskii (Moscow: Bol'shaia Sovetskaia Entsiklopediia, 1956), 314–15.

42. Andrei Azov, *Poverzhennye bukvalisty: Iz istorii khudozhestvennogo perevoda v SSSR v 1920–1960-e gody* (Moscow: Dom Vysshei Shkoly Ekonomiki, 2013), 40–41.

43. See, for instance, the article of Ivan Kashkin written in 1955 "V bor'be za realisticheskii perevod," (The struggle for realistic translation) where the author writes, "If formalism in its essence is dead statics, if impressionism is often unmotivated iniquity, and naturalism—a lifeless copy, realism is life in itself reflected in art." Ivan Kashkin, "V bor'be za realisticheskii perevod," in *Dlia chitatelia-sovremennika (Stat'i i issledovaniia)* (Moscow: Sovetskii Pisatel', 1968), 479.

44. Viktor Shklovskii, *O teorii prozy* (Moscow: Sovetskii Pisatel', 1983), 80.

45. *Bol'shoj tolkovyj slovar' russkogo iazyka,* ed. Sergei Kuznetsov (St. Petersburg: Norint, 1998), 101.

46. Ivan Kashkin, "Lozhnyi printsip i nepriemlemye rezul'taty (O bukvalizme v russkikh perevodakh Ch. Dikkensa)," in *Dlia chitatelia-sovremennika (Stat'i i issledovaniia),* 389.

47. Kashkin, "V bor'be za realisticheskii perevod," 476.

48. Kashkin, "V bor'be za realisticheskii perevod," 490.

49. Witt, "Between the Lines," 165.

50. Andrei Fedorov, *Vvedenie v teoriiu perevoda* (Moscow: Izdatel'stvo Literatury na Inostrannykh Iazykakh, 1953).

51. Andrei Fedorov, *Osnovy obshchei teorii perevoda (lingvisticheskie problemy)* (Moscow: Vysshaia Shkola, 1983).

52. Fedorov, *Vvedenie v teoriiu perevoda,* 14.

53. Fedorov, *Vvedenie v teoriiu perevoda,* 15.

54. Fedorov, *Vvedenie v teoriiu perevoda,* 12.

55. Oleksei Kundzich, "Perevodcheskii bloknot," in *Masterstvo perevoda,* ed. Kornei Chukovskii (Moscow: Sovetskii Pisatel', 1968), 219.

56. In the original, "by the book" (*po nauke*); see Nikolai Zabolotskii, "Zametki perevodchika," in *Perevod—sredstvo vzaimnogo sblizheniia narodov: Khudozhestvennaia publitsistika,* ed. Anatolii Klyshko (Moscow: Progress, 1987), 427. English text cited as in Nikolai Zabolotskii, "Translator's Notes," in *Russian Writers on Translation: An Anthology,* ed. Brian James Baer and Natalia Olshanskaya (Manchester: St. Jerome, 2013), 110.

57. Kundzich, "Perevodcheskii bloknot," 219.

58. Andrei Fedorov, *Osnovy obshchei teorii perevoda,* 104.

59. Efim Etkind, *Poeziia i perevod* (Moscow-Leningrad: Sovetskii Pisatel', 1963), 39.

60. Etkind, *Poeziia i perevod,* 133–42.

61. Etkind, *Poeziia i perevod,* 142.

62. Evgenii Iasin, "Shestidesiatniki: nostal'giia ili aktual'nost'?" in *Shestidesiatniki,* ed. Mark Barbakadze (Moscow: Fond "Liberal'naia Missiia," 2007), 8.

63. Mariia Zezina, *Sovetskaia khudozhestvennaia intelligentsiia i vlast' v 1950-e—60-e gody* (Moscow: Dialog MGU, 1999), 5.

64. Goriaeva, *Politicheskaia tsenzura v SSSR*, 318.

65. The term *Rump* comes from English history: the Rump Parliament of 1648 was what was left of the Long Parliament after it had been purged of those members who stood for the reinstatement of King Charles I, mainly Presbyterians. In the Soviet Union, the word was used now and then as a derogatory term to define any remaining adepts of the old regime and views.

66. RGANI. F. 89. Op. 6. Dok. 2.

67. Zoia Vodop'ianova and Tat'iana Goriaeva, eds., *Istoriia sovetskoi politicheskoi tsenzury: Dokumenty i kommentarii* (Moscow: ROSSPEN, 1997), 188–91.

Chapter 4: The Making of a Translator

1. Gennadii Zhirkov, *Istoriia tsenzury v Rossii XIX–XX vv.* (Moscow: Aspekt Press, 2001), 11.

2. Quoted in Zhirkov, *Istoriia tsenzury v Rossii*, 23.

3. Quoted in Zhirkov, *Istoriia tsenzury v Rossii*, 33.

4. Andrei Fedorov, *Osnovy obshchei teorii perevoda (lingvisticheskie problemy)* (Moscow: Vysshaia Shkola, 1983), 40–41.

5. Brian James Baer, Introduction to *Russian Writers on Translation: An Anthology*, ed. Brian James and Natalia Olshanskaya (Manchester: St. Jerome, 2013), iii.

6. The history of translation in Russia is described in detail in Efim Etkind, *Russkie poety-perevodchiki ot Trediakovskogo do Pushkina* (Leningrad: Nauka, 1973). Also, see Fedorov, *Osnovy obshchei teorii perevoda*, 43–52.

7. As was stated, for instance by Maksim Gor'kii, see Maxim Gorkii, "World Literature," in *Russian Writers on Translation: An Anthology*, 65–66.

8. Evgenii Nemirovskii and Viktor Kharlamov, *Istoriia knigi v SSSR. 1917–1921. T. 1* (Moscow: Kniga, 1983), 208–15.

9. Gorkii, "World Literature," 66.

10. For more on the activity of publishing house Vsemirnaia Literatura, its engagement in the World Literature project, as well as the development of Academia publishing house, see Samantha Sherry, *Discourses of Regulation and Resistance: Censoring Translation in the Stalin and Khrushchev Era Soviet Union* (Edinburgh: Edinburgh University Press, 2015), 19–22.

11. As in Vladimir Rossel's, "Estafeta slova," in *Skol'ko vesit slovo: Stat'i* by Vladimir Rossel's (Moscow: Sovetskii Pisatel', 1984), 19.

12. Katerina Clark, *Moscow, the Fourth Rome: Stalinism, Cosmopolitanism, and the Evolution of Soviet Culture, 1931–1941* (Cambridge, MA: Harvard University Press, 2011), 9–11.

13. Clark, *Moscow*, 10.

14. Clark, *Moscow*, 4.

15. Clark, *Moscow*, 8.

16. Clark, *Moscow*, 14.

17. The problem of literary personality cults in the Soviet Union was touched upon by Katerina Clark in Clark, *Moscow*, 325–29 and in Katerina Clark, *Petersburg: Crucible of Cultural Revolution* (Cambridge, MA: Harvard University Press, 1996), 288–89. Also see Susanna Witt, "Byron's *Don Juan* in Russian and the 'Soviet School

of Translation,'" *Translation and Interpreting Studies: The Journal of the American Translation and Interpreting Studies Association* 1 (2016).

18. Ivan Kashkin, "Voprosy perevoda," in *Dlia chitatelia-sovremennika (Stat'i i issledovaniia)* (Moscow: Sovetskii Pisatel', 1968), 447.

19. Dzhordzh G. Bairon, *Don Zhuan*, trans. Georgii Shengeli (Moscow: Goslitizdat, 1947).

20. Cited here through the collection of Kashkin's articles, *Dlia chitatelia-sovremennika*, 1968.

21. Ivan Kashkin, "Traditsiia i epigonstvo (Ob odnom perevode baironovskogo 'Don-Zhuana')," in *Dlia chitatelia-sovremennika*, 414–15.

22. George G. N. Byron, *The Works of Lord Byron. Poetry. Vol. VI*, ed. Ernest Hartley Coleridge (London: John Murray, 1903), 322.

23. Суворов в этот час, вновь командиром взводным, В рубашке, сняв мундир, калмыков обучал, Их совершенствуя в искусстве благородном Убийства. Он острил, дурачился, кричал На рохль и увальней. Философом природным, От грязи—глины он людской не отличал И максиму внушал, что смерть на поле боя, Подобно пенсии, должна манить героя (Bairon, *Don Zhuan*, trans. Shengeli, 268).

24. For the detailed description of Shengeli's translation approach, see Witt, "Byron's *Don Juan* in Russian."

25. Kashkin, "Traditsiia i epigonstvo," 419.

26. Суворов, сняв мундир, в одной рубашке, Тренировал калмыков батальон, Ругался, если кто-нибудь, бедняжка, Неповоротлив был иль утомлен. Искусство убивать штыком и шашкой Преподавал он ловко; верил он, Что человечье тело, без сомнения, -Лишь матерьял, пригодный для сражения! (Dzhordzh G. Bairon, *Don Zhuan*, trans. Tat'iana Gnedich [Moscow-Leningrad: Khudozhestvennaia Literatura, 1964], 302).

27. Galina Usova, *I Bairona v soavtory voz'mu. Kniga o Tat'iane Grigor'evne Gnedich* (St. Petersburg: DEAN, 2012), 54.

28. Kornei Chukovskii, *Sobranie sochinenii. T. 3* (Moscow: TERRA—Knizhnyi klub, 2001), 216–17.

29. As in, for instance, Rossel's, "Estafeta slova," 33.

30. Usova, *I Bairona v soavtory voz'mu*, 134–36, 155–57.

31. Etkind, *Russkie poety-perevodchiki*, 118.

32. Vil'iam Shekspir, *Tragicheskaia istoriia o Gamlete, printse datskom*, trans. Mikhail Lozinskii (Moscow: Goslitizdat, 1933).

33. Vil'iam Shekspir, *Gamlet, prints datskii*, trans. Boris Pasternak (Moscow: Goslitizdat, 1941).

34. Ignatii Ivanovskii, "Vospominaniia o Mikhaile Lozinskom," *Neva* 7 (2005): 197.

35. Boris Pasternak, "Zametki o perevode," in *Masterstvo perevoda*, ed. Kornei Chukovskii (Moscow: Sovetskii Pisatel', 1968), 110.

36. Mikhail Lozinskii, "Iskusstvo stikhotvornogo perevoda," in *Perevod—sredstvo vzaimnogo sblizheniia narodov: Khudozhestvennaia publitsistika*, ed. Anatolii Klyshko (Moscow: Progress, 1987), 103–4.

37. Chukovskii, *Sobranie sochinenii. T. 3*, 186–89.

38. Iurii Gavruk, "Nuzhen li novyi perevod 'Gamleta' na russkii iazyk?" in *Masterstvo perevoda*, 123–26.

39. Zhabotinskii, Leonid Ivanovich (1938–2016), Soviet weight lifter in the super-

heavyweight class, set seventeen world records, winner of gold medals at the 1964 and 1968 Olympic games; Vlasov, Iurii Petrovich (b. 1935), Soviet weight lifter in the heavyweight class, set thirty-one world records, winner of a gold medal at the 1960 Olympic games and a silver medal at the 1964 Olympic games.

40. Vil'gel'm Levik, "Nuzhny li novye perevody Shekspira?" in *Masterstvo perevoda*, 95.

41. Levik, "Nuzhny li novye perevody Shekspira," 97.

42. Levik, "Nuzhny li novye perevody Shekspira," 99–100.

43. Aleksei Semenenko, *Hamlet the Sign: Russian Translations of Hamlet and Literary Canon Formation* (Stockholm: Stockholm Universitet, 2007), 94–95, 98–99.

44. Semenenko, *Hamlet the Sign*, 99–100.

45. See, for instance, Nikolai Vil'iam-Vil'mont, "*Gamlet* v perevode Borisa Pasternaka," *Internatsional'naia literatura* 7–8 (1940); Mikhail Morozov, "*Gamlet* v perevode B. Pasternaka," *Teatr* 2 (1941).

46. Gavruk, "Nuzhen li novyi perevod," 131.

47. For a detailed account of the general tendencies and major events in Soviet literature of the period based on the example of Leningrad poetry, see Emily Lygo, *Leningrad Poetry, 1953–1975: The Thaw Generation (Russian Transformations: Literature, Culture and Ideas)* (Bern: Peter Lang, 2010).

48. LITO is an acronym for Literary Association (*Literaturnoe ob'edinenie*).

49. Mikhail Iasnov, "Uroki frantsuzskogo," *Sobaka.ru* 11 (2008), http://kn.sobaka.ru/n71/05.html.

50. Mikhail Iasnov, ed. *El'ga L'vovna Linetskaia (1909–1997). Materialy k biografii. Iz literaturnogo naslediia. Vospominaniia. Bibliografiia. Fotodokumenty* (St. Petersburg: Simpozium, 1999), 165.

51. Ol'ga Logosh, "My do sikh por sovetuemsia s El'goi L'vovnoi Linetskoi," *Viperson*, January 23, 2009, http://viperson.ru/wind.php?ID=608570.

52. Usova, *I Bairona v soavtory voz'mu*.

53. Etkind, *Razgovor o stikhakh* (Moscow, 1970).

54. Maria Tymoczko, *Enlarging Translation, Empowering Translators* (Manchester, UK, and Kinderhook, NY: St. Jerome, 2010), 213.

55. Lygo, *Leningrad Poetry*, 31–32.

56. Igor' Sukhikh, "Tynianov i Kiukhlia: izbiratel'noe srodstvo," *Zarubezhnye zapiski* 4 (2008): 174.

57. Lidiia Chukovskaia, *Zapiski ob Anne Akhmatovoi. V 3 tomakh* (Moscow: Vremia, 2013).

58. Vladimir Admoni and Tamara Sil'man, *My vspominaem* (St. Petersburg: Kompozitor, 1993), 209–10.

59. Admoni and Sil'man, *My vspominaem*, 201.

60. Nora Gal', *Slovo zhivoe i mertvoe* (Moscow: Vremia, 2007), 242–43, 263.

61. Mikhail Iasnov, "*Khranitel' chuzhogo nasledstva . . .* Zametki o leningradskoi (peterburgskoi) shkole khudozhestvennogo perevoda," *Inostrannaia literatura* 12 (2010): 238.

62. Inna Terterian and Lev Ospovat, eds., *Ispanskie poety XX veka* (Moscow: Khudozhestvennaia Literatura, 1977).

63. Lygo, *Leningrad Poetry*, 23.

64. Oleg Iur'ev, "Gorlitsa sovetskoi nochi," *Booknik*, January 23, 2009, http://booknik.ru/today/reports/gorlitsa-sovetskoy-nochi,

65. Founded in 1937, club *Derzanie* for children and teenagers at the Palace of Pioneers is still active.

Chapter 5: Literary Translation as a Profession

1. The Singer building in Nevsky Prospect, no. 28, still hosts the most famous bookstore in St. Petersburg. In Soviet times, it was also the location of the offices of several big publishing houses: Lendetgiz, Prosveshchenie (Uchpedgiz until 1964), Iskusstvo, Khudozhestvennaia Literatura (Goslitizdat), Khimiia, and Agropromizdat.

2. Irina Komarova worked in Uchpedgiz, which was engaged in publishing literature for education and science. Uchpedgiz hardly had any demand for literary translation, unlike Khudozhestvennaia Literatura and Iskusstvo, which specialized in fiction.

3. "Ustav Soiuza Sovetskih Pisatelei SSSR," in *Pervyi Vsesoiuznyi S'ezd Sovetskikh Pisatelei 1934: Stenograficheskii otchet* (Moscow: Khudozhestvennaia Literatura, 1934), 712–13.

4. *O partiinoi i sovetskoi pechati, radioveshchanii i televidenii. Sbornik dokumentov i materialov* (Moscow: Mysl', 1972), 413.

5. *O partiinoi i sovetskoi pechati*, 413.

6. In 1925, the organization was called the Central Committee of the Russian Communist Party—*ЦК РКП(б)*; in 1932, it already had the name the Central Committee of the All-Union Communist Party—*ЦК ВКП(б)*. For the text of the regulation see *O partiinoi i sovetskoi pechati*, 392–96.

7. *O partiinoi i sovetskoi pechati*, 395.

8. "Ustav Soiuza Sovetskih Pisatelei SSSR," 712.

9. It is notable that the structure of the Union of Writers was aligned with the structure of Glavlit (see chap. 3). This correspondence ensured closer control of all literary activity in the country and the awareness of all literary organizations of their being objects of surveillance.

10. The so-called labor book *(trudovaia knizhka)* with the record of all places of employment and positions held was introduced in the USSR. The book remains mandatory for every citizen of the Russian Federation.

11. *Ustav Soiuza pisatelei SSSR* (Moscow: Tipografiia "Literaturnoi gazety," 1971), 9–10, 22.

12. The Union of Writers of the USSR organized a special Literary Fund (hence the name—Litfond) in 1934 in order to manage its facilities and material resources. Dachas for the members of the Leningrad department of the Union of Writers were located in Komarovo—a famous resort in the suburbs of Leningrad/St. Petersburg on the coast of the Baltic Sea, which prides itself on a beautiful pine forest, sand beaches, and picturesque views. Komarovo is traditionally associated with Russian arts and literature: at different times, Komarovo was home to jeweler Carl Fabergé, ballet-dancer Matil'da Kshesinskaia, writer Evgenii Schwarz, and composer Dmitrii Shostakovich. The choice of the location for the Creativity Home and private dachas of the Leningrad Union of Writers was therefore historically predetermined.

13. *Ustav Soiuza pisatelei SSSR*, 12.

14. Ignatii Ivanovskii, "Fragmenty (iz knigi *Pochtovaia loshad'*)," *Zarubezhnye zapiski* 7 (2006): 141.

15. *Ustav Soiuza pisatelei SSSR*, 7.

16. *Ustav Soiuza pisatelei SSSR*, 12–13.

17. "Doklad tov. A. A. Zhdanova o zhurnalakh *Zvezda* i *Leningrad*," *Pravda*, 225 (10307), September 21, 1946.

18. Sakharov, Andrei Dmitrievich (1921–89), Soviet nuclear physicist who spoke against

nuclear proliferation in the 1960s. An open dissident, he regularly became the target of public bullying and Soviet media campaigns.

19. Ivanovskii, "Fragmenty," 7 (2006): 142–43.
20. The predecessor of Progress was Izdatel'stvo Inostrannoi Literatury. Founded in 1946, it regularly received foreign literature. In 1964, it was split into two publishing houses—Mir and Progress, and Progress became the one that was regularly provided with foreign literature. In 1982, Raduga publishing house split from Progress.
21. On overlapping of publishing plans see the regulation of the Central Committee of the Communist Party "Ob ustranenii nedostatkov v izdanii i retsenzirovanii inostrannoi khudozhestvennoi literatury" (Upon elimination of drawbacks in publication and reviewing of foreign literature) of April 5, 1958, see *O partiinoi i sovetskoi pechati*, 449–50.
22. St. Petersburg was renamed Petrograd in 1914 in the course of a massive anti-German campaign at the beginning of World War I. It was soon renamed again—this time to Leningrad, the renaming taking place five days after Lenin's death in 1924.
23. Katerina Clark, *Moscow, the Fourth Rome: Stalinism, Cosmopolitanism, and the Evolution of Soviet Culture, 1931–1941* (Cambridge, MA: Harvard University Press, 2011), 15.
24. Clark, *Moscow, the Fourth Rome*, 15.
25. Mikhail Iasnov, "Khranitel' chuzhogo nasledstva . . . Zametki o leningradskoi (peterburgskoi) shkole khudozhestvennogo perevoda," *Inostrannaia literatura* 12 (2010): 222.
26. Iasnov, "Khranitel' chuzhogo nasledstva," 222.
27. Uil'iam Folkner, "Avessalom, Avessalom!" trans. Meri Bekker, *Novyi mir* 9 &10 (1980).

Chapter 6: Poetry in Translation

1. Evgenii Evtushenko, *Vse poemy* (Moscow: Zebra E, 2015), 61.
2. Efim Etkind, *Russkie poety-perevodchiki ot Trediakovskogo do Pushkina* (Leningrad: Nauka, 1973), 3, 11–12, 22–30, 155–85, 246–47.
3. For open-air poetry sessions, see Robert Hornsby, *Protest, Reform and Repression in Khrushchev's Soviet Union* (Cambridge: Cambridge University Press, 2013), 257–60.
4. For military conflicts the Soviet Union took part in in 1960–91, see chap. 3.
5. See the Constitution of the Union of Soviet Socialist Republics, 1977. Konstitutsiia (Osnovnoi Zakon) Soiuza Sovetskikh Sotsialisticheskikh Respublik 1977, 16, 19, 46–47. Articles 34, 36, 45, 159.
6. David L. Cooper, "Vasilii Zhukovskii as Translator and the Protean Russian Nation," in *Contexts, Subtexts, Pretexts: Literary Translation in Eastern Europe and Russia*, ed. Brian James Baer (Amsterdam, Philadelphia: John Benjamins, 2011), 70–75.
7. Valerii Briusov, ed. *Poeziia Armenii s drevneishikh vremen do nashikh dnei v perevode russkikh poetov* (Moscow: Moskovskii Armianskii Komitet, 1916).
8. Vladimir Rossel's, "Znanie, talant, trud," in *Skol'ko vesit slovo: Stat'i* by Vladimir Rossel's (Moscow: Sovetskii Pisatel', 1984), 45–46.
9. Rossel's, "Znanie, talant, trud," 52–63.
10. Apparently, the reference to Stalin in the term alludes to the famous case of poet and translator Arsenii Tarkovskii, who was commissioned by Kremlin officials to trans-

late the collection of poems that Stalin had written in his youth. As the poems were written in Georgian, Tarkovskii was provided with highly detailed interlinear trots.

11. Anatolii Naiman, *Rasskazy o Anne Akhmatovoi* (Moscow: AST: Zebra E, 2008), 122.

12. Valentin Uvarov, "Paradoksy rolevogo povedeniia uchastnikov situatsii perevoda," in *Tetradi perevodchika. Vyp. 18*, ed. Leonid Barkhudarov (Moscow: Mezhdunarodnye Otnosheniia, 1981), 13.

13. Professor Efim Etkind was deprived of his academic titles and forced to emigrate in 1974 (see chap. 4).

14. Bella Akhmadulina, "Stikhotvorenie, podlezhashchee perevodu . . ." in *Perevod— sredstvo vzaimnogo sblizheniia narodov: Khudozhestvennaia publitsistika*, edited by Anatolii Klyshko (Moscow: Progress, 1987), 456–57.

15. Akhmadulina, Stikhotvorenie, podlezhashchee perevodu . . ." 457.

16. Elisaveta Bagryana, *Izbrani proizvedeniia v dva toma. Първи том* (Sofia: Bulgarski Pisatel, 1983), 14.

17. Elisaveta Bagriana, *Stikhi*, trans. from Bulgarian by Anna Akhmatova (Moscow: Khudozhestvennaia Literatura, 1979), 27.

18. Italics in this and the three quotations from Akhmatova below are mine.

19. Anna Akhmatova, *The Complete Poems of Anna Akhmatova. Vol. 1*, trans. Judith Hemschemeyer, ed. Roberta Reeder (Sommerville: Zephyr Press, 1990), 381. The Russian original goes, *И я закопала веселую птицу / За круглым колодцем у старой ольхи.*

20. See, for instance, Anna Akhmatova, "*V to vremia ia gostila na zemle . . .*" *Stikhotvoreniia. Poemy* (St. Petersburg: Lenizdat, 1995), 15, 63, 71, 72, 88, 121, 202, 204, 212, 281, 353, 460, 524, 554, 560.

21. Akhmatova, *Complete Poems*, 217. Russian original: *Мне холодно . . . Крылатый иль бескрылый, / Веселый бог не посетит меня.*

22. Akhmatova, *Complete Poems*, 323. Russian original: *Любо мне от глаз твоих зеленых / Ос веселых отгонять.*

23. Akhmatova, *Complete Poems*, 325. Russian original: *Прости меня, мальчик веселый, / Что я принесла тебе смерть.*

24. Viktor Toporov, *Dvoinoe dno. Priznaniia skandalista* (Moscow: Zakharov, AST, 1999), 184–86.

25. Efim Etkind, *Poeziia i perevod* (Moscow-Leningrad: Sovetskii Pisatel, 1963), 180–81.

26. Efim Etkind, *Poeziia i perevod*, 180.

27. Andrei Fedorov, *Iskusstvo perevoda i zhizn' literatury* (Leningrad: Sovetskii Pisatel, 1983), 41.

28. Fedorov, *Iskusstvo perevoda i zhizn' literatury*, 42.

29. Salomeja Neris (1904–45), Lithuanian poet, socialist realist.

Chapter 7: The Invisible Hand of Censorship

1. Susanna Witt, "Between the Lines: Totalitarianism and Translation in the USSR," in *Contexts, Subtexts, and Pretexts: Literary Translation in Eastern Europe and Russia*, ed. Brian James Baer (Amsterdam: John Benjamins, 2011), 155.

2. Arlen Blium, "Zarubezhnaia literatura v spetskhrane," *Inostrannaia literatura* 12 (2009): 137.

3. Polonnik here means the period of the Russian monarchy.

4. Tat'iana Goriaeva, *Politicheskaia tsenzura v SSSR. 1917–1991 gg.* (Moscow: ROSSPEN, 2009), 146–47.

5. Blium, "Zarubezhnaia literatura v spetskhrane," 134-35.
6. Arlen Blium, *Kak eto delalos' v Leningrade: Tsenzura v gody ottepeli, zastoia i perestroiki. 1953-1991* (St. Petersburg: Akademicheskii Proekt, 2005), 34-35.
7. Blium, *Kak eto delalos' v Leningrade*, 35.
8. Efim Etkind, *Zapiski nezagovorshchika* (Kharkiv: Prava Liudini, 2013), 23.
9. Etkind, *Zapiski nezagovorshchika*, 239.
10. Blium, "Zarubezhnaia literatura v spetskhrane," 132.
11. Blium, "Zarubezhnaia literatura v spetskhrane," 133.
12. Blium, "Zarubezhnaia literatura v spetskhrane," 133.
13. *Kratkaia literaturnaia entsiklopediia. T. 2*, ed. Aleksei Surkov (Moscow: Sovetskaia Entsiklopediia, 1964), 935-36.
14. *Literaturnaia entsiklopediia* (Moscow: Izdatel'stvo Kommunisticheskoi Akademii, 1931). http://dic.academic.ru/dic.nsf/enc_literature/2285.
15. Vasilii Betaki, "Red'iard Kipling i russkaia poeziia XX veka," concluding remarks to *Izbrannye stikhi iz vsekh knig* by Red'iard Kipling, ed. Vasilii Betaki (B.m.: Salamandra P.V.V., 2011), 285; Evgenii Vitkovskii, "Imperiia po imeni Red'iard Kipling," introduction to *Stikhotvoreniia. Roman. Rasskazy* by Red'iard Kipling, ed. Evgenii Vitkovskii (Moscow: Ripol Klassik, 1998), 12.
16. Red'iard Kipling, *Izbrannye stihi*, ed. Valentin Stenich (Leningrad: Khudozhestvennaia Literatura, 1936).
17. Rashel' Miller-Budnitskaia, "Poeziia Red'iarda Kiplinga," introduction to *Izbrannye stikhi* by Red'iard Kipling, 28.
18. Rudyard Kipling, *Mine Own People: The Works of Rudyard Kipling* (New York, Philadelphia, Chicago: Nottingham Society, 1909), 171.
19. Red'iard Kipling, *Stikhotvoreniia*, trans. Ada Onoshkovich-Iatsyna (Petrograd: Mysl', 1922).
20. Rudyard Kipling, *The Complete Verse* (London: Kyle Cathie Limited, 1990), 224-25.
21. Red'iard Kipling, *Red'iard Kipling v perevodakh Bena i Betaki* (Paris: Ritm, 1986), 89-91.
22. Vitkovskii, "Imperiia po imeni Red'iard Kipling," 9-10.
23. Red'iard Kipling, *Stikhotvoreniia. Roman. Rasskazy*, 167-68.
24. Robert Penn Uorren. "Potop," trans. Elena Golysheva, *Novyi mir* (1982): 4-8.
25. Narovchatov died in July 1981. The novel was published next year in five issues, the first of them—in April 1982.
26. Dzhanni Rodari, *Prikliucheniia Chipollino*, trans. Zlata Potapova (Moscow: Detgiz, 1955).
27. Aleks La Guma, *Skitaniia v nochi* (Moscow: Progress, 1964).
28. Aleks La Guma, *Izbrannoe* (Moscow: Pravda, 1985).
29. Goriaeva, *Politicheskaia tsenzura v SSSR*, 149.
30. *Dekrety Sovetskoi vlasti. T. I* (Moscow: Gosudarstvennoe Izdatel'stvo Politicheskoi Literatury, 1957), 24-25.
31. Ekaterina Kuznetsova, "Sposoby ideologicheskoi adaptatsii perevodnogo teksta: O perevode romana E. Khemingueia *Po kom zvonit kolokol*," *Logos* 3 (2012): 153-54.
32. A detailed and extremely live portrait of Mikhail Kol'tsov was drawn by Katerina Clark in her *Moscow, the Fourth Rome* (2011), where she describes his interests, character, personal life, prototypical linkage to Karkov, the details of his arrest, and subsequent death. The essay by Boris Efimov is extremely interesting as a memoir written by Kol'tsov's younger brother, a witness of many events of Kol'tsov's life. Katerina Clark, *Moscow, the Fourth Rome: Stalinism, Cosmopolitanism, and the*

Evolution of Soviet Culture, 1931–1941 (Cambridge, MA: Harvard University Press. 2011); Boris Efimov, *Sud'ba zhurnalista* (Moscow: Pravda, 1988).

33. Arlen Blium, *Sovetskaia tsenzura v epokhu total'nogo terrora. 1929–1953* (St. Petersburg: Akademicheskii Proekt, 2000), 226.

34. Kuznetsova, "Sposoby," 154–55.

35. For a more detailed analysis of the versions of 1941 and 1962, see Kuznetsova, "Sposoby."

36. Ernest Kheminguei, *Po kom zvonit kolokol*, in *Sobranie sochinenii. T. 3* by Ernest Kheminguei (Moscow: Khudozhestvennaia Literatura, 1968), 107–610.

37. Kuznetsova, "Sposoby," 168–69, 171.

38. Konstantin Simonov, "Ispanskaia tema v tvorchestve Khemingueia," introduction to *Sobranie sochinenii T. 3* by Ernest Kheminguei (Moscow: Khudozhestvennaia Literatura, 1968), 11–12.

39. The fear of the potential change in the political situation in the Soviet Union at the end of 1980s had a universal character and was not limited to literature. Until the end of the decade, Soviet universities still published research studies on "bourgeois ideology," "anticommunism," and "imperialism." See, for instance, Adel' Strizhenko, *Iazyk i ideologicheskaia bor'ba* (Language and ideological struggle) with its introduction insisting that "imperialistic ruling circles are not willing to accept that all the social development is subject to the ever growing influence of socialist ideas." Adel' Strizhenko, *Iazyk i ideologicheskaia bor'ba* (Irkutsk: Izdatel'stvo Irkutskogo Universiteta, 1988), 3. Also see Iasen Zasurskii and Alla Paroiatnikova, *Iazyk i stil' burzhuaznoi propagandy* (Language and style of bourgeois propaganda), which the authors devoted "to the criticism of methods and strategies of bourgeois propaganda, the unmasking of manipulative techniques of mass media of the biggest imperialistic states—the United States and the United Kingdom." Iasen Zasurskii and Alla Paroiatnikova, eds. *Iazyk i stil' burzhuaznoi propagandy* (Moscow: Moscow State University, 1988), 199.

40. Mir and Progress, in 1989.

41. In Russian, the nickname is based on a rhyme; the last word is grammatically distorted: *Chevychelov-kak-by-chego-ne-vychelov (Чевычелов-как бы чего не вычелов)*. This nickname apparently comes from the epigram "Pesnia rannikh ptits" (Early birds' song), which was written about Cevychelov by Samuel Marshak, who was aware of being controlled, censored, and reported on by Cevychelov: "Чево, чево, Чевычелов,Чево, чево, ты вычитал,Чево, чево, ты вычеркнул, Чевычелов, Чевычелов . . ."[What is there, what is there, Chevychelov / What is there, what is there that you have found, / What is there, what is there that you have crossed out / Chevychelov, Chevychelov . . .]. See Arlen Blium, *Sovetskaia tsenzura v epokhu total'nogo terrora. 1929–1953* (St. Petersburg: Akademicheskii Proekt, 2000), 220.

42. Blium, *Sovetskaia tsenzura*, 217–20.

43. Blium, *Sovetskaia tsenzura*, 278.

44. Markes, Gabriel' Garsiia, "Sto let odinochestva," *Inostrannaia literatura* 6 (1970): 54, 7 (1970): 151, 154.

45. Markes, "Sto let odinochestva," *Inostrannaia literatura* 6 (1970): 65.

46. Markes, Gabriel' Garsiia, *Sto let odinochestva* (Moscow: Khudozhestvennaia Literatura, 1971).

47. Markes, Gabriel' Garsiia, *Sto let odinochestva. Povesti i rakksazy* (Moscow: Progress, 1979).

48. William Styron, *Set This House on Fire* (New York: Random House, 1960), 150–51.

49. Uil'iam Stairon, *I podzheg etot dom*, trans. Viktor Golyshev, *Novyi mir* 2 (1985): 183–84.

50. Maria Tymoczko, *Enlarging Translation, Empowering Translators* (Manchester, UK, and Kinderhook, NY: St. Jerome Publishing, 2010), 257.

51. Tymoczko, *Enlarging Translation, Empowering Translators*, 258.

52. Styron, *Set This House on Fire*, 144–45, 151–2; Stairon [Styron], *I podzheg etot dom*, 180, 184.

53. See, for instance, Stairon, *I podzheg etot dom*, 184.

54. John Fowles, *The French Lieutenant's Woman* (London: Vintage, 1996), 293–95.

55. Dzhon Faulz, *Podruga frantsuzskogo leitenanta*, trans. Meri Bekker and Irina Komarova (Leningrad: Khudozhestvennaia literatura, 1985), 298.

56. Faulz, *Podruga frantsuzskogo leitenanta*, 297, 342.

57. English text: Fowles, *The French Lieutenant's Woman*, 296; Russian text: Faulz, *Podruga frantsuzskogo leitenanta*, 299.

58. Faulz, *Podruga frantsuzskogo leitenanta*.

59. Dzhon Faulz, *Liubovnitsa frantsuzskogo leitenanta*, trans. Meri Bekker and Irina Komarova (St. Petersburg: Khudozhestvennaia Literatura, 1993).

60. Quoted from the *King James Bible*.

61. The translation eventually reached the reader; see, for instance, Maiia Kviatkovskaia, trans., *Poesiás ibericas: Perevody Maii Kviatkovskoi s ispanskogo, portugal'skogo, katalanskogo i galisiiskogo iazykov* (St. Petersburg: Znak, 2013).

62. Gail W. Lapidus, "The Nationality Question and the Soviet System," *Proceedings of the Academy of Political Science* 3 (1984): 98–112.

63. Russian text: Truman Kapote, "Zavtrak u Tiffani," trans. Viktor Golyshev, *Moskva* 4 (1965): 97; English text: Truman Capote, *Breakfast at Tiffany's* (Harmondsworth: Penguin Books, 1977), 9–16.

64. Ken Kesey, *One Flew over the Cuckoo's Nest* (New York: Viking Press, 1970), 3–7.

65. Kurt Vonnegat, *Kolybel' dlia koshki*, trans. Rita Rait-Kovaleva (Moscow: Molodaia gvardiia, 1970).

66. Kurt Vonnegut, *Cat's Cradle* (New York: Delta Book, 1964), 26.

67. Vladimir Elistratov, *Slovar' russkogo argo* (Moscow: Russkie slovari, 2000).

68. Зика была лилипуткой, балериной иностранного ансамбля. Vonnegat, *Kolybel' dlia koshki*, 18.

69. *Bol'shoi akademicheskii slovar' russkogo iazyka. T. 9*, ed. Kirill Gorbachevich (Moscow–St. Petersburg: Nauka, 2007); *Slovar' sovremennogo russkogo literaturnogo iazyka. T. 6*, ed. Aleksandr Babkin (Moscow-Leningrad: Izdatel'stvo Akademii Nauk SSSR, 1957).

70. English text: Vonnegut, *Cat's Cradle*, 109. In the Russian text, see "... приятельницу-лилипутку, маленькую балерину" (Vonnegat, *Kolybel' dlia koshki*, 96).

71. English text: Vonnegut, *Cat's Cradle*, 198–99; Russian text: Vonnegat, *Kolybel' dlia koshki*, 180–81.

72. English text: Vonnegut, *Cat's Cradle*, 102; Russian text: Vonnegat, *Kolybel' dlia koshki*, 89.

73. Vonnegut, *Cat's Cradle*, 102.

74. Нестора Эймонса во время второй мировой войны сначала взяли в плен русские, а потом—немцы. Vonnegat, *Kolybel' dlia koshki*, 89.

75. Maiia Kviatkovskaia never reconciled with the changes forced into her translation of Zenea's poem. Her preferred version was finally published; see, for instance,

Maiia Kviatkovskaia, trans., *Poetas latinoamericanos: Poety Latinskoi Ameriki v perevodakh Maii Kviatkovskoi* (St. Petersburg: Znak, 2014), 28–34.

76. This process is described in detail, for instance, in Mikhail Shkarovskii, "Russkaia Pravoslavnaia Tserkov' i religioznaia politika sovetskogo gosudarstva v gody voiny," *Khristianskoe chtenie* 12 (1996).

77. See, for example, Khu Gao, *Perevodnaia kitaiskaia kniga v SSSR, 1949–1990 gg.: Problemy izdaniia i tematiko-tipologicheskii analiz*, PhD diss. abstract (Moskovskii gosudarstvennyi universitet kul'tury i iskusstv, 2001).

78. Anna Elistratova, *Bairon* (Moscow: AN SSSR, 1956), 21.

79. Now the situation is reverse: Irina Komarova does not need an official introduction and is widely known for her literary work, but the publication of her translations of Nash's poetry remains a difficult matter. Obtaining the rights from Nash's heirs turned out to be a complicated process, and Komarova's brilliant translations are currently available only in the twentieth-century editions.

80. For a description of the general outcry against the translation by Nemtsov, see Aleksandra Borisenko, "Selindzher nachinaet i vyigryvaet," *Inostrannaia literatura* 7 (2009): 224.

81. See Pamela Hunt Steinle, *In Cold Fear: The Catcher in the Rye Censorship Controversies and Postwar American Character* (Columbus: Ohio State University Press, 2000).

82. Aleksei Semenenko, "Smuggling the Other: Rita Rait-Kovaleva's Translation of J. D. Salinger's *The Catcher in the Rye*," *Translation and Interpreting Studies* 1 (2016): 65.

83. Alexander Burak, "The 'Americanization' of Russian Life and Literature through Translations of Hemingway's Works," *Translation and Interpreting Studies* 1 (2013).

84. Aleksandr Solzhenitsyn, *In the First Circle*, trans. Harry T. Willetts (New York: Harper Perennial, 2009), xxxi.

Chapter 8: A Farewell to Fear

1. Arlen Blium, *Kak eto delalos' v Leningrade: Tsenzura v gody ottepeli, zastoia i perestroiki. 1953–1991* (St. Petersburg: Akademicheskii Proekt, 2005), 64.

2. Arlen Blium, "Zarubezhnaia literatura v spetskhrane," *Inostrannaia literatura* 12 (2009): 139.

3. Efim Etkind, *Zapiski nezagovorshchika* (Kharkiv: Prava Liudini, 2013), 192.

4. Etkind, *Zapiski nezagovorshchika*, 193–95.

5. Nikita Bolotnikov, editor's concluding remarks to *Salamina* by Rockwell Kent (Moscow: Mysl', 1970), 377.

6. Aleksei Zverev, "Dzhek London: Velichie talanta i paradoksy sud'by," introduction to *Rasskazy* by Dzhek London (Moscow: Pravda, 1984), 4.

7. Vladimir Dzhanibekov, "Verit' budushchemu," introduction to *O skitan'iakh vechnykh i o Zemle* by Rei Bredberi (Moscow: Pravda, 1987), 3–4.

8. Nathanael West, *The Complete Works of Nathanael West* (New York: Farrar, Straus and Cudahy, 1957), 346.

9. Oldos Khaksli, "O divnyi, novyi mir," trans. Osiia Soroka, in *Antiutopii XX veka: Evgenii Zamiatin, Oldos Khaksli, Dzhordzh Oruell* (Moscow: Knizhnaia Palata, 1989), 131–271.

10. The female derivative of the name *Lenin* actually exists in the Russian language; it is *Lenina* [lenina] and not *Lenaina* [lenaina]. The etymology of this female name is unmistakably recognized by most Russian speakers.

11. Irina Komarova, translator's note to *Vse, krome nas s toboi: Sto izbrannykh stikhot-vorenii* by Ogden Nesh, trans. Irina Komarova (Leningrad: Lenizdat, 1988), 8.

12. Michel Foucault, *The History of Sexuality. Volume 1: An Introduction* (New York: Random House, 1978), 95.

13. For the question of everyday resistance, see Stellan Vinthagen and Anna Johansson, "Everyday Resistance: Exploration of a Concept and Its Theories," *Resistance Studies Magazine* 1 (2013). www.rsmag.org. For space of resistance, see Athina Karatzogianni and Andrew Robinson, *Power, Resistance and Conflict in the Contemporary World: Social Movements and Hierarchies* (London and New York: Routledge, 2009), 127.

14. Gennadii Zhirkov, *Istoriia tsenzury v Rossii XIX—XX vv.* (Moscow: Aspekt Press, 2001), 355.

Appendix A: Literary Translation under Restrictions

1. Ernest Kheminguei, "Po kom zvonit kolokol," in *Sobranie sochinenii. T. 3* by Ernest Kheminguei (Moscow: Khudozhestvennaia Literatura, 1968), 107–610.

2. Ekaterina Kuznetsova, "Sposoby ideologicheskoi adaptatsii perevodnogo teksta: O perevode romana E. Khemingueia *Po kom zvonit kolokol*," *Logos* 3 (2012): 157–58.

3. English text quoted as in Ernest Hemingway, *For Whom the Bell Tolls* (Harmondsworth: Penguin Books, 1966), 338–39; Russian text cited through its first edition: Kheminguei, "Po kom zvonit kolokol," 488.

4. Ernest Kheminguei, *Po kom zvonit kolokol. Na angliiskom iazyke* (Moscow: Progress, 1981), 388.

5. English text: Hemingway, *For Whom the Bell Tolls*, 392; Russian text: Kheminguei, "Po kom zvonit kolokol," 549.

6. English text: Hemingway, *For Whom the Bell Tolls*, 399; Russian text: Kheminguei, "Po kom zvonit kolokol," 558.

7. English text: Hemingway, *For Whom the Bell Tolls*, 400; Russian text: Kheminguei, "Po kom zvonit kolokol," 559.

8. Kheminguei, "Po kom zvonit kolokol," 555.

9. Kheminguei, *Po kom zvonit kolokol. Na angliiskom iazyke*, 455.

10. Kheminguei, "Po kom zvonit kolokol," 556.

11. Kheminguei, "Po kom zvonit kolokol," 356, 490.

12. J. D. Salinger, *The Catcher in the Rye* (New York: Modern Library, 1958), 70.

13. И вдруг в Трентоне вошла дама и села рядом со мной. Вагон был почти пустой, время позднее, но она все равно села рядом со мной, а не на пустую скамью, потому что я сидел на переднем месте, а у нее была громадная сумка. И она выставила эту сумку прямо в проход, так что кондуктор или еще кто мог об нее споткнуться. Должно быть, она ехала с какого-нибудь приема или бала—на платье были орхидеи. Лет ей, вероятно, было около сорока—сорока пяти, но она была очень красивая. Я от женщин балдею. Честное слово. Нет, я вовсе не в том смысле, вовсе я не такой бабник, хотя я довольно-таки впечатлительный. Просто они мне нравятся. Dzherom Selindzher, *Nad propast'iu vo rzhi*, trans. Rita Rait-Kovaleva, in *Nad propast'iu vo rzhi; Povesti; Deviat' rasskazov* by Dzherom Selindzher (Moscow: Khudozhestvennaia Literatura, 1983), 60.

14. Salinger, *The Catcher in the Rye*, 72.

15. Salinger, *The Catcher in the Rye*, 71.

16. А сын ее был самый что ни на есть последний гад во всей этой мерзкой школе. Всегда он после душа шел по коридору и бил всех мокрым полотенцем. Вот какой гад. (Selindzher, *Nad propast'iu vo rzhi*, 61).

17. Selindzher, "*Nad propast'iu vo rzhi*."

INDEX

www.ingramcontent.com/pod-product-compliance
Lightning Source LLC
Chambersburg PA
CBHW020648030726
47498CB00002B/419